# Approaches to Work-Based Learning in Higher Education

*Approaches to Work-Based Learning in Higher Education* provides a comprehensive introduction to the delivery of university-level work-based learning (WBL) for educators and policymakers. The contributing authors draw from their wealth of experience of developing apprenticeships, placement programmes and other work-based learning opportunities, advising on best practice when delivering learning in partnership with industry.

Supported by a unique balance of practical and theoretical insight, including international perspectives on how common challenges may be addressed, this essential volume explores the following key themes:

- Pedagogies – this section outlines established best practice in delivery of WBL for higher education and offers suggestions for how readers may continue to develop and improve their provision.
- Projects – this section covers a range of approaches to work-based learning within higher education and explores examples of this in practice, including live briefs, work placements and industrial project-based learning.
- Apprenticeships – this section focuses specifically on work-based degree programmes, covering their design, delivery, implementation and assessment.

A must-read for anyone working within higher education policy or practice, this book provides readers with the tools to successfully navigate work-based learning, as well as strategies for ensuring and enhancing the quality of the learning experience.

**Matthew Barr** is Head of Education and Practice at the University of Glasgow's School of Computing Science and Programme Director for the Graduate Apprenticeship in Software Engineering. He serves as Director of Education for the Scottish Informatics and Computer Science Alliance and as Director of the Ada Scotland Festival.

# Approaches to Work-Based Learning in Higher Education

## Improving Graduate Employability

**Edited by Matthew Barr**

LONDON AND NEW YORK

Designed cover image: Getty Images

First published 2025
by Routledge
4 Park Square, Milton Park, Abingdon, Oxon OX14 4RN

and by Routledge
605 Third Avenue, New York, NY 10158

*Routledge is an imprint of the Taylor & Francis Group, an informa business*

© 2025 selection and editorial matter, Matthew Barr; individual chapters, the contributors

The right of Matthew Barr to be identified as the author of the editorial material, and of the authors for their individual chapters, has been asserted in accordance with sections 77 and 78 of the Copyright, Designs and Patents Act 1988.

All rights reserved. No part of this book may be reprinted or reproduced or utilised in any form or by any electronic, mechanical, or other means, now known or hereafter invented, including photocopying and recording, or in any information storage or retrieval system, without permission in writing from the publishers.

*Trademark notice*: Product or corporate names may be trademarks or registered trademarks, and are used only for identification and explanation without intent to infringe.

*British Library Cataloguing-in-Publication Data*
A catalogue record for this book is available from the British Library

ISBN: 978-1-032-80419-4 (hbk)
ISBN: 978-1-032-80376-0 (pbk)
ISBN: 978-1-003-49677-9 (ebk)

DOI: 10.4324/9781003496779

Typeset in Galliard
by Apex CoVantage, LLC

# Contents

*List of Contributing Authors* — vii

1  Introduction — 1
   MATTHEW BARR

2  The Design and Delivery of Work-Based Degree
   Programmes: Challenges and Solutions — 5
   MATTHEW BARR

3  Higher Education Apprenticeship Pedagogies:
   A Multilateral Approach — 24
   JESSICA LOMAS

4  The Dual Study Programme in Germany – Concept,
   Strengths and Challenges — 45
   UTE HIPPACH-SCHNEIDER

5  GUSS at 5: A Retrospective of Work-Based Learning
   Within an In-House Student-delivered Software Service — 64
   NADER AL HAFFAR, SAYAN BANDYOPADHYAY, LEN LUKOWSKI,
   NIHANTH MANYAM, AHMAD SALMAN, DEREK SOMERVILLE,
   TIM STORER, STELLA EVA TSIAPALI AND TESS VAUGHAN

6  Bringing the Real World Into the Classroom Through
   Team-Based Live Brief Projects — 81
   JONATHAN JACKSON, NICHOLAS DAY AND KEVIN MAHER

7 Moving From Industry-Sponsored Academic Projects to
Supporting Student Learning in Industry 106
REBECCA BATES, RON ULSETH, CODY MANN AND LIN CHASE

8 Integrated Professional Development Pathways:
Learning-Integrated Work? 125
STAN LESTER

9 From Inception to Delivery: The UK's First Degree
Apprenticeship in Diagnostic Radiography 142
DEMELZA GREEN

10 Quality Metrics: Navigating the Quality Landscape of
Degree Apprenticeships in Higher Education Institutions 159
SAMANTHA REIVE HOLLAND AND ERNEST EDEM EDIFOR

11 The Role of Reflection in Effective Work-Based Learning
and Assessment 179
SYED WAQAR NABI AND DEREK SOMERVILLE

12 Advancing Work-Based Learning in Higher Education 197
MATTHEW BARR

*Index* 201

# Contributing Authors

**Nader Al Haffar** Mohammed Nader Al Haffar is a student pursuing a master's degree in cyber security, privacy, and trust at the University of Edinburgh. He holds a BSc Honours in computer science from the University of Glasgow. Mohammed has worked with the Glasgow University Software Service (GUSS) for a year. His research focuses on the intricacies of crypto forensics, including the investigation of blockchain transactions, digital evidence collection and development of forensic tools for cryptocurrency analysis. Mohammed is also looking forward to becoming a project manager in the future.

**Sayan Bandyopadhyay** Sayan is an engineer with a diverse background in biomedical engineering, computer science and integrated quantum photonics. He has previously worked in the telecommunications sector as a senior software developer and has spearheaded a start-up focused on creating a modular upper-limb prosthetics platform. Sayan has worked part-time with the Glasgow University Software Services and is actively engaged in research within the domain of quantum nanophotonics. Currently pursuing a PhD at the University of Glasgow, his work in developing photonic chips through machine learning techniques has broad implications for the design of biomedical sensors, quantum computation, and more.

**Matthew Barr** Dr Matthew Barr is Head of Education and Practice at the University of Glasgow's School of Computing Science and Programme Director for the Graduate Apprenticeship in Software Engineering. He is Director of Education for the Scottish Informatics and Computer Science Alliance (SICSA) in 2021 and a founding editor of the journal *Open Scholarship of Teaching and Learning*. Matt is also the founder of the Ada Scotland Festival, which aims to improve gender balance in computing science education. He serves on a number of national education-related committees, including the Scottish Apprenticeship Approvals Group and the Scottish Government's Digital Economy Skills Group.

**Rebecca Bates** Rebecca Bates is Professor and Founding Chair of Integrated Engineering at Minnesota State University, Mankato, home of Iron Range Engineering and Twin Cities Engineering. These project- and practice-based programs articulate with two-year colleges and partner with industry. She has been a program officer at the National Science Foundation in the Division of Equity for Excellence in STEM. She is a fellow of the American Society for Engineering Education. She earned her BS in biomedical engineering and MS in electrical engineering from Boston University, an MTS (theological studies) from Harvard Divinity School, and her PhD in electrical engineering from the University of Washington.

**Lin Chase** Lin Chase, PhD, served as founding Director of the zomputer Science (CS) program at Minnesota State University, Mankato. The CS program is an entirely project-based upper division program in which industry and research partners provide real-world, full-scale projects for student teams as the core of the curriculum. Lin joined MSU Mankato to lead the launch of this program after working for 35 years in the software industry in roles that included engineering, sales, marketing and serving as CEO of a Silicon Valley company. She has led software development and enterprise deployments globally, and she earned her PhD at the School of Computer Science at Carnegie Mellon University in Pittsburgh, PA, USA.

**Nicholas Day** Nicholas Day is a senior lecturer and programmer leader for Buckinghamshire New University's (BNU) undergraduate computing course. He completed his PhD in computer science education (CSEd) in 2020 and now applies his pedagogical research to the development and delivery of BNU's undergraduate, postgraduate and apprenticeship degrees. Furthermore, Nicholas is a departmental lecturer at Oxford University's Department for Continuing Education (OUDCE), teaching on data science courses and contributing to their AI Steering Group. He is also a fellow of the Higher Education Academy (FHEA), a member of the British Computing Society (MBCS) and an external examiner for Cardiff University's postgraduate computing degrees.

**Ernest Edem Edifor** Dr Ernest Edem Edifor, a reader in digital education at Manchester Metropolitan University, serves as the Director of the Digital Technology Solutions (DTS) degree apprenticeship with over 600 apprentices from over 70 employers across the UK. Ernest is a book author and has published numerous peer-reviewed articles in prestigious journals and conferences. Notably, he co-authored a recent national report on degree apprenticeships, which received a foreword from the Minister for Skills, Apprenticeships, and Higher Education. His contributions extend to trailblazer groups, talks, training sessions and a widening participation initiative related to degree apprenticeships.

**Demelza Green** Demelza Green, a senior lecturer at the University of Exeter, is a radiographer by profession who entered academia in 2003. Since then she has worked at several higher education institutions across the UK. During her academic career, Demelza Green has taken several roles including programme lead and academic assessment officer. In 2019 Demelza Green and her colleague Christine Heales developed and in 2020 launched the first degree apprenticeship in diagnostic radiography; she has spoken widely about the experiences of introducing apprenticeship training into radiography. Demelza Green is currently undertaking her education doctorate, exploring the use of progress testing in radiography education.

**Ute Hippach-Schneider** Ute Hippach-Schneider is Senior Researcher at Federal Institute for Vocational Education and Training (Bundesinstitut für Berufsbildung, BIBB). Ute is a member of BIBB's "International VET Comparison, Research and Monitoring" section, where she is examining the dynamics and flexibility of VET systems. Her focus is on governance and mainly on the role of actors. The current interest is particularly focused on the perspective of learners in vocational education and training and their role in the governance systems of VET systems. Furthermore, she is National Coordinator of the European network ReferNet.

**Samantha Reive Holland** Dr Samantha Reive Holland is a distinguished scholar and author, and received both her MA and PhD from the University of Leeds. Samantha's current work explores the socio-economic impact of degree apprenticeships, and in her role of Apprentice and Employer Engagement Fellow at Manchester Metropolitan University, she has collaborated on key projects and international networks. She has also co-authored numerous publications, including peer-reviewed journal articles and national reports, and presented her research at major conferences both nationally and internationally.

**Jonathan Jackson** Jonathan Jackson completed his degree in computer science (BSc) at Brunel University before going into industry as a web programmer and entrepreneur. He embarked on a teaching career in higher education in 2015 and most recently has held a position as Senior Lecturer and Programme Lead for the Digital and Technology Solutions degree apprenticeship at Buckinghamshire New University. Jon is a chartered IT professional (CITP) with BCS, is a fellow of the Higher Education Authority (FHEA), and has a postgraduate certificate in academic practice (PgCAP). His scholarly interests include digitally enhanced teaching and learning; large language models (LLMs); and authentic assessment.

**Stan Lester** Dr Stan Lester started his career in vocational education in the 1980s. He has worked since 1993 as a consultant, researcher and systems developer in professional and work-related education and development and has been described as a leading expert on professional competence as well as one of the world's most important thought-leaders and most cited authors on university-level work-based learning. Stan is currently an associate with the University Vocational Awards Council, where he is currently working on the use of degree and similar apprenticeships as professional entry and progression routes.

**Jessica Lomas** Jessica Lomas is a lecturer in global innovation at the University of Winchester and an associate lecturer in international business and strategy at Henley Business School, University of Reading. Jessica is a fellow of the Higher Education Authority (FHEA) and holds a postgraduate certificate in learning and teaching in higher education (PgCert) in addition to her MSc in international business. Her specialisms include social responsibility, banking, business ethics and microfinance, while her PhD explores the origins of corporate social responsibility (CSR) in early financial systems and social enterprises.

**Len Lukowski** Len Lukowski is an administrator at GUSS.

**Kevin Maher** Kevin Maher completed an apprenticeship as a laboratory technician in the petrochemical industry, gaining an HNC in chemistry. He subsequently completed a BSc and PhD in chemistry at UMIST. His research focused on the use of chromatographic methods for the analysis and synthesis of compounds that could inspire the production of new medicinal drugs. He has worked at Buckinghamshire New University since 1994, making contributions in various roles and departments, most recently as Deputy Head of School for Creative and Digital Industries. He was original lead for the development of the University's Digital and Technology Solutions L6 Apprenticeship Degree programmes.

**Cody Mann** Cody Mann is the Director of Operations at Iron Range Engineering (IRE). He helped to create unique facilitator staff positions and served as a facilitator and then the coordinator of facilitators for four years before becoming the Director of Operations. His work consists of program development, fiscal and operational management, supervision of staff, partnership coordination, student experience satisfaction, and recruitment. His research interests include work-based learning and program evaluation, focusing on staffing. He earned his BS in engineering from the original project-based IRE program at Minnesota State University, Mankato, and his MEng from the University of Minnesota Duluth.

**Nihanth Manyam** Nihanth Manyam is a project manager at Glasgow University oftware Service. His role involves managing teams, ensuring project timelines and objectives are met and liaising with stakeholders and clients to deliver successful software solutions. He completed his master's degree at the University of Glasgow. His research interests focus on the integration of real and virtual environments to create new applications to enhance perception, interaction capabilities in robots and advanced mission planning with simulations in defence using mixed reality.

**Syed Waqar Nabi** Dr Syed Waqar Nabi is Lecturer at the School of Computing Science, University of Glasgow. He is a member of the Education & Practice and Computer Systems research sections in the School. He teaches primarily for the BSc (Hons) Software Engineering (Graduate Apprenticeship) program, covering foundational courses in the area of: logic design, computer architecture, operating systems, network systems, data structures, algorithms, and discrete maths. His research interests include competency-based and mastery learning, use of AI and LLMs in software engineering education, and higher education in Low-and-Middle Income Countries (LMICs). He is also interested in heterogenous, high-performance, and sustainable computing.

**Ahmad Salman** Ahmad Salman is a current MSc data science student at the University of Glasgow. Before joining Glasgow, Ahmad completed his high school education partially in Jordan and Turkey. He then proceeded to get a bachelor's degree in computer engineering from Bilkent University in Turkey. Ahmad's interests revolve around developing software, with a particular interest in developing products for the banking sector. He is currently working as a data scientist at a fintech start-up in Turkey. Moreover, he is interested in hardware design and embedded systems with a focus on IoT devices.

**Derek Somerville** Derek Somerville is an experienced developer and programme manager with over 20 years in computing. As a consultant, he has worked in a variety of technical roles across Europe, Asia, Africa and the US. In 2018 Derek moved from industry to academia to bring his experience to the newly created Graduate Apprenticeship programme at the University of Glasgow. Based in the School of Computing Science, he is currently the Programme Lead for the BSc and MSci Software Engineering and the summer and year internship programmes. Derek's current area of research is software engineering education, particularly how new developers explore codebases.

**Tim Storer** Dr Tim Storer is a senior lecturer in software engineering at the University of Glasgow, in the School of Computing Science. He is the Academic Director of the Glasgow University Software Service and Deputy Director and Director of Knowledge Exchange of the Scottish Informatics and Computer Science Alliance (SICSA). His research interests focus on the practice of software engineering, with particular interest in studying the perspectives and behaviours of software practitioners, as well as proposing, building and testing new methods and tools for them. His research focuses in particular on quality assurance, requirements engineering, team coordination and software engineering education.

**Stella Eva Tsiapali** Stella Eva Tsiapali is a software engineer at the Glasgow University Software Service (GUSS) and works as a demonstrator for the School of Computing Science at the University of Glasgow.

**Ron Ulseth** Ron Ulseth, PhD, PE, is the Founding Director of the project-based and work-based learning models at Iron Range Engineering. IRE has been named an emerging world leader in engineering education and has won the ABET Innovation Award. He has been the PI or Co-PI on seven NSF grants. His research interests include the intersection of self-directed learning and PBL/WBL. He has taught eight or more engineering courses per year for the past 32 years on the faculty of Minnesota North College. He is also an adjunct professor at Minnesota State University, Mankato, and adjunct associate professor at Aalborg University.

**Tess Vaughan** Tess Vaughan joined the Glasgow University Software Service (GUSS) as Assistant Manager in 2021 having held other roles at the university. Tess manages a range of projects for GUSS and loves supporting student developers to deliver professional project work for customers. Working at GUSS has provided great learning opportunities; in terms of the tech stacks used and the challenges of developing GUSS as a service whilst ensuring that student development teams are well looked after. Tess enjoys learning about customers' fields of work and appreciates how the service's projects can inform students of wider opportunities available to them on graduation.

# Chapter 1

# Introduction

*Matthew Barr*

Work-based learning (WBL) has emerged as a powerful approach to bridging the gap between academic learning and professional practice in higher education. By integrating theoretical knowledge with real-world experience, WBL programmes aim to equip university students with the skills, competencies, and mindsets necessary to thrive in their chosen careers. This book explores the diverse landscape of work-based learning in higher education, presenting insights, case studies, and recommendations from scholars and practitioners across a range of disciplines and contexts. Here, work-based learning is taken to mean courses and opportunities that are designed and developed in partnership with employers and students, consisting of structured, authentic learning activities – a broad definition based on the guiding principles for work-based learning established by the UK Quality Assurance Agency for Higher Education (QAA).

The book is organised into three sections: Pedagogies, Projects, and Apprenticeships. With reference to specific examples, the Pedagogies section looks at established best practice in delivering WBL in higher education, as well as offering suggestions for how we continue to develop and improve our provision. The remaining sections are organised around the two most prevalent forms of WBL in university contexts: work-based projects and degree-level apprenticeships. The Projects section covers a range of approaches, including projects based on live briefs, work placements, and industrial project-based learning. The Apprenticeships chapters offer a similarly broad view of work-based degree programmes, including how they are designed, delivered, and assessed.

The chapters in this book highlight the growing importance of WBL in meeting the evolving needs of students, employers, and society. As the demand for highly skilled, adaptable, and professionally competent graduates continues to rise, universities are increasingly partnering with industry to design and deliver programmes that blend academic rigour with practical relevance. From degree-level apprenticeships to project-based learning and reflective practice, the contributions in this volume showcase the innovative approaches being adopted to enhance student employability and address skills gaps in the workforce.

DOI: 10.4324/9781003496779-1

One of the key themes that emerges across the chapters is the importance of collaboration and partnership in the design and delivery of effective WBL programmes. Ute Hippach-Schneider's chapter on dual study programmes in Germany highlights the critical role of employers in shaping curricula and providing students with meaningful work experiences. Similarly, in my own chapter, Sharon Green's account of launching a diagnostic radiography degree apprenticeship at the University of Exeter emphasises the importance of close collaboration with health providers to ensure the programme meets workforce needs and regulatory requirements.

The chapter by Rebecca Bates and Minnesota State University colleagues on the evolution of an engineering programme from project-based to practice-based learning further underscores the value of deep engagement with industry partners. By involving employers in the design of authentic assessments and providing students with extensive opportunities for work-based learning, the programme has achieved high levels of student motivation, low attrition rates, and strong graduate outcomes. The authors also highlight the importance of a supportive learning community and the role of facilitators in guiding students' professional development.

Another key theme is the need for pedagogical innovation and flexibility in WBL programmes. As Jessica Lomas argues in her chapter on apprenticeship pedagogies, educators must adopt a multilateral approach that integrates theory-driven and traditional teaching practices, fosters collaborative partnerships, promotes reflective practice, and leverages technology to enhance the learning experience. The chapter presents a framework for understanding the unique needs and challenges of apprentice learners and offers practical strategies for supporting their academic and professional growth.

Jonathan Jackson and colleagues' chapter on live brief projects also emphasises the importance of authentic, team-based learning experiences in preparing students for the demands of the modern workplace. By engaging with real-world clients and stakeholders, students develop valuable transferable skills such as collaboration, communication, and problem-solving, while also gaining exposure to industry practices and networks. Indeed, Tim Storer, Derek Somerville, and their students identify similar positive outcomes in their chapter on a student software service that carries out development work on behalf of real-world clients. Elsewhere, authors also highlight the potential of generative AI tools to support the design and delivery of live brief projects, as well as the importance of considering ethical factors such as intellectual property and developer remuneration – all very real concerns.

The quality assurance and regulatory landscape of WBL programmes is another important theme addressed in the book. Samantha Reive Holland and Ernest Edifor's chapter on navigating the quality landscape of degree apprenticeships in England provides a comprehensive overview of the formal and informal quality metrics that shape programme design, assessment, and delivery. The authors emphasise the need for a streamlined and holistic approach to quality assurance, with recommendations for centralising oversight, involving employers in course design, and embedding quality standards in day-to-day operations.

The chapter by Stan Lester on integrated professional development pathways further explores the challenges and opportunities of aligning academic learning with professional competencies. Drawing on examples from teaching, nursing, and degree apprenticeships, the author highlights the importance of genuine integration between theory and practice at a pedagogical and practical level, as well as the need to maintain a balance between workplace and academic concerns. The chapter also offers insights into the organisational and partnership structures that support effective integrated learning, as well as the role of digital technologies in overcoming boundaries between learning spaces.

Reflective practice emerges as a critical component of effective WBL throughout the book. Waqar Nabi and Derek Somerville's chapter on the role of reflection in work-based learning and assessment presents a compelling case study of a graduate apprenticeship programme in software engineering that incorporates structured reflection throughout the curriculum. The authors provide examples of student work that demonstrates the power of reflection in cementing connections between theoretical knowledge and practical application, developing self-awareness, and articulating subtle aspects of learning. They argue that structured reflection should be integral to WBL programmes to encourage deliberate reflection-on-action and enhance learning outcomes.

Taken together, the chapters in this book offer a rich and diverse portrait of work-based learning in higher education. They highlight the transformative potential of WBL in preparing students for the complex and rapidly changing world of work, while also acknowledging the challenges and tensions inherent in designing and delivering effective programmes. From the need for close collaboration with industry partners to the importance of pedagogical innovation, quality assurance, and reflective practice, the contributions provide valuable insights and recommendations for educators, policymakers, and practitioners.

As the landscape of higher education continues to evolve, work-based learning is likely to play an increasingly important role in bridging the gap between academia and industry. The examples and perspectives presented in this book demonstrate the vitality and creativity of the field, as well as the commitment of educators and partners to providing students with meaningful, transformative learning experiences. By embracing the opportunities and challenges of WBL, universities can position themselves as leaders in developing the workforce of the future, while also contributing to the social and economic wellbeing of their communities.

In conclusion, this book provides a timely and valuable contribution to the growing literature on work-based learning in higher education. It offers a comprehensive overview of the key issues, trends, and practices shaping the field, while also providing practical guidance and inspiration for those seeking to design, deliver, or enhance WBL programmes. As the authors demonstrate, effective work-based learning requires a commitment to collaboration, innovation, and student-centred approaches that recognise the unique needs and aspirations of learners. By embracing these principles and practices, higher education institutions can unlock the full potential of WBL to transform lives, careers, and communities.

# Chapter 2

# The Design and Delivery of Work-Based Degree Programmes

## Challenges and Solutions

*Matthew Barr*

## Introduction

Degree-level apprenticeship programmes, which blend work-based experience with academic learning, have gained increasing recognition as a powerful model for developing skilled professionals. From a student point of view, apprenticeships have been shown to increase earning potential (Wolter and Ryan, 2011), enhance the development of professional skills (Barr *et al.*, 2024), lower the likelihood of unemployment, and increase job satisfaction (Fuller and Unwin, 2017). Employers, meanwhile, report that apprentices contribute to productivity gains (Fuller and Unwin, 2017) and help address skills shortages (Muehlemann and Wolter, 2014). At a societal level, apprenticeships have been found to not only improve productivity, but also increase social mobility (Nawaz *et al.*, 2022) and widen access to higher education (Barr *et al.*, 2023). However, challenges persist in the design and delivery of work-based degree programmes. This chapter aims to address these challenges, drawing on existing literature and in-depth interviews with experienced higher education practitioners.

## The Alignment Challenge

The central challenge in apprenticeships is what Sauli *et al.* (2021) describe as the "non-alignment and uselessness" of learning experiences across institutional and workplace settings. Sauli (2021) elaborates, stating "there are issues with helping apprentices connect the experiences they have gained from school and training company and aligning the content learned in the two locations".

Misalignment can stem from various factors. Lynsey Joyce, Head of Work Based Learning at the University of Stirling, points to the traditional autonomy of academic institutions in determining curriculum, observing that industry involvement in the design of degree apprenticeship standards "was quite a change for many academic colleagues, who were very used to them defining what was taught within the programme". Sharon Green, Professor and Dean of Executive Education and Skills at the University of Lincoln, makes a similar point about the traditional autonomy of academic institutions in determining curricula:

> Traditionally, I think where universities might have gone wrong is where they've taken their existing provision, bolted the apprenticeship onto it. But this is taking curriculum development to a different level and saying "teach to the standard" rather than what we can do internally.

Green also highlights that aligning apprenticeship standards with the reality of university teaching is not always straightforward, especially if the standard is too specific to a particular employer:

> The very first challenge we have is making sure that we can work collaboratively with IfATE [the Institute for Apprenticeships and Technical Education, responsible for the occupational standards on which apprenticeships in England are based] and with the employer groups to understand that sometimes the things they ask for aren't generic enough for us as a university to be able to exploit that standard.

Dr Ernest Edifor, Director of Manchester Metropolitan University's Digital and Technology Solutions Degree Apprenticeship, also highlights the diversity of employer contexts as a challenge: "You're working with multiple employers who are in different sectors. Some are big, some are small, public sector, private sector, you name it. You're working to meet their needs, and it's challenging to make it very applicable to everyone".

Moreover, Edifor notes the varying levels of expertise among apprentices themselves:

> The learners coming in, of course, are all not eighteen-year olds. Some have worked but they just need that extra edge to move up . . . they've been in the field but they just need to reskill. So you have [different backgrounds] to contend with, so when you're making it applicable you have to have that featured in, otherwise you will not be as inclusive as you want to be.

Jonathan Jackson, Programme Lead for the digital and technology degree apprenticeships at Buckinghamshire New University, points out that the breadth of some apprenticeship standards can also pose challenges for direct workplace alignment:

> The digital and technology solutions professional programme is quite broad, all those core skills. So, even if you're on the software engineering pathway, you still have to cover things like cyber and networking and things

like that. There's inevitably some of the content that isn't directly aligned with what they do in their workplace.

### Conceptualising Alignment

To address these challenges, some have argued for a reconceptualisation of apprenticeships. Billett (2016) proposes seeing apprenticeships not just as an educational model, but also as a mode of learning through practice and work activities. He advocates for enriching learning experiences through practice curricula, pedagogies, and engaging apprentices' personal epistemologies. In other words, it is less about adapting existing university provision and more about embracing the realities of the workplace. This aligns with Lynsey Joyce's experience of degree apprenticeship development in the UK, where "industry was involved very heavily in terms of designing the programmes". She notes that while the opportunity for students to undertake a degree whilst also working was quite unique, "the degree had then very much been tailored to the needs of the sector and the needs of the industry".

However, this shift in thinking is not always easy. Joyce goes on to acknowledge "challenges, particularly with academic colleagues who were maybe not as keen, or more reluctant, to be completely responsive to the needs of industry". Matt Bungay, Head of Apprenticeships at City, University of London, similarly notes the difficulty in persuading faculty to understand that "they needed to adapt some delivery to make sure that knowledge skills were being taught, but also to try and re-emphasise the behaviours".

### Strategies for Integration

The literature offers some guiding principles and strategies for better integrating academic content with workplace activities. Messmann and Mulder (2015), for example, found that apprentices' work-based learning was facilitated by their perception of institution-based learning as work-oriented and by complex, autonomous, and supportive work environments.

Meanwhile, Sauli *et al.* (2021) suggest that differences between educational and workplace settings can be harnessed as learning opportunities through boundary-crossing processes. For example, apprentices can be supported to apply academic learning in work contexts or to draw on diverse peer experiences from different workplaces. Billett (2015, cited in Billett, 2016) argues for the importance of actively facilitating and supporting apprentices' processes of experiencing, suggesting:

> there is likely to be value in engaging with them before, during and after their workplace experiences to prepare them for those experiences, to support them during their engagement and, perhaps most importantly, to assist them to reconcile, share and compare with others what they have experienced in practice settings.

The interviewed practitioners offer further practical strategies. Ann Minton is an independent consultant on work-based learning in higher education, with 20 years' experience of designing, delivering, and quality assuring a range of work-based learning programmes across the UK and internationally. She advocates starting with a thorough understanding of the workplace activities and required knowledge, skills, and behaviours and designing the academic programme around these. Ernest Edifor emphasises co-creation, "involving the employers every step of the way" in design, delivery, and assessment of the programme. According to Edifor, continuous evaluation and review, through mechanisms including employer advisory boards, is seen as crucial for maintaining alignment over time.

Jonathan Jackson highlights the value of authentic assessments that allow flexibility to incorporate workplace contexts, as well as fostering collaborative learning environments where apprentices "can learn from each other". On a more granular level, Jackson advocates providing detailed information to line managers about academic projects to ensure workplace fit, while Matt Bungay describes offering bespoke employer webinars to clarify programme alignment with organisational needs. Referring to computing-related apprenticeships, Jackson goes on to explain how Buckinghamshire New University uses employers' technologies in academic modules, to ensure applicability in the workplace. Where relevant, then, universities should aim to mirror the technologies, processes, and platforms used by their employer partners. Of course, as Manchester Metropolitan's Edifor alludes to earlier, working with a range of employers may render such efforts impracticable.

### Fostering Collaboration

Underpinning all of these strategies is the need for close collaboration between educators and employers. Sauli (2021) found that weak collaboration between vocational education and training (VET) partners in Switzerland often left apprentices unsupported in connecting their learning across contexts, while networks with an integrative vision improved partnerships.

The interview respondents offer several insights into fostering such collaboration. Consultant Ann Minton advises simply showing "a willingness to listen" to employers and accepting the value of workplace learning, moving towards a genuine partnership rather than a provider-client model.

Lynsey Joyce suggests demonstrating the mutual benefits of collaboration and leveraging industry-engaged academic colleagues as exemplars to bring others on board. She notes:

> There might be initially an engagement on one particular area, but we have seen that then broadening out into research and broadening out into other opportunities. It's not just for the sole purpose of delivering these work-based style degrees or work-based style modules. It's about

broadening out those industrial relationships which are so beneficial and so crucial now for universities to progress with all aspects of their business.

A range of practical collaboration mechanisms are described by the respondents:

- Frequent meetings between university business development managers and employers;
- Regular employer advisory boards to review programmes;
- Guest lectures and joint events such as open days and conferences with industry partners;
- Bespoke employer webinars to understand organisational needs and context;
- Tripartite reviews involving the apprentice, line manager, and university skills staff responsible for apprentices' academic development;
- Specific information sharing and three-way calls for work-based academic projects.

## *The Importance of Communication*

Ultimately, ongoing open communication between all stakeholders emerges as the essential ingredient for alignment and collaboration. As Ernest Edifor puts it, "communication is key. . . . Having very, very strong communication links with the employers helps us. . . . I think we should actually elevate it to the strategic level and see how we can strategically foster stronger partnerships".

Lynsey Joyce similarly emphasises the importance of "having those bodies, having those boards, those opportunities where industry and academia can engage openly and freely" to share needs and shape responsive programmes. She advises "engaging with industry in as many ways as we possibly can and consistently doing that throughout the process", not just in initial programme establishment.

In a similar vein, Sharon Green refers to the importance of the tripartite relationship between the apprentice, employer, and university – a recurring theme in this chapter. She emphasises effective communication and collaboration: "Keeping those channels open, the personal tutor and the review process is so important to that and stepping in early enough if the wheel's going to fall off".

In summary, apprenticeship programmes face a significant challenge in integrating and aligning the learning experiences of apprentices across educational institutions and workplaces. The literature and practitioner insights, however, point to a range of strategies and principles that can foster greater connectivity.

At a conceptual level, it is crucial to approach apprenticeships as a mode of learning through practice, and to design curricula, pedagogies, and assessments that engage with and enrich work-based learning. In practice, this requires deep industry involvement and co-creation throughout the apprenticeship lifecycle, from initial design to ongoing delivery and review.

Supporting apprentices to connect and apply their learning across contexts is key, through techniques like authentic and flexible assessments, collaborative peer learning, workplace-oriented projects, regular tripartite progress reviews, and active facilitation of boundary crossing.

Fundamentally, the success of all these strategies rests on a foundation of strong, strategic partnerships between educators and employers. Open and frequent communication, formalised through regular touchpoints and governance structures, allows for a genuine integration of academic and workplace learning to the benefit of all stakeholders.

By implementing these principles, the full potential of apprenticeship programmes' unique learning model may be realised, developing professionals with the knowledge, skills, and behaviours to thrive in their chosen occupations and drive innovation and productivity in their industries.

## Ensuring Appropriate Work for Apprentices

The task of ensuring that apprentices engage in appropriate and meaningful work during their placements is multifaceted, encompassing identifying suitable tasks, providing adequate mentoring and support, fostering collaboration between employers and educational institutions, and ensuring the overall quality of the workplace experience. Both the literature and interview data offer a view of the challenges and solutions related to these aspects.

### Identifying Suitable Workplace Tasks and Projects

A recurring theme is the difficulty in identifying appropriate tasks for apprentices. According to Rowe et al. (2017), over 60% of employers find it challenging to identify suitable projects and tasks for apprentices. Similarly, Jackson et al. (2017) note that host organisations struggle with this aspect, which is crucial for the apprentices' development and integration into the workplace.

Jonathan Jackson from Buckinghamshire New University (BNU) highlights a specific challenge where apprentices are delayed in starting meaningful work due to requirements such as security clearance. He observes, "months in, some are still onboarding, not having to do much. Some of that is maybe caused by security clearance. They can't work on any projects yet because they haven't got security clearance". This underscores the need for flexibility and the provision of alternative learning opportunities during such delays.

The complexity of aligning the needs of various stakeholders is another challenge, as noted by Manchester Metropolitan's Ernest Edifor: "You have different employers who have different needs . . . different students who have different needs . . . you have to make sure that everything aligns with the occupational standard". This highlights the importance of careful planning and coordination to ensure that tasks are both relevant and appropriately challenging.

### Providing Adequate Mentoring and Support

Effective mentoring is critical for the success of apprenticeships. Roberts et al. (2019) emphasise that effective mentoring involves providing inductions, setting workplace expectations, facilitating learning, and supporting apprentices in achieving their qualification. However, mentoring can be constrained by time and resources, as noted by Furness and Gilligan (2004), who draw parallels with teacher training, where "practice teachers need sufficient time and training to assess students' practice adequately" but face challenges due to resource constraints.

The interview data corroborate these findings, with several participants emphasising the importance of continuous support and mentoring. For instance, Edifor advises that "the line manager and the academic supervisor come together to ensure that the work is appropriately challenging for the apprentice". Such collaboration helps align the academic requirements with practical tasks in the workplace.

### Fostering Collaboration Between Employers and Educational Institutions

Strong partnerships between employers and educational institutions are essential for integrating on- and off-the-job learning. Roberts et al. (2019) argue that such partnerships are vital for ensuring the effectiveness of apprenticeships. Lester and Bravenboer (2020) also highlight the need for improvement in collaboration between these stakeholders.

The interviewees echoed the importance of collaboration in ensuring appropriate work for apprentices. Ernest Edifor described the process of involving employers in the design of assessments and learning modules: "We had a very long consultation with employers to actually have a look at the content and comment". A consultation process, such as that outlined by Barr and Parkinson (2019), ensures that the curriculum is relevant and meets the needs of both the apprentices and their employers.

Moreover, the use of employer advisory boards has been beneficial in addressing emerging needs, such as the demand for skills in artificial intelligence (AI). As Edifor notes, "The employers are like, look, we want a lot more AI stuff, and so we've managed to have various other sessions for the apprentices where they can improve on their skills when it comes to AI".

### Ensuring the Overall Quality of the Workplace Experience

The workplace experience is a critical component of an apprenticeship. Jackson *et al.* (2017) suggest that placements should provide expansive learning environments that support development beyond basic competence. Inadequate learning opportunities or poorly designed placements can be detrimental to apprentices, as highlighted by Furness and Gilligan (2004).

To ensure the quality of the workplace experience, monitoring and assessing the work-based learning environment is essential. Matt Bungay from City, University of London explains their approach: "It must place equal value on the underpinning theory and the application and evidence of the application in practice". Clearly, a rigorous quality assurance process helps in maintaining high standards and relevance in the apprentices' work.

The role of skills coaches – sometimes referred to as personal tutors or academic advisers – is also significant in monitoring and supporting apprentices. These university staff help in identifying gaps in skills and ensuring that apprentices meet the knowledge, skills, and behaviours (KSBs) required for the apprentices' roles. As Manchester Metropolitan University's Edifor explains, "They provide that coaching . . . helping them meet the KSBs . . . they meet with their learners and the employers to review".

### Balancing Employer Needs With Academic Requirements

Balancing the needs of employers with the academic requirements of the apprenticeship programme is a delicate task. University of Stirling's Lynsey Joyce emphasises the importance of managing employer expectations: "It's managing those expectations on the employer's side of what a student can achieve being mindful as well that they're also students". This balance ensures that apprentices are not overwhelmed and that their work remains aligned with their academic goals.

Ernest Edifor highlights the challenges of managing diverse requirements from multiple employers, especially in open cohorts with small and medium-sized enterprises (SMEs): "SMEs may have different requirements . . . we try to be as generic as we can in various aspects so that we are not being too specific". Such an approach helps in catering to a wide range of needs while maintaining the relevance and applicability of the learning outcomes.

In summary, then, ensuring that apprentices engage in appropriate and meaningful work involves addressing multiple challenges. These challenges relate to identifying suitable tasks, providing adequate mentoring and support, fostering collaboration between employers and educational institutions, and ensuring the overall quality of the placement experience. Both the literature and the interviews conducted here underscore the importance of a coordinated and flexible approach that considers the diverse needs of apprentices, employers, and educational institutions.

By addressing these challenges through effective planning, continuous support, and strong partnerships, stakeholders can create enriching and valuable apprenticeship experiences that benefit both the apprentices and their employers. It may seem obvious, but such a holistic approach is essential for the success and sustainability of apprenticeship programmes.

## Adapting Assessment Approaches

Much of the literature on assessing apprenticeships highlights the importance of aligning assessments with the unique workplace context and intended learning outcomes. Key themes include the use of authentic assessment methods, the challenges posed by workplace variability, the need for flexible and innovative assessment strategies, and ensuring parity of assessment across different employers. Each of these themes is discussed next.

### Authentic Work-Based Assessment Methods

The literature emphasises the significance of authentic work-based assessment methods. Rowe (2018) discusses the importance of workplace projects, reflective practice, and employer mentoring in degree apprenticeships, while Scholtz (2020) examines the use of portfolios and performance appraisals for assessing work-based learning. In a similar vein, Lester and Costley (2010) and Lillis and Bravenboer (2020) highlight the role of reflective practice, self-managed learning, and employer involvement in WBL assessment. Meanwhile, Costley and Armsby (2007) argue for the use of generic work-based assessment criteria that capture the transdisciplinary nature of WBL as opposed to traditional subject-based criteria.

In line with scholars such as Rowe, interviewees support the use of authentic assessment methods. As experienced work-based learning consultant Ann Minton emphasises, "Your assessment strategy should draw on authentic sources of work that arise in the workplace . . . real work activity is used to inform and drive the assessment process". Buckinghamshire New University's Jonathan Jackson concurs:

> In as many of the modules as possible, we try to shoot for authentic assessments that have some flexibility built in. So, if they're learning theories, or learning content in a module, at the end completing an assignment, if that assignment is based on an organisational context – which can be their own – I think that adds depth and helps with the alignment.

An authentic assessment approach, then, ensures that assignments are relevant and contextualised to the apprentices' actual work experiences.

### Challenges in Assessing Workplace Activities

Assessing workplace activities presents several challenges due to the variability and complexity of different work environments. Scholtz (2020) found misalignment between portfolio evidence and intended learning outcomes as a result of variations in workplace contexts and limited collaboration between academic and workplace supervisors. Similarly, Costley and Armsby (2007) and Doherty and Stephens (2020) highlight the challenges of assessing WBL across diverse workplace settings, underscoring the need for flexible assessment criteria.

Interviewees echoed these challenges. Ernest Edifor notes the difficulties posed by security constraints and administrative burdens: "Security has been a massive one . . . students have to go through various hoops to get work . . . it's quite messy when you're assessing some workplace activities". Another challenge mentioned by programme director Matt Bungay is aligning end-point assessments[1] with academic qualifications to prevent apprentices from completing one without the other: "You can't achieve one without the other so you can't get your MSc unless you've completed your EPA".

### Flexible and Innovative Assessment Strategies

To address the challenges of WBL assessment, several authors advocate for flexible and innovative strategies. Saville *et al.* (2020), for example, found that a strengths-based curriculum and assessment approach contributed to higher grades for apprentices compared to traditional degree students. Mulkeen *et al.* (2019) suggest integrating academic and professional assessments to streamline degree apprenticeships. Lillis and Bravenboer (2020) emphasise the interconnection between successful WBL practices and valid workplace-based assessment to build "pedagogical resilience" in post-pandemic higher education.

Interviewees provided examples of innovative assessment practices. Consultant Ann Minton describes how healthcare students produce materials that benefit their organisations, as part of their assessment: "Healthcare students are involved in health promotion activity . . . they might produce health promotion leaflets artefacts that can be used by their patients". Meanwhile, programme leader Jonathan Jackson highlights the use of reflective essays, personal development plans, and action inquiries as part of the assessment strategy: "We've historically used . . . action inquiry . . . we've kind of evolved that to a more flexible work-based research project".

Finally, the University of Lincoln's Sharon Green stresses the importance of leaving assessment strategies flexible enough to adapt to industry changes:

> I'm always disappointed in validation events with our own university or externally where I just see death by assignment because that's not what an apprenticeship is about. It's about innovative methods of assessment that align with industry needs and can be adapted to change with the currency of those sectors.

### Ensuring Parity of Assessment Across Employers

Ensuring comparable assessment across different employers is crucial for maintaining academic rigour and fairness. Perusso and Wagenaar (2022) note disparities in WBL adoption across European countries and disciplines, pointing out a lack of quality assurance methods. Costley (2007) and Lester and Costley (2010), meanwhile, stress the importance of recognising the unique forms of knowledge developed in WBL and adapting assessment accordingly.

Interviewees stressed the importance of maintaining parity through robust assessment frameworks. Ann Minton suggests using learning contracts to ensure consistency in negotiated modules: "You need to have very clear criteria that you're sticking to . . . so that somebody's not looking at something very simple and somebody else is looking at something very complex". Meanwhile, Ernest Edifor describes how Manchester Metropolitan's verification and moderation processes help ensure assessments are fair and unbiased: "We have a very robust moderation system . . . the programmes team, the internal verifier, and the external examiner ensure that there is parity".

Meanwhile, Sharon Green suggests using case studies to decouple assessment from specific employer contexts: "We do use a lot of case studies because the moment you lift it away from the employer domain and put it back into a case study scenario . . . you're teaching across a range of disciplines, you're helping individuals to be multifaceted". Green also recommends involving employers in setting case studies: "We get the employers to set the case studies with us . . . and the employers come in and look at the presentations with us".

In summary, then, the literature and interview data reveal a consensus on the need to adapt assessment approaches to the specific context of apprenticeships, using authentic work-based methods that align with intended learning outcomes. However, several challenges persist, including workplace variability, the need for effective academic–employer collaboration, and ensuring parity of assessment across different employers. To address these challenges, a number of recommendations may be made.

Above all, perhaps, it is clear that effective collaboration is essential for aligning assessments with workplace activities and ensuring that they meet both academic and professional standards. As such, regular consultations and the use of employer advisory boards can help in designing relevant assessments.

Next, assessment methods should be flexible and contextualised: by utilising a variety of assessment methods, such as reflective essays, action inquiries, and workplace projects, the diverse contexts of apprenticeships may be accommodated and the relevance of assessments enhanced. At the same time, robust quality assurance frameworks are essential. Establishing clear criteria and rigorous verification and moderation processes can ensure parity of assessment across different employers and sectors. This includes using learning contracts and involving external examiners to validate assessments.

It is also recommended that those involved in assessing apprentices' work should be offered continuous professional development. Clearly, providing training for academic staff and workplace mentors on effective assessment practices can improve the quality and consistency of assessments. This might include training on reflective practice, self-managed learning, and the use of authentic assessment methods.

Finally, institutions should leverage technology to deliver innovative assessment solutions. Matt Bungay advocates for the use of virtual reality (VR) on apprenticeships, for example, while other digital tools can facilitate innovative assessment practices, especially in situations where physical presence is challenging. Such tools can enable peer-to-peer assessment and provide a platform for interactive and immersive learning experiences, as well as help to develop a sense of community that is otherwise difficult to cultivate.

By adopting these recommendations, educational institutions and employers can improve the assessment of apprenticeships, ensuring that the process is meaningful, fair, and aligned with the intended learning outcomes. It might also be suggested that such a holistic approach will contribute to the overall success and sustainability of work-based learning programmes, benefiting both apprentices and their employers.

## Providing Academic and Pastoral Support

Successful apprenticeship programmes rely heavily on comprehensive academic and pastoral support systems that address the unique needs of apprentices. For one thing, apprentices spend a significant amount of their time at their workplace, which can lead to feelings of disconnection from the university. Hughes and Saieva (2021) and Wenham *et al.* (2020) stress the importance of creating a sense of community despite limited face-to-face interactions. Interviewees here noted similar challenges. For example, Sharon Green observes, "[apprentices] spend more time with the employers . . . most of them don't have that strong learning community".

Both the literature and interview data emphasise key elements such as the tripartite relationship between the apprentice, employer, and university, the need for flexibility, the importance of pastoral care, and the role of ongoing mentoring. Each of these elements is discussed next.

### The Tripartite Relationship

The literature consistently highlights the crucial role of the tripartite relationship between the apprentice, employer, and university. Hughes and Saieva (2021) and Wenham *et al.* (2020) emphasise that effective support requires close collaboration and communication among all three parties. This partnership approach ensures that each party respects the others' needs, which is fundamental to providing holistic support to apprentices.

Interviewees echoed this sentiment, noting that effective communication between these groups is essential for maintaining support structures. Consultant Ann Minton describes the importance of establishing a personal tutor relationship that facilitates ongoing communication and support: "You need a personal tutor relationship . . . the student may be studying a number of different modules but they've got a key point of contact who maintains oversight of their programme throughout the time". This approach ensures that apprentices receive consistent support tailored to their individual needs.

## Flexible Delivery

Flexibility in training delivery is another recurring theme in the literature. Hughes and Saieva (2021) argue that universities must recognise the constraints under which employers operate, particularly SMEs, and adapt provision accordingly. The need for flexibility is also emphasised by Saville *et al.* (2020), who call for funding and policies that enable providers to offer a tailored approach to delivery, especially for apprentices from disadvantaged backgrounds.

Interview data highlight the practical challenges of maintaining this flexibility, however. Manchester Metropolitan's Ernest Edifor notes the difficulties in integrating apprentices into university life due to their limited time on campus: "They spend more time with the employers . . . most of them don't have that strong learning community". This challenge underscores the need for universities to develop flexible support mechanisms that accommodate the varied schedules and commitments of apprentices.

## Pastoral Care

The importance of pastoral support, particularly for apprentices' wellbeing and resilience, is highlighted by several authors. Marsden and Youde (2012) emphasise the role of tutors in being proactively available and approachable, helping apprentices navigate the challenges of balancing employment with study. Indeed, Gambin *et al.*'s (2011) analysis found a statistically significant association between higher apprenticeship completion rates and the provision of pastoral care.

Interviewees here reinforced the need for robust pastoral support. Ann Minton describes how ongoing communication is crucial for supporting apprentices effectively: "I think it's having a regular meeting . . . you have to check in with your student between every eight to twelve weeks . . . it gives you the carrot and it gives you the stick". Such a structured approach ensures that apprentices receive consistent support and any challenges they face may be addressed promptly.

## Ongoing Mentoring

Previous authors have suggested that mentorship is a key component of successful apprenticeship programmes. Wenham *et al.* (2020) report that apprentices highly value face-to-face mentoring, and Hughes and Saieva (2021) identify mentoring as a crucial factor influencing completion rates. Marsden and Youde (2012) discuss how frequent mentor meetings create a sense of "transactional presence" and connection for remote learners.

Interviewees also emphasised the importance of mentoring. Manchester Metropolitan's Ernest Edifor describes the crucial role that their skills coaches play in a cohesive system of support for apprentices: "The skills coach is the glue who holds everything together so they make sure that right from the unit level to the programme level everything is working smoothly". Edifor argues that such continuous mentoring ensures that apprentices receive guidance and support throughout their training.

### Communication and Engagement

Effective communication is crucial for supporting apprentices – especially so, given the remote nature of their situation. The literature suggests the use of formal systems for monitoring progress and engagement, as described by Marsden and Youde (2012) and Wenham *et al.* (2020). Meanwhile, interviewees here highlighted the importance of clear and consistent communication. Ann Minton advocates for an iterative process of maintaining contact: "You keep in contact with them . . . checking in, you know, are you OK, is everything going well?"

Technology also plays an important role in facilitating communication. Minton, who was involved in the use of virtual learning environments in work-based learning as far back as the early 2000s, points to the use of tools like Blackboard Collaborate and ePortfolios to maintain engagement and monitor progress: "You can use things like OneDrive, PebblePad, discussion boards . . . so if your students are remote, they can share ideas". Matt Bungay also notes that the use of technology such as virtual and mixed reality can help widen participation in apprenticeships: "you give them a VR headset, it's much more accessible for them to achieve the training and they don't miss out because this particular course is only delivered in London, so you rule out a lot of people".

### Tailored Support

Adapting support mechanisms to meet individual needs is another important consideration. Wenham *et al.* (2020), for example, suggest that academic tutors should receive training on supporting apprentices' diverse needs. Indeed, effective delivery of apprenticeships requires that both tutors and line managers are adequately trained (Taylor-Smith *et al.*, 2024). Such training ensures that they understand the specific needs and regulatory requirements associated with apprenticeships. Ernest Edifor points out the necessity of staff training to ensure that apprentices' university experience is comparable to that of traditional students: "If teachers don't really understand apprenticeships then it becomes very, very difficult to deliver".

Interviewees similarly stressed the importance of personalised support. Edifor explains how Manchester Metropolitan University uses various data-driven systems to flag high-risk apprentices, again highlighting the role of technology:

"We have mechanisms to monitor apprentices' progress at unit level . . . to identify high-risk apprentices and how to support them". The University of Lincoln's Sharon Green, meanwhile, stresses the importance of contextualising individual plans, despite the challenges posed by fixed degree curricula. She provides an example from their social work programme: "In the first module it's actually written into the curriculum and it's the first assignment – they develop themselves a five-year plan . . . From that moment, that person can take very early responsibility for their learning".

To summarise, providing comprehensive academic and pastoral support is essential for the success of apprenticeship programmes. The literature and interview data highlight the importance of the tripartite relationship, flexibility in training delivery, robust pastoral care, and ongoing mentoring. Addressing challenges such as reduced time on campus, while maintaining effective communication, leveraging technology, and personalising support can enhance the apprentice experience.

By integrating these elements through a holistic approach, universities and employers can create supportive environments that foster the academic and professional growth of apprentices.

## Institutional Challenges

While many of the challenges raised by interviewees here are relatively well documented, the interview data also reveal some important institutional issues that are less prominent in the existing literature.

The first of these issues is the need for apprenticeships to be established as a strategic priority within the host university. Such a commitment often involves significant investment and a shift in institutional culture, which cannot be taken for granted. Ernest Edifor explains how Manchester Metropolitan integrated apprenticeships into university strategy to help ensure that the quality of their delivery was on a par with their existing programmes: "We've set degree apprenticeships as a strategic priority for the institution and we invest very, very heavily in it". Matt Bungay reinforces this idea by highlighting the alignment of apprenticeships with university strategy at University of London: "I think the apprenticeships have to meet the strategy of the university. That's the biggest thing".

Implementing work-based programmes often involves overcoming significant internal challenges within universities, which is perhaps why the positioning of apprenticeships as a strategic priority is so important. Such challenges include aligning existing systems and processes with the needs of work-based learning, as Lynsey Joyce elaborates: "There were lots of internal challenges for us to address and overcome at different stages . . . it was bringing in a more flexible approach to how we were designing and delivering degrees".

It is also clear that the complexity of regulatory and legislative requirements is a significant challenge for apprenticeship programmes, and universities must be prepared to navigate these. Jonathan Jackson highlights the importance of considering the regulatory environment from the start: "So, right from the programme design, before the first teaching session, we were thinking about the regulatory environment and building that in so that we have systems in place to capture the metrics or the milestones or the KPIs we need".

Managing the governance and reporting requirements for apprenticeship programmes can be complex and time-consuming, and institutions need robust systems to handle these aspects effectively. Joyce provides one example: "We had the external reporting that you had to do to the funder . . . there was lots of learning to be done internally for us to be able to effectively deliver". Edifor also notes the burden of regulatory requirements: "It is costly, in terms of the regulatory burden. If care is not taken and things keep going the way they are going I think it's just a matter of time before a lot of training providers say it's not worth it".

## Conclusion

The design and delivery of work-based degree programmes present unique challenges that can only be effectively addressed through close collaboration between universities and employers. This chapter has highlighted the critical importance of deep, strategic partnerships in aligning the academic and workplace components of apprenticeships.

Successful programmes are characterised by co-creation at every stage, from initial design through to delivery, assessment, and review. As Ann Minton asserts, "it starts with the employers. You can't do it without the employers. The employers and the learners are at the heart of it". Employers must be actively involved in shaping curricula and pedagogies that integrate theory and practice, and that meet the evolving needs of their industries. Universities, in turn, must be responsive and adaptable, working closely with employers to ensure that programmes remain relevant and valuable.

Effective collaboration rests on a foundation of open, regular communication and a shared commitment to the apprentice experience. Mechanisms such as employer advisory boards, workplace mentoring, and tripartite progress reviews are essential for fostering alignment, identifying challenges and opportunities, and supporting apprentices to connect their learning across contexts.

Assessment is another key area where university-employer collaboration is vital. Authentic, work-based assessment methods must be designed in partnership to ensure they are robust, relevant, and consistent across diverse workplace settings. This requires flexibility and innovation on the part of universities, as Lynsey Joyce suggests: "It's being prepared to be agile. It's being prepared to change and to move and to be responsive". Meanwhile, employers must also demonstrate willingness to engage in the assessment process.

More broadly, the success of work-based degrees depends on establishing apprenticeships as a shared strategic priority, with buy-in and investment from both university leadership and employers. Both parties must work together to navigate complex regulatory requirements, ensure appropriate resourcing, and build the organisational capabilities to deliver high-quality programmes.

Ultimately, close collaboration between universities and employers is the key to unlocking the full potential of apprenticeships. By working in partnership to design and deliver programmes that integrate academic learning with meaningful workplace experience, universities and employers can develop the skilled professionals needed to drive innovation, productivity, and social mobility. The challenges are not insignificant, but through genuine collaboration and a shared vision, they can be transformed into opportunities for apprentices, employers, universities, and society as a whole.

## Note

1 In England, the end-point assessment (EPA) is the final, independent assessment of whether an apprentice has developed the skills, knowledge, and behaviours specified in the industry-defined apprenticeship standard.

## References

Barr, M., Andrei, O. and Kallia, M. (2023) 'Widening Access to Higher Education through Degree-Level Apprenticeships in Software Engineering', in *2023 IEEE Frontiers in Education Conference (FIE). 2023 IEEE Frontiers in Education Conference (FIE)*, pp. 1–8. Available at: https://doi.org/10.1109/FIE58773.2023.10343199.

Barr, M. and Parkinson, J. (2019) 'Developing a Work-based Software Engineering Degree in Collaboration with Industry', in *Proceedings of the 1st UK & Ireland Computing Education Research Conference*. Canterbury, United Kingdom: Association for Computing Machinery (UKICER), pp. 1–7. Available at: https://doi.org/10.1145/3351287.3351292.

Barr, M. et al. (2024) 'The Development of Students' Professional Competencies on a Work-Based Software Engineering Program', in *Proceedings of the 55th ACM Technical Symposium on Computer Science Education V. 1*. New York, NY, USA: Association for Computing Machinery (SIGCSE 2024), pp. 81–87. Available at: https://doi.org/10.1145/3626252.3630944.

Billett, S. (2016) 'Apprenticeship as a Mode of Learning and Model of Education', Edited by E. Smith. *Education + Training*, 58(6), pp. 613–628. Available at: https://doi.org/10.1108/ET-01-2016-0001.

Costley, C. (2007) 'Work-Based Learning: Assessment and Evaluation in Higher Education', *Assessment & Evaluation in Higher Education* [Preprint]. Available at: https://doi.org/10.1080/02602930600848184.

Costley, C. and Armsby, P. (2007) 'Work-Based Learning Assessed as a Field or a Mode of Study', *Assessment & Evaluation in Higher Education*, 32(1), pp. 21–33. Available at: https://doi.org/10.1080/02602930600848267.

Doherty, O. and Stephens, S. (2020) 'The Cultural Web, Higher Education and Work-Based Learning', *Industry and Higher Education*, 34(5), pp. 330–341. Available at: https://doi.org/10.1177/0950422219879614.

Fuller, A. and Unwin, L. (2017) 'Apprenticeship Quality and Social Mobility', in *Better Apprenticeships: Access, Quality and Labour Market Outcomes in the English Apprenticeship System*. London, UK: The Sutton Trust, pp. 9–36. Available at: www.suttontrust.com/our-research/better-apprenticeships-quality-access-social-mobility/.

Furness, S. and Gilligan, P. (2004) 'Fit for Purpose: Issues from Practice Placements, Practice Teaching and the Assessment of Students' Practice', *Social Work Education*, 23(4), pp. 465–479. Available at: https://doi.org/10.1080/0261547042000245053.

Gambin, L., Hasluck, C. and Hogarth, T. (2011) 'Maximizing Apprenticeship Completion Rates in England', *Canadian Apprenticeship Journal*, 4. Available at: http://journals.sfu.ca/caj/index.php/caj-jca/article/view/59 (Accessed: 6 May 2024).

Hughes, C. and Saieva, G. (2021) 'The Journey of Higher Degree Apprenticeships', in D.A. Morley and M.G. Jamil (eds) *Applied Pedagogies for Higher Education: Real World Learning and Innovation across the Curriculum*. Cham: Springer International Publishing, pp. 243–266. Available at: https://doi.org/10.1007/978-3-030-46951-1_11.

Jackson, D. *et al.* (2017) 'Employer Understanding of Work-Integrated Learning and the Challenges of Engaging in Work Placement Opportunities', *Studies in Continuing Education*, 39(1), pp. 35–51. Available at: https://doi.org/10.1080/0158037X.2016.1228624.

Lester, S. and Bravenboer, D. (2020) *Sustainable Degree Apprenticeships*. London, UK: Middlesex University.

Lester, S. and Costley, C. (2010) 'Work-Based Learning at Higher Education Level: Value, Practice and Critique', *Studies in Higher Education*, 35(5), pp. 561–575. Available at: https://doi.org/10.1080/03075070903216635.

Lillis, F. and Bravenboer, D. (2020) 'The Best Practice in Work-Integrated Pedagogy for Degree Apprenticeships in a Post-Viral Future', *Higher Education, Skills and Work-Based Learning*, 10(5), pp. 727–739. Available at: https://doi.org/10.1108/HESWBL-04-2020-0071.

Marsden, F. and Youde, A. (2012) 'Fostering a Transactional Presence: A Practical Guide to Supporting Work-Based learners', in B. Jones and S. Oosthuizen (eds) *Part-Time Study: The New Paradigm for Higher Education? A Selection of Papers Presented at the 2011 Conference of the Universities Association for Lifelong Learning*. Leicester, UK: UALL. Available at: www.uall.ac.uk/part-time-study (Accessed: 6 May 2024).

Messmann, G. and Mulder, R.H. (2015) 'Conditions for Apprentices' Learning Activities at Work', *Journal of Vocational Education & Training*, 67(4), pp. 578–596. Available at: https://doi.org/10.1080/13636820.2015.1094745.

Muehlemann, S. and Wolter, S.C. (2014) 'Return on Investment of Apprenticeship Systems for Enterprises: Evidence from Cost-Benefit Analyses', *IZA Journal of Labor Policy*, 3(1), p. 25. Available at: https://doi.org/10.1186/2193-9004-3-25.

Mulkeen, J. *et al.* (2019) 'Degree and Higher Level Apprenticeships: An Empirical Investigation of Stakeholder Perceptions of Challenges and Opportunities', *Studies in Higher Education*, 44(2), pp. 333–346. Available at: https://doi.org/10.1080/03075079.2017.1365357.

Nawaz, R. *et al.* (2022) 'The Impact of Degree Apprenticeships: Analysis, Insights and Policy Recommendations', *Transforming Government: People, Process and Policy*, 17(3), pp. 372–386. Available at: https://doi.org/10.1108/TG-07-2022-0105.

Perusso, A. and Wagenaar, R. (2022) 'The State of Work-Based Learning Development in EU Higher Education: Learnings from the WEXHE Project', *Studies in Higher Education*, 47(7), pp. 1423–1439. Available at: https://doi.org/10.1080/03075079.2021.1904233.

Roberts, A., Storm, M. and Flynn, S. (2019) 'Workplace Mentoring of Degree Apprentices: Developing Principles for Practice', *Higher Education, Skills and Work-Based Learning*, 9(2), pp. 211–224. Available at: https://doi.org/10.1108/HESWBL-10-2018-0108.

Rowe, L. (2018) 'Managing Degree Apprenticeships Through a Work Based Learning Framework: Opportunities and Challenges', in D.A. Morley (ed) *Enhancing Employability in Higher Education through Work Based Learning*. Cham: Springer International Publishing, pp. 51–69. Available at: https://doi.org/10.1007/978-3-319-75166-5_4.

Rowe, L. et al. (2017) 'The Challenges of Managing Degree Apprentices in the Workplace: A Manager's Perspective', *Journal of Work-Applied Management*, 9(2), pp. 185–199. Available at: https://doi.org/10.1108/JWAM-07-2017-0021.

Sauli, F. (2021) 'The Collaboration between Swiss Initial Vocational Education and Training Partners: Perceptions of Apprentices, Teachers, and In-Company Trainers', *Empirical Research in Vocational Education and Training*, 13(1), p. 10. Available at: https://doi.org/10.1186/s40461-021-00114-2.

Sauli, F., Wenger, M. and Berger, J.-L. (2021) 'Supporting Apprentices' Integration of School- and Workplace-Based Learning in Swiss Initial Vocational Education and Training', *Research in Post-Compulsory Education*, 26(4), pp. 387–409. Available at: https://doi.org/10.1080/13596748.2021.1980660.

Saville, K.-M. et al. (2020) 'Using Strength-Based Approaches to Fulfil Academic Potential in Degree Apprenticeships', *Higher Education, Skills and Work-Based Learning*, 10(4), pp. 659–671. Available at: https://doi.org/10.1108/HESWBL-02-2019-0024.

Scholtz, D. (2020) *Assessing Workplace-Based Learning*. Available at: http://digital-knowledge.cput.ac.za/handle/11189/7926 (Accessed: 6 May 2024).

Taylor-Smith, E. et al. (2024) 'Investigating Induction Training for CS Work-Based Learning Workplace Mentors', in *Proceedings of the UK & Ireland Computing Education Research Conference*. Manchester, UK: Association for Computing Machinery (UKICER).

Wenham, K.E., Valencia-Forrester, F. and Backhaus, B. (2020) 'Make or Break: The Role and Support Needs of Academic Advisors in Work-Integrated Learning Courses', *Higher Education Research & Development* [Preprint]. Available at: www.tandfonline.com/doi/abs/10.1080/07294360.2019.1705254 (Accessed: 6 May 2024).

Wolter, S.C. and Ryan, P. (2011) 'Apprenticeship', in E.A. Hanushek, S. Machin and L. Woessmann (eds) *Handbook of the Economics of Education*. Elsevier, pp. 521–576. Available at: https://doi.org/10.1016/B978-0-444-53429-3.00011-9.

# Chapter 3

# Higher Education Apprenticeship Pedagogies
## A Multilateral Approach

*Jessica Lomas*

## Introduction

In the ever-changing and dynamic landscape of higher education, the diversity of students and learners within academic ecosystems continues to expand. Traditional students, with their varied backgrounds, experiences, and intellectual approaches, coexist alongside a distinct cohort: apprentice learners. Unlike their counterparts, apprentice learners are tasked not only with achieving academic excellence but also with meeting the demands of their respective workplaces and industries. This convergence of academic and professional expectations necessitates a re-evaluation of pedagogical approaches within higher education institutions so as to better equip educators with the pedagogic tools to teach the next generation of learners. This chapter intends to explore the intricate intersection of higher education and apprenticeship pedagogies, aiming to shed light on the complex nature of supporting apprentice learners, effectively. Through a threefold approach, this chapter considers pedagogical adaptations and the integration of theory-driven and traditional teaching practices, alongside the enhancement of the overall learner experience.

Firstly, this chapter confronts the notion of juxtaposing learning pathways. The first part attempts to scrutinise the distinctions between traditional student learning and apprenticeship learning. It also probes how these pathways are inherently different and how educators can navigate these variances to support apprentice learners through pedagogical adaptations better. Central to this discussion are concepts of belonging and compassionate approaches, acknowledging the unique challenges apprentice learners face in reconciling academic pursuits whilst managing their professional obligations. Additionally, we explore the pivotal role of student partnerships in fostering a supportive learning environment conducive to the academic and professional growth of apprentices. In this exploration, the chapter considers the challenges and opportunities of apprenticeships, albeit applied to a higher education context, whilst drawing on Fuller and Unwin's (2011) insights into expansive learning environments. In doing so, this section aims to provide valuable insights into

DOI: 10.4324/9781003496779-3

the unique requirements and experiences of apprentice learners, informing a discussion on adapting pedagogical approaches to meet their diverse needs.

The second part evaluates the integration of theory-driven and traditional teaching practices as mechanisms to support the apprentice learner best. Recognising the dynamic nature of pedagogy, this portion of the chapter examines traditional and institutional student partnerships, dissecting their relevance in the context of apprentice learners. Tripartite relationships involving institutions, students, and employers come under scrutiny as this section unravels the intricacies of adapting pedagogical approaches. Emphasis is placed on the flexibility and adaptability required to navigate the complex landscape of apprentice education effectively. Drawing upon the works of Biggs *et al.* (2022), this part of the chapter explores the concept of constructive alignment and its application in designing pedagogical approaches that resonate with and support apprentices. Additionally, Hattie and Timperley's (2007) research on the power of feedback further informs the discussion on the importance of providing timely and meaningful feedback to apprentice learners in order to enhance their learning outcomes.

Finally, in the third part, the chapter advocates for the expansion of pedagogical lenses to encompass a holistic view of apprentice learning, emphasising the importance of fostering inclusive and engaging learning environments constructed around industry requirements. Moreover, building upon the work of Boud and Falchikov (2006), the discussion delves into the concept of "assessment for learning" and its relevance in evaluating both incoming and outgoing knowledge among apprentice learners. Furthermore, insights from Bovill *et al.* (2011) on student co-creation of teaching approaches and curricula provide a guiding framework for the exploration of strategies to enhance the learner experience for apprentice learners. Embracing peer-to-peer and near-to-peer engagement models, the chapter suggests the creation of a truly dynamic learning environment nestled within the evolving landscape of higher education: a setting that promotes collaboration, critical thinking, practical application, and reflective practice among apprentices. Through these initiatives, educators and institutions can empower apprentice learners to take ownership of their learning journey, ultimately nurturing their academic and professional development.

## Understanding Apprentice Learners

Apprentice learners represent a unique cohort within higher education, blending academic pursuits with professional responsibilities. To comprehend their learning needs and challenges, it is imperative to contrast traditional student learning with apprenticeship learning, explore the concept of a compassionate approach (Gibbs, 2017), and highlight the significance of student partnerships in supporting their academic development.

## Differences Between Traditional Student Learning and Apprenticeship Learning

Traditional student learning predominantly occurs within the confines of academic institutions, focusing on theoretical knowledge acquisition and assessment. In contrast, apprenticeship learning intertwines academic study with on-the-job training, emphasising practical skills acquisition and real-world application (Billett, 2002). This distinction underscores the dual nature of apprentice learners' educational journey, where they must navigate academic rigours alongside workplace demands. Moreover, apprenticeship learning often entails a more experiential and hands-on approach, with learning outcomes closely aligned with industry standards and job requirements (Eraut, 2004; Fuller and Unwin, 2011). Unlike traditional students who may prioritise grades and academic achievements, apprentice learners are driven by the pursuit of professional competence and career advancement, shaping their learning motivations and priorities.

There exist other apparent differences between students and learners. For example, students are tasked with meeting their module learning outcomes, eventually attaining a degree. In contrast, apprentice learners must meet the exact expectations whilst simultaneously addressing their requisite knowledge, skills, and behaviours (KSBs) and working, often full time, in their given profession. KSBs are foundational elements in the development and assessment of apprentices within the context of apprenticeship learning (Roberts *et al.*, 2019). KSBs encompass a broad range of competencies, including both technical skills specific to the apprenticeship trade or profession and transferable skills essential for success in the workplace. The ideology is that the apprentice programme should be designed and taught in a way to support the development of these competencies.

Furthermore, at a modular level, it should be evident to apprentices how these KSBs are connected to their professional environment. By delineating the critical knowledge areas, technical skills, and behavioural attributes required for proficiency in a particular field, KSBs provide a framework for curriculum development, assessment, and ongoing skills development throughout the apprenticeship journey (Pius, 2024). This transparency ensures that KSBs are transferable, thereby enhancing career development opportunities. The KSBs also act as measurable outcomes, which contribute to a successful end-point assessment and competition of the apprenticeship. Given the importance of these competencies, it then becomes vital that institutions, working in tandem with apprenticeship employers, regularly update their learning materials in line with both industry standards and requisite KSBs. A study undertaken by Hughes and Saieva (2019) highlighted the need to incorporate employers within the development process in order to ensure not only the viability of a programme but also success. In general, integrating KSBs into apprenticeship programmes ensures that apprentices are equipped with the multifaceted competencies needed to excel professionally within their degree apprenticeship and contribute meaningfully to their respective industries (Pius and English, 2023).

Another critical difference between traditional students and apprentices, beyond KSBs, is the tripartite relationship. The tripartite collaboration in apprenticeship learning is not only logistical but also social. Degree-level apprentices rely on interest and support from their employers and colleagues to foster meaningful integration between their work and studies (Roberts *et al.*, 2019). This collaboration extends beyond peer support into meaningful connections and informs both their work and academic pursuits. The university plays a crucial role in facilitating these essential connections, serving as a bridge between the academic and professional realms.

Furthermore, effective work-based learning hinges on a partnership among apprentices, employers, and universities, as outlined by Smith and Betts (2000). This partnership is characterised by collaborative self-interest, transparency in requirements, and negotiation to establish an agreed program of learning. The success of this collaboration is contingent upon all parties engaging actively and ensuring a mutually beneficial outcome. However, barriers such as employer disengagement, cultural mismatches, and challenges in aligning learning outcomes with workplace objectives can disrupt this delicate balance (Fuller and Unwin, 2011).

## Concepts of Belonging and Compassionate Approaches

Belonging and compassionate approaches play pivotal roles in fostering a supportive learning environment for apprentices. Cultivating a sense of belonging, wherein apprentice learners feel valued, included, and supported, is essential for their academic and personal well-being (Hager and Hodkinson, 2009; Fuller and Unwin, 2011). Compassionate approaches, therefore, are characterised by empathy, understanding, and flexibility and are equally crucial in addressing the diverse needs and challenges of apprentice learners. By this, it is meant that the learners come from varying educational backgrounds and personal circumstances, often varying greatly from a mainstream student. Smith *et al.*'s (2021) study touches on other disadvantages; for example, feeling stigmatised (Mallman and Lee, 2016) or the notion of imposter syndrome, whereby individuals who externally may appear high-performing internally may not feel successful, which could lead to anxiousness around acceptance and belonging (Ramsey and Brown, 2018).

Recognising the competing demands placed on apprentice learners, educators must adopt a compassionate stance, accommodating their unique circumstances and providing tailored support (Eraut, 2004). This compassionate ethos fosters trust, rapport, and collaboration, facilitating meaningful learning experiences for apprentice learners.

In the context of higher education apprenticeships, where learners' ambitions and goals diverge from traditional academic pathways, a compassionate approach to teaching and learning is paramount. Maxwell (2017) discusses the concept of compassionate empathy, emphasising its significance in professional practice and ethical obligations. As apprentice learners navigate the dual demands of academic study and workplace responsibilities, they require support that acknowledges their unique journey and aspirations. Gibbs (2017) advocates for compassionate pedagogy, recognising the importance of empathy and care in educational settings. This notion resonates deeply in the context of apprentice learning, where learners are striving to achieve different objectives compared to their counterparts in traditional academia. The pedagogy of compassion includes three essential concepts (Vandeyar and Swart, 2018):

1. Overcoming binary thinking and examining deeply held convictions entails disrupting accepted ideas.
2. Shifting perspectives by empathetically interacting with diverse individuals in educational contexts.
3. Cultivating optimism and nurturing long-lasting harmony.

The compassionate approach can acknowledge the multifaceted challenges faced by apprentice learners and seeks to provide them with the necessary support and understanding. Ultimately, apprentices need to feel cared for and about, which can occur through compassionate support.

## *Significance of Student Partnerships*

Student partnerships serve as a cornerstone of apprentice learners' academic development, facilitating collaboration, peer learning, and mutual support. Within the context of apprenticeship learning, student partnerships extend beyond traditional classroom interactions to encompass collaborative endeavours within the workplace and academic settings (Fuller and Unwin, 2011). These partnerships enable apprentice learners to leverage collective expertise, share best practices, and navigate complex challenges collectively. Moreover, student partnerships bridge the gap between academic theory and practical application, empowering apprentice learners to contextualise their learning within real-world scenarios. One way in which this can occur is by fostering the care theory (Noddings, 1984). This can occur in a twofold approach, through those who are "cared for" and those who are "cared about" (Vandeyar, 2021). The former is characterised by meetings, offering "attention and motivational displacement" (Vandeyar, 2021, 2163). In the instance of apprentices, such meetings may occur within tripartite reviews, where both the teacher and employer can care for the learning needs and well-being of the apprentice. The latter helps build social capital through informal education, which expands the concept of education beyond just the curriculum and teaching methods. In contrast, informal education can include activities such as career meetings, student services, fairs, workshops, social events, and peer mentoring. It is important to note that where a tripartite meeting is regulated and therefore formalised, it would align with the "cared for" approach.

In the context of understanding the significance of student partnerships within apprenticeship learning, peer learning emerges as a vital tool for fostering collaborative engagement and enhancing apprentices' comprehension of course content (Boud and Falchikov, 2006). Apprentices, like traditional university students, benefit from various forms of peer, collaborative, or cooperative learning, mainly through small group activities. These approaches not only promote the development of collaborative skills but also encourage apprentices to take responsibility for their own learning journey within the workplace and academic settings. However, the effectiveness of peer learning in apprenticeships can be hindered by assessment practices that prioritise individual achievement over collaborative effort (Boud and Falchikov, 2007). Further, although Johnson *et al.*'s (2014) study concerned students, the analysis also has implications for apprentices. Specifically, their work highlights how students may be hesitant to participate in group activities if they believe their individual contributions are not adequately recognised. This same dynamic applies to apprentices, who may perceive collaborative work as undervalued, potentially leading to a reluctance to engage in cooperative learning.

Moreover, unproductive competition within and between apprentice groups may arise if assessment practices foster a sense of rivalry rather than collaboration (Dochy *et al.*, 1999). Thus, fostering a supportive learning environment that values collaborative effort and meaningful engagement among apprentices is essential to optimise the benefits of student partnerships and promote a deeper understanding of course content within apprenticeship programs. In essence, understanding apprentice learners necessitates an exploration of their distinct learning pathways, socio-emotional needs, and collaborative dynamics. That being said, understanding and supporting degree apprentices within the context of higher education presents challenges for academics and scholars, who often operate within capacity constraints and competing demands. However, establishing robust internal university systems and support mechanisms can facilitate the adequate provision of tailored support to degree-level apprentice learners.

Firstly, universities can invest in professional development opportunities for lecturers to enhance their understanding of apprentice education and develop relevant pedagogical skills (Billett, 2002). Workshops, seminars, and training programs focused on apprenticeship pedagogies, socio-emotional support strategies, and collaborative dynamics can equip lecturers with the knowledge and tools needed to engage with apprentice learners effectively. Secondly, universities can establish dedicated support teams or units tasked with providing targeted assistance to degree apprentices (Fuller and Unwin, 2011). These support teams may consist of academic advisors, learning mentors, career departments, and industry liaisons, who work collaboratively to address the diverse needs of the apprentices. This can occur through offering personalised guidance, mentorship, and advocacy. As a result, these support teams can help apprentice learners navigate academic challenges, overcome barriers, and maximise their learning potential. Furthermore, universities can implement comprehensive support systems that leverage technology to enhance communication and facilitate access to resources for both lecturers and apprentice learners (Garrison and Kanuka, 2004). Virtual learning environments, online forums, and digital repositories can serve as platforms for sharing best practices, exchanging ideas, and accessing relevant materials related to apprentice education (Arkorful and Abaidoo, 2015). Additionally, the integration of data analytics and learning analytics tools can enable universities to monitor apprentice learners' progress, identify areas of concern, and provide targeted interventions as needed (Siemens and Long, 2011; Ferguson, 2012). Moreover, universities can foster a culture of collaboration and partnership among lecturers, employers, and apprentice learners to create a supportive ecosystem conducive to learning and growth, thus underpinning and strengthening the tripartite relationship (Hughes and Saieva, 2019). By establishing channels for regular communication, feedback, and collaboration, universities can facilitate meaningful interactions and mutual support among stakeholders, ultimately enhancing the apprentice learning experience.

In summary, supporting apprentice learners within the constraints of academic roles and university systems requires a multifaceted approach that prioritises professional development, dedicated support structures, technological innovation, and collaborative partnerships. By investing in these practical strategies, universities can create inclusive, supportive, and empowering learning environments that meet the unique needs of apprentice learners and foster their academic and professional success. Moreover, by embracing the complexities inherent in apprentice education and leveraging concepts of belonging and compassionate approaches and student partnerships, educators can create inclusive, supportive, and empowering learning environments that resonate with the unique aspirations and challenges of apprentice learners.

## Integrating Theory-Driven and Traditional Teaching Practices

This section delves into the integration of theory-driven and traditional teaching practices, a crucial venture in supporting the unique needs of degree apprentices. It explores traditional and institutional student partnerships and tripartite relationships involving institutions, students, and employers and considers the adaptation of pedagogical approaches most relevant to supporting the apprentice learner journey.

## Traditional and Institutional Partnerships

Traditional student partnerships typically revolve around collaborative learning activities within academic settings, fostering peer support and knowledge exchange (Topping, 2005). However, within the context of apprenticeship learning, partnerships extend far beyond the confines of the classroom to encompass collaborative endeavours within both the workplace and academic environments (Billett, 2002; Fuller and Unwin, 2011). Unlike traditional student partnerships, which primarily focus on academic collaboration, apprentice learners engage in multifaceted partnerships that integrate theoretical knowledge with practical experience. Apprentices collaborate with colleagues and mentors in the workplace to apply classroom concepts to real-world scenarios, gaining invaluable insights into industry practices and developing critical thinking skills essential for professional growth (Evans *et al.*, 2010; Billett, 2002). Additionally, apprentices form collaborative partnerships with academic educators who play a pivotal role in bridging the gap between theoretical learning and practical application. These educators provide guidance, feedback, and support to apprentice learners, facilitating their navigation of complex learning environments and ensuring the integration of academic and workplace learning experiences. As a result, apprenticeship partnerships not only enhance academic learning but also foster the development of essential professional competencies and networks crucial for career advancement.

## Tripartite Relationships: Institutions, Students, and Employers

Tripartite relationships involving institutions, students, and employers are fundamental to the success of apprentice learners. This is because institutions with degree-awarding powers serve as catalysts for learning, providing academic resources, guidance, and accreditation pathways. Employers, on the other hand, offer valuable workplace experiences, mentorship, and opportunities for skill development (Fuller and Unwin, 2011). Navigating these interconnected relationships requires effective communication, collaboration, and mutual understanding among all stakeholders. As a result, universities in many jurisdictions have a legislative obligation to align their curricula with industry standards and expectations, ensuring that degree apprentices acquire relevant skills and competencies (Eraut, 2004). Employers, in turn, play an active role in mentoring apprentice learners, providing meaningful work experiences, and offering feedback to enhance their professional development (Billett, 2002; Hager and Hodkinson, 2009). Moreover, degree apprentices also play a vital role as active participants in the tripartite relationship, bridging the gap between academic theory and workplace practice.

Indeed, within the tripartite relationship, reflective practice emerges as a critical component, facilitating the development of apprentice learners into effective managers and leaders within contemporary organisational environments. Reflective practice enables apprentice learners to cultivate self-awareness, receptiveness, and adaptability, essential skills for navigating the complexities of 21st-century employment (Helyer and Price, 2016). As emphasised by Rowe *et al.* (2020), engaging in reflective practice empowers employees to become more resilient, cope with change effectively, and maintain currency in their skills. Furthermore, reflective practice encourages individuals to learn from both successes and mistakes, fostering continuous improvement and growth. In the context of apprenticeship standards, evidence of applying academic knowledge and theories within the workplace necessitates that learners become critically reflective, identifying how their skills have evolved within their roles (Hughes and Saieva, 2020). While critical self-reflection may pose challenges, its outcomes can be profound, offering individuals the opportunity to gain insights into their professional practice and inform future actions (Rowe *et al.*, 2020). Consequently, the role of the university representative becomes pivotal in actively supporting the development of apprentice learners' reflective capabilities, guiding them in using reflection as a tool for learning and informing their progression toward senior positions. By leveraging reflective practice within the tripartite relationship, apprentices, employers, and the university representative can collaboratively foster a culture of continuous learning and development, ultimately enhancing individual and organisational effectiveness in the dynamic landscape of contemporary business and management. Overall, through reflective practice, apprentice learners integrate theoretical knowledge with practical experiences, drawing connections between classroom learning and real-world applications (Billett, 2002; Eraut, 2004). This reciprocal relationship fosters a deeper understanding of industry dynamics, enhances professional development, and promotes lifelong learning among apprentice learners (Goodman and Kooner-Evans, 2024).

### Adaptation of Pedagogical Approaches

Adapting pedagogical approaches to meet the diverse needs of apprentice learners is paramount for their academic success and professional growth. While specific pedagogical examples tailored for higher education apprentices may be limited, there are overarching principles and adaptable approaches that can be applied. For example, principles of experiential learning, problem-based learning, and situated cognition are highly relevant to the apprenticeship context (Collins *et al.*, 1991; Billett, 2002). These approaches emphasise active engagement, real-world problem-solving, and contextualised learning, aligning closely with the needs of apprentice learners who seek to integrate theoretical knowledge with practical skills.

In adapting these pedagogical approaches, educators can incorporate elements of authentic assessment and workplace simulation to enhance the relevance and applicability of learning experiences (Gibbs and Simpson, 2004). Authentic assessment tasks, such as workplace projects and case studies based on real industry scenarios, allow apprentice learners to demonstrate their understanding and application of knowledge in authentic contexts (Boud and Falchikov, 2006). Similarly, workplace simulations provide immersive learning experiences that replicate authentic work environments, enabling apprentice learners to develop practical skills in a controlled setting (Sanchez et al., 2023). Additionally, incorporating principles of adult learning theory/andragogy (see Knowles, 1984), such as self-directed learning and relevance to learners' experiences, can enhance the effectiveness of pedagogical approaches for apprentice learners (Merriam et al., 2007). Take, for example, self-directed learning; apprentices may prefer to take responsibility for their learning process, setting their own goals and determining the pace of learning, that is, set reading and exercises. By empowering apprentice learners to take ownership of their learning journey and contextualising learning experiences within their professional contexts, educators can create meaningful and impactful learning environments. This approach promotes autonomy and self-efficacy among apprentice learners, fostering a sense of responsibility and commitment to their academic and professional development (Tough, 1971).

Furthermore, the integration of technology-enhanced learning tools and resources can facilitate flexible and interactive learning experiences for apprentice learners (Garrison and Kanuka, 2004). Virtual learning environments, online collaborative platforms, and multimedia resources offer opportunities for apprentice learners to engage with course content, interact with peers and instructors, and access learning materials at their own pace and convenience (Salmon, 2011). This is particularly the case after the COVID-19 pandemic, where institutions had to rapidly adapt and deliver apprenticeships remotely. A study conducted by Barr et al. (2020) highlighted a new model of delivery to software engineering degree apprenticeships through the merging of module content and condensed block learning over a short time period, alongside prerecorded sessions complemented by online learning programmes such as Zoom. While specific examples may vary depending on the disciplinary context and industry requirements, the overarching principles of learner-centeredness, active engagement, and relevance remained a central component to this effective adaptation of learning for the apprentices. In conclusion, this part underscores the importance of integrating theory-driven and traditional teaching practices to support the diverse needs of apprentice learners within higher education. By fostering collaborative partnerships, nurturing tripartite relationships, and adapting pedagogical approaches, educators can create inclusive, supportive, and empowering learning environments that empower apprentice learners to succeed in both academic and professional domains.

## Enhancing the Learning Experience for Apprentice Learners

The need to continually adapt and refine pedagogical approaches is not uncommon. In the wake of technological changes, for example, the integration of augmented reality, virtual reality, and artificial intelligence within learning environments and the rising need to train apprentices in an ever-evolving industry, it is pragmatic to adapt pedagogies to support degree-level apprentice learners better. By expanding the pedagogical lens, redefining assessment practices, and embracing innovative engagement models, educators can create dynamic and enriching learning environments that empower apprentice learners to thrive academically and professionally.

### *Expanding the Pedagogical Lens*

To better support apprentices, it is imperative to expand the pedagogical lens beyond traditional approaches and embrace a holistic framework that integrates theory-driven practices with real-world applications. This entails incorporating and adapting differing pedagogy and principles. For example, Kolb's (2014) notion of experiential learning could be adapted to address the needs of the learners by designing tasks that mirror workplace challenges and promoting hands-on skill development. Barrows (1986) stated that problem-based learning could be enhanced further by structuring courses around real-world problems, facilitating collaborative problem-solving discussions, and providing guidance for critical thinking and reflection. Specifically, the apprentice's employers need to work in tandem with the university to facilitate a tangible programme that addresses realistic industry needs. Finally, situated cognition into curriculum design and delivery (Lave and Wenger, 1991) can occur through embedding learning in authentic contexts like simulated work environments. Moreover, universities can foster collaboration through knowledge-sharing platforms and encourage reflective documentation of learning experiences. By providing degree apprentice learners with opportunities to engage in authentic tasks, workplace simulations, and collaborative projects, educators can facilitate the integration of theoretical knowledge with practical skills, thereby enhancing the relevance and applicability of learning experiences (Billett, 2002).

Moreover, adopting a learner-centred approach that prioritises individualised support, self-directed learning, and reflective practice is essential for meeting the diverse needs of apprentice learners (Knowles, 1984). By empowering apprentice learners to take ownership of their learning journey and encouraging them to reflect on their experiences, educators can foster a sense of agency and autonomy, ultimately enhancing motivation, engagement, and academic achievement (Merriam *et al.*, 2007). Additionally, integrating collaborative learning strategies, such as peer teaching and group projects, can foster a supportive and interactive learning environment where apprentice learners can learn from each other's experiences, share insights, and collaborate on challenging tasks (Topping, 2005). Furthermore, incorporating technology-enhanced learning tools and resources, such as online simulations, virtual laboratories, and multimedia presentations, can enhance the accessibility and effectiveness of learning experiences for apprentice learners (Means *et al.*, 2009). In addition, providing opportunities for apprentices to engage in real-world projects and internships can further enrich their learning experiences and enhance their employability skills (Fuller and Unwin, 2011).

### *Assessment for Learning*

Assessment plays a crucial role in shaping the learning experience of apprentice learners, serving as a means to evaluate progress, provide feedback, and guide future learning (Black and Wiliam, 1998). In the context of apprentice learners, assessment for learning (AFL) takes on added significance, as it encompasses not only the evaluation of outgoing knowledge but also the assessment of incoming knowledge and skills acquired through workplace experiences (Fuller and Unwin, 2011). Within the context of this book chapter, outgoing knowledge will be considered as learnt knowledge gained throughout the apprenticeship. In contrast, incoming knowledge is pre-existing and present at the commencement of learning.

AFL involves a multilayered approach that includes formative assessment, peer assessment, self-assessment, and authentic assessment tasks (Sadler, 1989). Assessment is a fundamental component of the learning process, providing valuable feedback to both students and instructors to inform teaching and learning practices (Black and Wiliam, 1998). Formative assessments are an ongoing process that occurs throughout a course or unit, offering timely feedback to students to improve their understanding and performance (Black and Wiliam, 1998). They encompass various strategies such as quizzes, class discussions, and peer feedback, aiming to identify areas of strength and weakness alongside guiding academics' decisions throughout the teaching process (Sadler, 1989). Peer assessment, on the other hand, involves students evaluating the work of their peers based on predetermined criteria (Topping, 1998). This approach fosters critical thinking skills, enhances understanding of course concepts, and promotes communication and collaboration abilities (Falchikov and Goldfinch, 2000). Moreover, peer assessment can take the form of peer grading, peer review of writing or presentations, or peer evaluation of group projects, thus creating opportunities for active engagement and the development of a supportive learning community (Falchikov and Goldfinch, 2000).

Similarly, self-assessment encourages students to reflect on their learning progress, strengths, and areas for improvement (Boud, 1995). By engaging in self-reflection activities such as journals, quizzes, and goal-setting exercises, students develop metacognitive skills and become more autonomous and self-directed learners (Boud, 1995). Self-assessment also promotes intrinsic motivation and a growth mindset by emphasising the importance of effort and perseverance in learning (Hattie and Timperley, 2007). Furthermore, authentic assessment tasks mirror real-world contexts and require students to apply their knowledge and skills to solve complex, real-world problems or tasks (Wiggins, 1990). Unlike traditional assessments focused on rote memorisation, authentic assessment tasks emphasise the application and transfer of learning to authentic situations (Wiggins, 1990). Examples include case studies, simulations, projects, performances, and portfolios, which promote higher-order thinking skills and prepare students for success in real-world settings.

## Stretch and Challenge

In addition to assessment for learning, enhancing the learning experience for apprentice learners requires a commitment to stretch and challenge them to reach their full potential (Schunk and Zimmerman, 1998). This entails providing apprentice learners with opportunities to engage in intellectually stimulating tasks, pursue independent inquiry, and explore complex problems relevant to their field of study (Biggs *et al.*, 2022). Moreover, establishing a benchmark in learning at a modular level is essential to ascertain the progression of apprentice learners and to ensure that they are appropriately challenged throughout their educational journey.

Peer-to-peer and near-to-peer engagement models offer practical strategies for promoting stretch and challenge among apprentice learners (Topping, 2005). Peer mentoring programs, collaborative learning communities, and interdisciplinary projects enable apprentice learners to learn from each other, share insights, and tackle challenging problems collaboratively (Boud and Falchikov, 2006). By fostering a culture of intellectual curiosity, collaboration, and innovation, educators can inspire apprentice learners to push the boundaries of their knowledge and skills. Furthermore, the use of differentiated instruction techniques, such as tiered assignments and choice boards, can provide apprentice learners with opportunities to engage with course material at varying levels of complexity, ensuring that each student is appropriately challenged based on their individual abilities and learning preferences. In particular, choice boards, as an instructional tool, provide the opportunity for apprentices to take control of their learning by offering a variety of ways in which they can be assessed in a module (whether this be formative or summative). For example, learners could investigate a successful project case study, create a project timeline, develop a project plan, write a reflective essay, design a project management role-playing game, or deliver a presentation on project management skills (Maloy, 2020).

Additionally, incorporating project-based learning and problem-based learning (PBL) approaches into the curriculum can offer apprentice learners authentic opportunities to apply their knowledge and skills to real-world challenges (Barrows, 1986; Blumenfeld *et al.*, 1991). PBL and PBL tasks present apprentice learners with complex, ill-structured problems that require critical thinking, problem-solving, and collaboration to resolve. By engaging in these types of tasks, apprentice learners develop valuable skills such as analytical reasoning, creativity, and communication, while also gaining a deeper understanding of course content and its practical applications. Moreover, leveraging technology-enhanced learning tools and resources can provide apprentice learners with access to interactive simulations, virtual laboratories, and online collaborative platforms, enriching their learning experiences and expanding their opportunities for stretch and challenge (Means *et al.*, 2009). Virtual reality (VR), augmented reality (AR), and gamification techniques can also be integrated into the learning environment to create immersive and engaging experiences that motivate and inspire apprentice learners to explore new ideas and concepts (Limbu *et al.*, 2018).

Given this, enhancing the learning experience for apprentice learners requires a multifaceted approach that integrates innovative pedagogical practices, assessment strategies, and engagement models. By expanding the pedagogical lens, redefining assessment practices, and promoting stretch and challenge, educators can create caring, compassionate, and empowering learning environments that equip apprentice learners with the knowledge, skills, and mindset needed to succeed in both academic and professional domains.

## Recommendations: Moving to a Multilateral Approach

This section will outline a comprehensive set of recommendations, drawing upon the insights and strategies discussed throughout the chapter and providing actionable guidance for higher education institutions seeking to enhance the learning experience for apprentice learners. By embracing multifaceted pedagogical approaches, fostering collaborative partnerships, promoting reflective practice and assessment for learning, cultivating a compassionate and inclusive learning environment, and leveraging technology-enhanced learning, universities can create dynamic learning environments that empower apprentice learners to succeed in both academic and professional domains.

### *Embrace Multifaceted Pedagogical Approaches*

Higher education institutions should adopt a multifaceted approach to pedagogy that recognises the diverse needs of apprentice learners. They should blend traditional teaching methods with emerging theory-driven practices to create effective learning environments. They should incorporate experiential learning opportunities, problem-based learning approaches, and situated cognition strategies to engage learners in active inquiry and practical application of knowledge (Lave and Wenger, 1991; Billett, 2002). By embracing a multilateral approach to pedagogy, universities can cater to the unique aspirations and challenges of apprentice learners.

### Foster Collaborative Partnerships

Cultivate collaborative partnerships between higher education institutions, employers, and apprentices to enhance the relevance and applicability of learning experiences. Collaborate on curriculum design, work placements, and professional development initiatives to ensure alignment with industry needs and standards (Fuller and Unwin, 2011). Foster a culture of mutual support and shared responsibility, where all stakeholders are actively engaged in the educational process (Billett, 2002). By fostering collaborative partnerships, universities can create meaningful and impactful learning environments that empower apprentice learners to succeed in both academic and professional domains.

### Promote Reflective Practice and Assessment for Learning

Encourage reflective practice and assessment for learning to support apprentice learners' academic development and professional growth. Provide opportunities for apprentices to reflect on their learning experiences, identify strengths and areas for improvement, and set personal learning goals (Knowles, 1984). Implement formative assessment strategies that focus on continuous feedback and improvement, rather than just summative evaluation (Black and Wiliam, 1998). By promoting reflective practice and assessment for learning, universities can empower apprentice learners to take ownership of their learning journey and develop the skills needed for lifelong learning and career success.

### Cultivate a Compassionate and Inclusive Learning Environment

Create a compassionate and inclusive learning environment that values diversity, fosters belonging, and supports the socio-emotional needs of apprentice learners. Implement compassionate pedagogy approaches that prioritise empathy, care, and understanding in the educational process (Maxwell, 2017). Foster a sense of belonging and community among apprentice learners, where they feel valued, respected, and supported in their academic and professional endeavours (Tinto, 1993). By cultivating a compassionate and inclusive learning environment, universities can enhance apprentice learners' well-being, motivation, and academic achievement.

### Leverage Technology-Enhanced Learning

Harnessing the power of technology to enhance the learning experience for apprentice learners can occur in different ways. Nevertheless, the underlying current that draws them together is an exploration of differing innovative digital tools and platforms to facilitate flexible and accessible learning opportunities (Billett, 2022). Provide training and support for both educators and learners to effectively navigate digital learning environments and maximise the benefits of technology-enhanced learning (Barr *et al.*, 2020). By leveraging technology-enhanced learning, universities can expand access to education, enhance engagement, and facilitate personalised learning experiences for apprentice learners.

By employing these recommendations, higher education institutions can adopt a multilateral approach to apprenticeship pedagogies that meets the diverse needs of apprentice learners, fosters collaborative partnerships, promotes reflective practice and assessment for learning, cultivates a compassionate and inclusive learning environment, and leverages technology to enhance the learning experience.

## Conclusion

### *Moving to a Multilateral Approach*

To summarise, this exploration of higher education apprenticeship pedagogies underscores the imperative of adopting a multifaceted approach to meet the diverse needs of apprentice learners. As academic teachers navigate the complexities of apprentice education, it becomes increasingly evident that a singular, one-size-fits-all approach is inadequate. Instead, a multilateral approach that integrates theory-driven and traditional teaching practices fosters collaborative partnerships and promotes reflective practice is essential in creating a caring, compassionate, and empowering learning environment.

This chapter has delved into the intricacies of degree-level apprentice education, recognising the unique characteristics and learning pathways of learners. From the blending of academic study with workplace training to the socio-emotional needs and collaborative dynamics inherent in apprenticeships, we have highlighted the nature of apprentice education. It is imperative that educators embrace this complexity and tailor their pedagogical approaches to meet the diverse needs and aspirations of apprentice learners. Central to our discussion is the integration of theory-driven and traditional teaching practices. By leveraging principles of experiential learning, problem-based learning, and situated cognition, educators can bridge the gap between theory and practice, enhancing the relevance and applicability of learning experiences for apprentices. Moreover, fostering collaborative partnerships between institutions, students, and employers is crucial in creating supportive learning environments. Through these partnerships, apprentice learners can engage in authentic tasks, workplace simulations, and collaborative projects, gaining insights into industry practices and developing critical thinking skills essential for their professional growth.

Reflective practice somewhat emerges as a cornerstone in this exploration, offering apprentice learners the opportunity to critically assess their learning experiences and chart their academic and professional development. By promoting reflective practice, educators empower apprentice learners to become active participants in their learning journey, fostering a deeper understanding of themselves and their professional roles. As we look ahead, it is essential that higher education institutions prioritise the enhancement of the learning experience for apprentice learners. This entails expanding the pedagogical lens to encompass diverse learning approaches, such as peer-to-peer and near-to-peer engagement models. By fostering collaborative learning environments and promoting peer interaction, educators can create opportunities for apprentice learners to learn from one another, share experiences, and collectively solve problems. Furthermore, assessment for learning emerges as a critical component in enhancing the learning experience for apprentice learners. By adopting innovative assessment practices that evaluate both incoming and outgoing knowledge, educators can provide meaningful feedback and support apprentice learners in their academic and professional development. As such, a multilateral approach to higher education apprenticeship pedagogies is essential in meeting the diverse needs and aspirations of apprentices.

Table 3.1 Employing pedagogy to support the degree-level apprenticeship experience

| Pedagogy | Expanded to benefit the apprentice |
| --- | --- |
| **Experiential Learning Opportunities (Kolb, 2014):** | a) Design authentic tasks and projects that mirror workplace challenges and scenarios, providing learners with hands-on experience and practical skills development (Kolb, 2014). |
| | b) Organise site visits, industry tours, or field trips to expose learners to different workplace environments and practices other than their own, fostering a deeper understanding of their field of study (Kolb, 1984). |
| **Problem-Based Learning (PBL) Approaches (Barrows, 1986):** | a) Structure modules or courses around real-world problems and incorporate contemporary case studies relevant to the learners' professional context, encouraging them to analyse, synthesise, and solve complex problems collaboratively. |
| | b) Facilitate supplementary small-group discussions, workshops, or seminars where learners can explore and discuss challenging issues, applying theoretical concepts to practical situations (McTighe and Thomas, 2003). |
| | c) Provide scaffolding and guidance as learners work through problems, encouraging them to think critically, propose solutions, and reflect on their decision-making processes. |
| **Situated Cognition Strategies (Lave and Wenger, 1991):** | a) Embed learning activities within authentic contexts that mirror workplace settings, such as simulated work environments and virtual reality simulations. |
| | b) Foster collaboration and knowledge sharing among learners by creating communities of practice or online forums where they can interact, exchange ideas, and learn from each other's experiences (Wenger, 1998). |
| | c) Encourage apprentices to document and reflect on their learning experiences in workplace journals, blogs, or reflective essays, highlighting connections between theory and practice. |

## References

Arkorful, V. and Abaidoo, N., 2015. The role of e-learning, advantages and disadvantages of its adoption in higher education. *International Journal of Instructional Technology and Distance Learning*, 12(1), pp. 29–42. Available at: www.ijern.com/journal/2014/December-2014/34.pdf

Barr, M., Nabi, S.W. and Somerville, D., 2020, November. Online delivery of intensive software engineering education during the COVID-19 pandemic. In *2020 IEEE 32nd Conference on Software Engineering Education and Training (CSEE&T)* (pp. 1–6). IEEE. https://doi.org/10.1109/CSEET49119.2020.9206196

Barrows, H.S., 1986. A taxonomy of problem-based learning methods. *Medical Education*, 20(6), pp. 481–486. https://doi.org/10.1111/j.1365-2923.1986.tb01386.x

Biggs, J., Tang, C. and Kennedy, G., 2022. *Teaching for Quality Learning at University 5e*. McGraw-Hill Education (UK).

Billett, S., 2002. Toward a workplace pedagogy: Guidance, participation, and engagement. *Adult Education Quarterly*, 53(1), pp. 27–43. https://doi.org/10.1177/074171302237202

Black, P. and Wiliam, D., 1998. Inside the black box: Raising standards through classroom assessment. *Phi Delta Kappan*, 80(2), pp. 139–148. https://doi.org/10.1177/003172171009200119

Blumenfeld, P.C., Soloway, E., Marx, R.W., Krajcik, J.S., Guzdial, M. and Palincsar, A., 1991. Motivating project-based learning: Sustaining the doing, supporting the learning. *Educational Psychologist*, 26(3–4), pp. 369–398. https://doi.org/10.1080/00461520.1991.9653139

Boud, D., 1995. *Enhancing Learning through Self-Assessment*. London: Kogan Page.

Boud, D. and Falchikov, N., 2006. Aligning assessment with long-term learning. *Assessment & Evaluation in Higher Education*, 31(4), pp. 399–413. https://doi.org/10.1080/02602930600679050

Boud, D. and Falchikov, N., 2007. Developing assessment for informing judgement. In *Rethinking Assessment in Higher Education* (pp. 191–207). Routledge.

Bovill, C., Cook-Sather, A. and Felten, P., 2011. Students as co-creators of teaching approaches, course design, and curricula: Implications for academic developers. *International Journal for Academic Development*, 16(2), pp. 133–145.

Collins, A., Brown, J.S. and Holum, A., 1991. Cognitive apprenticeship: Making thinking visible. *American Educator*, 15(3), pp. 6–11. Available at: www.psy.lmu.de/isls-naples/intro/all-webinars/collins/cognitive-apprenticeship.pdf

Dochy, F.J.R.C., Segers, M. and Sluijsmans, D., 1999. The use of self-, peer and co-assessment in higher education: A review. *Studies in Higher Education*, 24(3), pp. 331–350. https://doi.org/10.1080/03075079912331379935

Eraut, M., 2004. Informal learning in the workplace. *Studies in Continuing Education*, 26(2), pp. 247–273. https://doi.org/10.1080/158037042000225245

Evans, K., Guile, D., Harris, J. and Allan, H., 2010. Putting knowledge to work: A new approach. *Nurse Education Today*, 30(3), pp. 245–251. https://doi.org/10.1016/j.nedt.2009.10.014

Falchikov, N. and Goldfinch, J., 2000. Student peer assessment in higher education: A meta-analysis comparing peer and teacher marks. *Review of Educational Research*, 70(3), pp. 287–322. https://doi.org/10.2307/1170785

Ferguson, R., 2012. Learning analytics: Drivers, developments and challenges. *International Journal of Technology Enhanced Learning*, 4(5–6), pp. 304–317. https://doi.org/10.1504/IJTEL.2012.051816

Fuller, A. and Unwin, L., 2011. Expansive learning environments: Integrating organisational and personal development. In: *The SAGE Handbook of Workplace Learning* (pp. 205–218). Sage Publications Ltd. https://doi.org/10.4324/9780203571644

Garrison, D.R. and Kanuka, H., 2004. Blended learning: Uncovering its transformative potential in higher education. *The Internet and Higher Education*, 7(2), pp. 95–105.

Gibbs, G. and Simpson, C., 2004. Conditions under which assessment supports students' learning. *Learning and Teaching in Higher Education*, (1), pp. 3–31. https://doi.org/10.1007/978-3-8348-9837-1

Gibbs, P. ed., 2017. *The Pedagogy of Compassion is at the Heart of Higher Education*. Springer. https://doi.org/10.1007/978-3-319-57783-8

Goodman, D. and Kooner-Evans, P., 2024. Tripartite relationships between students, employers and the university: A conversation about degree apprenticeships. In: *The Impact of a Regional Business School on its Communities: A Holistic Perspective* (pp. 109–140). Cham: Springer International Publishing. https://doi.org/10.1007/978-3-031-47254-1_5

Hager, P. and Hodkinson, P., 2009. Moving beyond the metaphor of transfer of learning. *British Educational Research Journal*, 35(4), pp. 619–638.

Hattie, J. and Timperley, H., 2007. The power of feedback. *Review of Educational Research*, 77(1), pp. 81–112. https://doi.org/10.3102/003465430298487

Helyer, R. and Price, A., 2016. Learning to learn. In: *Facilitating Work-based Learning* (pp. 207–226). London: Palgrave.

Hughes, C. and Saieva, G. (2019). Degree apprenticeships – an opportunity for all? *Higher Education, Skills, and Work-Based Learning*, 9(2), pp. 225–236. https://doi.org/10.1108/heswbl-10-2018-0113.

Hughes, C. and Saieva, G., 2020. The journey of higher degree apprenticeships. In: *Applied Pedagogies for Higher Education: Real World Learning and Innovation Across the Curriculum* (pp. 243–266). Cham: Springer International Publishing. https://doi.org/10.1007/978-3-030-46951-1_11

Johnson, D.W., Johnson, R.T. and Smith, K.A., 2014. Cooperative learning: Improving university instruction by basing practice on validated theory. *Journal on Excellence in University Teaching*, 25(4), pp. 1–26.

Knowles, M.S., 1984. *Andragogy in Action: Applying Modern Principles of Adult Education*. Jossey-Bass.

Kolb, D.A., 1984. *Experiential Learning: Experience as the Source of Learning and Development*. Englewood Cliffs, NJ: Prentice Hall.

Kolb, D.A., 2014. *Experiential Learning: Experience as the Source of Learning and Development*. FT press.

Lave, J. and Wenger, E., 1991. *Situated Learning: Legitimate Peripheral Participation*. Cambridge University Press.

Limbu, B.H., Jarodzka, H., Klemke, R. and Specht, M., 2018. Using sensors and augmented reality to train apprentices using recorded expert performance: A systematic literature review. *Educational Research Review*, 25, pp. 1–22. https://doi.org/10.1016/j.edurev.2018.07.001

Mallman, M. and Lee, H., 2016. Stigmatised learners: Mature-age students negotiating university culture. *British Journal of Sociology of Education*, 37(5), pp. 684–701. https://doi.org/10.1080/01425692.2014.973017

Maloy, R., 2020, October. Designing high-quality choice boards for student-centred explorations of content. In *SITE Interactive Conference* (pp. 311–314). Association for the Advancement of Computing in Education (AACE).

Maxwell, N., 2017. *Handbook of Philosophy of Science: Philosophy of Science: Volume 1*. Philosophy of Science Association.

McTighe, J. and Thomas, R.S., 2003. Backward design for forward action. In *Understanding by Design*. ASCD.

Means, B., Toyama, Y., Murphy, R., Bakia, M. and Jones, K., 2009. *Evaluation of Evidence-Based Practices in Online Learning: A Meta-Analysis and Review of Online Learning Studies*. US Department of Education.

Merriam, S.B., Caffarella, R.S. and Baumgartner, L.M., 2007. *Learning in Adulthood: A Comprehensive Guide*. John Wiley & Sons.

Noddings, N., 1984. *Caring, a Feminine Approach to Ethics & Moral Education*. Berkeley: University of California Press.

Pius, A., 2024. Exploring the Experience of Degree Apprentices and Academics in Fostering Managerial-Level Competencies: A Case of Vocational Degrees within the UK Higher Education. http://doi.org/10.59268/taas/010520242

Pius, A. and English, V., 2023, August 1. Apprentices' educational decisions and the choice of vocational degrees for masters' qualifications: An emerging frontier. In *Proceedings of the International Conference on Innovations in Education and Technology (ICIET 2023)*. http://dx.doi.org/10.2139/ssrn.4549129

Ramsey, E. and Brown, D., 2018. Feeling like a fraud: Helping students renegotiate their academic identities. *College & Undergraduate Libraries*, 25(1), pp. 86–90. https://doi.org/10.1080/10691316.2017.1364080

Roberts, A., Storm, M., & Flynn, S. (2019). Workplace mentoring of degree apprentices: Developing principles for practice. *Higher Education, Skills and Work-Based Learning*, 9(2), pp. 211–224. https://doi.org/10.1108/heswbl-10-2018-0108.

Rowe, L., Moore, N. and McKie, P., 2020. The reflective practitioner: The challenges of supporting public sector senior leaders as they engage in reflective practice. *Higher Education, Skills and Work-Based Learning*, 10(5), pp. 783–798. https://doi.org/10.1108/HESWBL-03-2020-0038

Sadler, D.R., 1989. Formative assessment and the design of instructional systems. *Instructional Science*, 18, pp. 119–144.

Salmon, G., 2011. *E-Moderating: The Key to Online Teaching and Learning*. Routledge.

Sanchez, D.R., Rueda, A., Kawasaki, K., Van Lysebetten, S. and Diaz, D., 2023. Reviewing simulation technology: Implications for workplace training. *Multimodal Technologies and Interaction*, 7(5), p. 50. https://doi.org/10.3390/mti7050050

Schunk, D.H. and Zimmerman, B.J., 1998. *Self-Regulated Learning: From Teaching to Self-Reflective Practice*. Guilford Press.

Siemens, G. and Long, P., 2011. Penetrating the fog: Analytics in learning and education. *Educause Review*, 46(5), p. 30. http://dx.doi.org/10.17471/2499-4324/195

Smith, R. and Betts, M., 2000. Learning as partners: Realising the potential of work-based learning. *Journal of Vocational education and Training*, 52(4), pp. 589–604.

Smith, S., Taylor-Smith, E., Fabian, K., Zarb, M., Paterson, J., Barr, M. and Berg, T., 2021. A multi-institutional exploration of the social mobility potential of degree apprenticeships. *Journal of Education and Work*, 34(4), pp. 488–503. https://doi.org/10.1080/13639080.2021.1946494

Tinto, V., 1993. *Leaving College: Rethinking the Causes and Cures of Student Attrition*. University of Chicago Press.

Topping, K., 1998. Peer assessment between students in colleges and universities. *Review of Educational Research*, 68(3), pp. 249–276. https://doi.org/10.3102/00346543068003249

Topping, K.J. (2005) Trends in peer learning. *Educational Psychology*, 25(6), pp. 631–645. https://doi.org/10.1080/01443410500345172.

Tough, A.M., 1971. *The Adult's Learning Projects: A Fresh Approach to Theory and Practice in Adult Learning*. Toronto, Canada: Ontario Institute for Studies in Education.

Vandeyar, S., (2021) Educational transmogrification: From panicgogy to pedagogy of compassion. *Teaching in Higher Education*, 28(8), pp. 2160–2172. https://doi.org/10.1080/13562517.2021.1952568.

Vandeyar, S. and Swart, R., (2018) Shattering the silence: Dialogic engagement about education protest actions in South African university classrooms. *Teaching in Higher Education*, 24(6), pp. 772–788. https://doi.org/10.1080/13562517.2018.1502170.

Wenger, E., 1998. *Communities of Practice: Learning, Meaning, and Identity*. Cambridge University Press. https://doi.org/10.1017/CBO9780511803932

Wiggins, G., 1990. The case for authentic assessment. *Practical Assessment, Research, and Evaluation*, 2(1), p. 2. https://doi.org/10.7275/ffb1-mm19

Chapter 4

# The Dual Study Programme in Germany – Concept, Strengths and Challenges

*Ute Hippach-Schneider*

## Introduction

Over the last 50 years, hybrid education programmes have developed in Germany's tertiary education sector, combining the strengths of both vocational and academic education. Their importance in the tertiary education sector has increased continuously. The combination of theory and practice as well as a quick entry into the labour market make them attractive for students. But they also have advantages for companies, as the hybrid form of the dual study programme ensures the availability of academically trained employees who are already familiar with practical work processes.

## Emergence of the Dual Study Programmes

Dual study programmes emerged in Germany in the 1970s. The idea was to offer practice-oriented training in order to better prepare higher education graduates for the needs of the economy (Brünner *et al.*, 2016) and to close a gap between academic education and the requirements of the world of work. The approach of systematically combining theory and practice was not new in Germany. The well-established dual vocational education and training (VET) programme at secondary level – an apprenticeship system – also combines practical work-based learning in a company with technical and theoretical learning at school and coordinates the learning content of the two learning venues.

There were several reasons for the emergence of dual study programmes. In the 1970s, for example, the number of people in Germany with a higher education entrance qualification increased significantly. This led to a large influx of students to universities and the newly established universities of applied sciences.[1] At the same time, a shortage of qualified skilled labour became noticeable in various sectors. In some cases, companies had difficulties finding well-trained staff.

In 1971, the automotive corporation Daimler-Benz AG proposed a new form of training: in order to increase the attractiveness of training for high school graduates, the dual training system – actually a secondary education programme – was to be combined with a type of "university course system". In-company training should not be supplemented by a vocational school but by a higher education partner. Supporters of the idea were found in the Stuttgart companies Robert Bosch GmbH and Standard Elektrik Lorenz AG. This new form of dual training was intended to offer a genuine alternative to conventional higher education studies.

In cooperation with the Württembergische Verwaltungs- und Wirtschaftsakademie and the Mittlerer Neckar Chamber of Industry and Commerce, the three companies developed the so-called Stuttgart Model in 1972. The following year, the minister of education and cultural affairs for the state of Baden-Württemberg announced a plan to create a vocational academy, and the first vocational academy was founded in 1974 (Bauer-Hailer and Wezel, 2008). In this way, the dual VET system was effectively transferred to the tertiary sector. The former Berufsakademie has since developed into the Baden-Württemberg Cooperative State University (DHBW), today one of the largest providers of dual study programmes in Germany. Other federal states followed suit and further dual study programmes were developed.[2] There are still vocational academies in many federal states. These are part of the tertiary education sector in Germany and have the same status as higher education institutions, but are not formally part of the higher education sector.

Companies therefore played a decisive role in the development of the dual study programme, as well as in its content and organisation. Thanks to the close cooperation between higher education institutions and companies, practical course content was developed that met the current, particularly regional, requirements of the labour market. As a result, the dual study programme enabled students to integrate into the world of work at an early stage and made it easier for companies to recruit well-trained skilled labour. In terms of its impact on the entire education system, the dual study programme was also seen as a vehicle for fundamentally strengthening the idea of duality in vocational training in Germany, including traditional dual VET in secondary education.

In contrast to conventional university programmes, the central structural feature of dual study programmes is the interlinking of theory and practice. According to the definition of the German Council of Science and Humanities (Wissenschaftsrat), a degree programme only qualifies as a dual study programme if it has a structural, institutional and/or content-related interlocking of the academic and vocational learning aspects. However, the forms and intensity of this interlinking can vary (Wissenschaftsrat, 2013).

## Types of Dual Study Programmes and Features of Dual Study Programmes Compared to Conventional University Study Programmes

### Types of Dual Study Programmes

The area of dual study programmes is characterised by great heterogeneity, in terms of both the range of content and the structural implementation. This is also due to the fact that responsibility for the regulations for dual study programmes lies with the 16 federal states. Three types of dual study programmes have now emerged, with a distinction made between training-integrated, practice-integrated and work-integrated dual study programmes. The remainder of this chapter refers exclusively to the two study programmes that can be assigned to initial training; that is, training-integrated and practice-integrated study programmes. The continuing education model focusses on adults who are already in employment.

Training-integrated degree programmes are dual degree programmes that integrate full VET into the course of study. The graduate thus acquires two degrees, the academic degree and the vocational degree. This degree programme also means combining three places of learning: the higher education institution, the company and the vocational school.

Practice-integrated dual study programmes have an increased practical component that goes far beyond the practical requirements and practical relevance of conventional study programmes. Students on these programmes are also employed in companies but only obtain a bachelor's degree rather than a second degree. The practical components are structurally and institutionally interlinked with the degree programme. Usually, students complete their practical training at one specific company throughout their studies. They can therefore be classified as dual study programmes according to the definition of the German Council of Science and Humanities.

In addition, mixed forms have also become established, with higher education institutions offering a degree programme in both a training and a practice-integrated format.

In the case of work-integrated degree programmes, the full-time or part-time study programme is linked to the related professional activity and has interlocking content.

Even if part-time study programmes for employed adults are not referred to as dual study programmes due to the lack of systematic dovetailing of academic and company-based learning, they are a central format for universities to open up higher education to working people. Dual master's degree programmes are now also on the increase. The distinction between these and part-time study programmes is often blurred.

Dual study programmes and conventional higher education degree programmes therefore differ in various aspects, from the structure and process to

Table 4.1 Overview of the three main types of dual study programmes

| Form of the programme | Educational level | Company integration | Curricular concept | Qualification | Duration | Entry qualification |
|---|---|---|---|---|---|---|
| **Training-integrated** | Initial education | Training or internship contract | Interlocking of training and study programme in terms of content and time | Vocational qualification, bachelor's degree | 3–5 years | (specialised) university entrance qualification |
| **Practice-integrated** | Initial education | Internship, traineeship or (part-time) employment contract | Content-related links between company practice and study programme | Bachelor's or master's degree | 3/2 years | (specialised) university entrance qualification |
| **Work-integrated** | Continuing education | (Part-time) employment contract (company grants leave of absence) | Content-related links between company practice and bachelor's degree programme | Bachelor's degree | generally 3 years | vocational training and professional experience |

Sources: Bundesinstitut für Berufsbildung, 2023; Wissenschaftsrat, 2013

the objectives and the integration of practical experience. As a rule, dual study programmes are structured in such a way that students complete both components in a predetermined alternation between higher education and practical phases over a period of three to five years. This allows them to develop both academic and professional skills. In conventional degree programmes, the focus is primarily on imparting theoretical knowledge. Practical experience is gained in the form of internships or as part of final theses, but it is not as integral a part of the degree programme as it is in the dual model. The high level of practical relevance is in fact also a key reason why first-year students opt for this study model (Woisch and Mentges, 2018).

In principle, all those with a higher education entrance qualification have the opportunity to study on a dual study programme. However, it is notable that dual students are predominantly motivated and high-achieving young adults who expect better entry-level positions and opportunities for rapid career development in companies through the dual study programme (Woisch and Mentges, 2018, p. 4). One reason for this is that the requirements of a dual study programme, with its shortened learning phases and company phases to be completed, tend to attract performance-motivated first-year students. Another factor is that the companies decide who is accepted onto a dual study programme: a training or study contract with a company is a prerequisite for admission to a dual study programme. Companies therefore play a central role in regulating access to dual study programmes.

### Interlocking Theory and Practice

The constitutive feature of the dual study programme is the interlinking of theory and practice. Three dimensions can be distinguished in this regard, each of which may be organised in slightly different ways and with different intensity, as follows.

*The relationship between higher education institutions and company partners*

Various models have developed as to how the two places of learning, the higher education institution and the company, are interlinked. One of the reasons for this is that the individual federal states are responsible for the legal frameworks of the higher education institutions and these regulate the involvement of companies in dual study programmes differently or, in some cases, leave the form of cooperation completely up to the higher education institutions (Nickel *et al.*, 2022). In the federal state of Hesse, for example, interested companies can contact the providers of dual study programmes and jointly design a study programme or cooperation. Once an agreement has been reached, a contractual agreement follows. This then forms the basis for the implementation and funding (Hessisches Ministerium für Wirtschaft, Energie, Verkehr und Wohnen, 2020) [Hessian Ministry of Economics, Energy, Transport and Housing]. The further integration of the companies then takes place via membership in various organisational and committee structures. This enables the so-called dual partners to participate in the strategic development of the higher education institution.

In Baden-Württemberg, for example, the cooperating companies can participate in the university council, the senate, the local university council and the commission for quality assurance at the Cooperative State University (DHBW). The company partners also have the opportunity to send experienced employees to the higher education institution as lecturers. As part of this institutionalised cooperation, the curricula, learning objectives and examination forms of the two learning locations are also coordinated. The operational design of the dual study programme also requires a regular exchange of information between the learning locations, both at an organisational level and at the level of teachers and company supervisors (Gerstung and Deuer, 2021b).

It can be observed that larger companies participate more frequently in university committees, although 52.7% of all company partners stated in a survey that they have not yet been involved in university committees (Bundesministerium für Bildung und Forschung, 2022) [Federal Ministry of Education and Research].

The dual study programme creates a close network between the company and the higher education institution. This facilitates further cooperation and can lead to further synergy effects. Companies can benefit from the knowledge and technology transfer of the higher education institution.

### i. The Relationship Between the Students and the Companies

In the dual study programme, the relationship between the students and the cooperating companies is very close. The companies select the students; that is, a contract with a cooperating company is a prerequisite for admission to a dual study programme. For degree programmes at the DHBW, this has a duration of three years for a dual bachelor's degree. As a rule, students are paid a training allowance, usually also during the theory phases. European Credit Transfer System (ECTS) points are also earned during the practical phases.

### ii. The Relationship Between the Students and the Higher Education Institution

This relationship is also based on a contract, the study contract. The higher education institution teaches the academic foundations, application-orientated methodological knowledge and the ability to think theoretically and systematically. During the practical phases, what has been learnt is put into practice in everyday working life in the company. The theoretical and practical phases are closely harmonised through framework plans. In the final bachelor's thesis, students work on a practical problem using practical and scientific knowledge and methods.

The exact organisation of the alternation between the theoretical and practical phases is regulated by the higher education institutions individually and in some cases specifically for individual subject areas. The DHBW, for example, defines the organisation of learning locations in study plans, the learning content and the skills to be acquired and in module handbooks.[3] In order to optimise the dovetailing of the learning locations in the course of studies, the DHBW conducted a survey of the dual partners – the contact persons for dual students.[4]

Overall, the so-called block model is still the dominant model (Bundesinstitut für Berufsbildung, 2023) [Federal Institute for Vocational Education and Training]. This involves alternating phases of roughly equal length at the company partner and at the higher education institution in weekly or monthly blocks over the entire semester. Rotation models also exist. These involve alternating between the university and company phases on different days of the week. A third model is distance learning, with or without occasional attendance at the higher education institution.

## Provider and Subject Structure

Universities of applied sciences offer the largest number of dual study programmes,[5] providing almost 70% of dual study programmes in 2022. They are followed by the three dual universities: the DHBW, the Duale Hochschule Schleswig-Holstein (DHSW) and the Duale Hochschule Gera-Eisenach (DHGE) with a share of approximately 16%. The DHBW alone offers 240 degree programmes, the DHGE 27 and the DHSH five. In addition, vocational academies offer 152 dual study programmes, or approximately 9% of the total. Universities and other higher education institutions continue to offer only a small number of programmes in this format, at 59 (3.4%) and 48 (2.7%) respectively (Bundesinstitut für Berufsbildung, 2023, p. 21).

Most dual study programmes are offered in the subject groups of engineering (46.0%), law, economics and social sciences (44.8%) and health sciences (6.9%) (Bundesinstitut für Berufsbildung, 2023, p. 16). If differentiated according to the number of students, business administration/economics is clearly ahead of computer science, followed by administrative sciences, health and therapy, mechanical engineering/process engineering and electronics as well as numerous other fields of study. For training-integrated dual study programmes, in which a second full vocational qualification is acquired in dual VET (upper secondary level), professions from the fields of electrical engineering and information technology, office and administration as well as installation and metal construction technology predominate. Two-thirds of the training-integrated degree programmes last between seven and nine semesters, while more than 80% of the practice-integrated programmes have standard study periods of six or seven semesters (Bundesinstitut für Berufsbildung, 2023, p. 15).

In 2022, a total of 56,852 companies were involved as partners in dual study programmes. Large companies with more than 250 employees invest in dual study programmes in particular. However, companies with fewer than 50 employees are also involved (Deloitte and Stifterverband, 2015). In some cases, companies also work together with two or more higher education institutions. There are three main reasons why companies get involved in dual study programmes. Firstly, they hope to transfer new content and ideas from the universities to their company and expect to gain access to this through their involvement. The recruitment of new employees also plays a major role. Through their commitment and willingness to integrate students into work processes and to see the company as a place of learning, they want to secure particularly high-performing students who are a good fit for the company as future specialists at an early stage. In this way, and this is the third reason, they also address the shortage of skilled labour, particularly in the fields of engineering and computer science (Konegen-Grenier and Winde, 2017).

## *Financial Aspects*

In addition to the individual federal states, which provide the basic funding for the higher education institutions, industry contributes to the funding of dual study programmes in a variety of ways. This takes place in both monetary and non-monetary form, for example through the provision of equipment or human resources.

Students receive remuneration from the company during their studies, including during the theoretical phases. The amount of this remuneration can vary from around €700 to €1,500 per month in the first year of study. The subject studied, the industry, the specific company and the study model all play a role. It is possible, for example, that companies pay a higher salary for a training-integrated programme than for a practice-integrated programme, because an additional VET qualification has to be prepared and acquired. There may also be additional benefits, such as digital devices, coverage of costs for study materials, holiday and Christmas bonuses, bonus payments, shareholdings and even (partial) coverage of tuition fees.

German companies increasingly invest in academic education, particularly in dual study programs. In 2015, the industrial and service sectors invested €1.4 billion in dual study programs, up from €675 million in 2009, accounting for 42% of all corporate education investments (Konegen-Grenier and Winde, 2017, p. 13). While industrial sector funding remained stable since 2012, the service sector significantly increased investments in dual students (Konegen-Grenier and Winde, 2017, p. 22). Reasons for this investment are discussed later.

## Institutional and Quantitative Development of Dual Study Programmes

Since their introduction, dual study programmes have experienced considerable development in Germany. After the idea of such programmes emerged in the 1970s on the initiative of the business community, with its implementation driven forward by education policy in Baden-Württemberg, vocational academies were also founded in other federal states.

Institutionally, however, it was initially not easy for the dual study programme to find its place in the education system. Due to its strong practical orientation and the direct influence of business on the content, it stood in contrast to the traditional self-image of higher education institutions, especially universities. However, despite initial scepticism from the higher education sector, the dual study program model has proven successful. The steady growth in student enrolment and the ongoing expansion of available specialisations and programmes have firmly established dual study programs as a viable and attractive option within the German higher education landscape.

However, it has taken time to get to this point. In some federal states, additional vocational academies were founded after Baden-Württemberg. In others, however, there was resistance to permitting another type of higher education institution alongside the already established universities of applied sciences. Instead, dual study programmes were set up at the existing universities of applied sciences. This approach was also supported by the German Council of Science and Humanities (Wissenschaftsrat, 1993).

In Baden-Württemberg, it was also established by law in 1989 that the degrees awarded by vocational academies are equivalent to those awarded by universities of applied sciences. This was an important step in clarifying the relationship between universities of applied sciences and vocational academies, which were not formally categorised as higher education institutions. In 1993, a further four federal states followed suit and enacted comparable regulations. However, this lack of uniformity in the regulations in Germany impaired the educational mobility of graduates; for example, if they wanted to gain admission to a master's degree programme at a university of applied sciences after completing a bachelor's degree at a university of cooperative education.

Not least for this reason, the Baden-Württemberg University of Cooperative Education sought official university status in 2009. The vocational academy, which now has several locations, became Baden-Württemberg Cooperative State University (DHBW). This change in status also allowed the possibility of offering master's degree programmes, a mandate for cooperative research and the ability to award academic degrees. Overall, an increased academisation of dual study programmes was a defining trend in the 2000s due to the growing number of dual study programmes at universities of applied sciences.

In the 2010s, the popularity and diversification of the dual study programme continued to grow. While dual study programmes were traditionally strongly represented in the fields of technology and business administration, there has been a diversification into other sectors and subject areas in recent years. For example, dual study programmes have increasingly been offered in the fields of health, social sciences and media. Advancing digitalisation and technologisation have led to an adaptation of dual study programmes to the changing requirements of the labour market. New degree programmes in the fields of information technology, digitalisation and engineering were increasingly offered.

*Table 4.2* Development of the number of dual study programmes, cooperation partners and dual students in 2004, 2011 and 2022 (absolute figures)

| Year | Number of dual study programmes | Number of cooperation partners | Number of students** |
|---|---|---|---|
| 2004 | 512 | 18,168 | 40,982 |
| 2011* | 879 | 40,555 | 59,628 |
| 2022 | 1749 | 56,862 | 120,517 |

* Since 2011, the data relates exclusively to initial study programmes.
** Not all higher education institutions enter student numbers in the database, so it can be assumed that the number of students is higher than recorded in the database.

Source: Bundesinstitut für Berufsbildung, 2023, p. 11

In 2011, there were 879 dual study programmes in Germany, rising to 1,749 in 2022, and 40,630 companies were involved as cooperation partners in 2011, increasing to 56,862 in 2022. The number of dual students has doubled in the last ten years, representing 4.2% of all first-semester students across Germany. This growth has led to the dual study programme being described as a model for success (Konegen-Grenier and Winde, 2017; Stifterverband, 2018).

A comparison between training-integrated programmes, which include full VET and a corresponding dual qualification, and practice-integrated degree programmes shows a different trend. While training-integrated degree programmes still accounted for a good half of all programmes in 2011, they have fallen by 18.4% since then and only account for a third of all programmes in 2022. In contrast, practice-integrated degree programmes increased by 7.7% in the same period, now accounting for half of the degree programmes offered. A striking increase of 10.7% can be seen in the mixed programmes, which have more than tripled their share since 2011. One explanation for the increase of the mixed forms is the growing differentiation in the design of dual study programmes (Bundesinstitut für Berufsbildung, 2023, p. 13), which allows such programmes to meet the needs of the companies and a wider range of students. The decline in training-integrated programmes may be explained by the high time burden for students and the coordination required between the higher education institution, company partner and the vocational school

There are many reasons for the growth and attractiveness of the dual study programme. For example, the importance of employability for graduates is increasing. The opportunity to come into contact with the world of work during their studies, the prospect of having a secure job after graduation and having professional experience that promotes flexibility on the labour market as a whole make dual study programmes attractive. The continuously growing number of school leavers with a higher education entrance qualification is also likely to have contributed to the growth of these degree programmes. In addition, as part of the European Bologna Process, the differentiation of university degrees has been abolished, meaning that bachelor's and master's degrees from universities, universities of applied sciences and vocational academies can be regarded as formally equivalent. This has given further impetus to universities of applied sciences, which offer the largest proportion of dual study programmes.

## Challenges and Points of Criticism

Although dual study programmes are considered a successful model in Germany and offer many advantages, there are also some points of criticism and challenges. A source of criticism is often the comparison with the dual VET system in secondary education. The dual VET system has grown over a long period of time and is highly regarded in society and the economy. As a result, it is the template for how the theory–practice link should be organised and for how governance structures are conceptualised.

### *Possible Marginalisation of Dual VET*

However, there is one fundamental point of discussion relating to the educational system as a whole: to what extent do dual study programmes weaken the dual VET system at secondary level (Ertl, 2020)? It should be noted in this context that over 25% of those who complete a dual VET programme at secondary level in Germany now have a higher education entrance qualification. In this respect, the dual study programmes with their identical or very similar hybrid approach are in direct competition with dual VET, which traditionally produces skilled workers at middle management level. The dual study programmes additionally have the prestige of a higher education degree course and at the same time offer the advantages of vocational training, for example the remuneration, the theory–practice connection and the easy transition into the labour market.

A trend towards higher education in general has been observed since the 1960s and thus a continuous convergence in the number of new entrants to VET and higher education (Baethge and Wolter, 2015). In 1992, almost twice as many young people started VET compared to higher education. Since 2011, the figures have converged and in 2020, for the first time, the number of new university entrants exceeded the number of newly concluded training contracts for dual VET.[6] The specific impact of the expansion of dual study programmes cannot be clearly measured. However, it is likely to be inconsistent, depending in particular on occupations, sectors and company-specific recruitment practices (Krone *et al.*, 2019; Wolter, 2016).

### *Governance Aspects*

In Germany, the trade unions have traditionally been an important player in the organisation of the dual training system. Alongside the other three institutional players, the employer representatives, the federal government and the federal states, they are involved in all VET policy decisions. They are represented in all important public decision-making bodies at both federal and state level, for example on the main committee of the Federal Institute for Vocational Education and Training, the central competence centre for vocational education and training in Germany (Section 92 Vocational Training Act).[7] They are also regularly involved in the design of training regulations, which are the standards that describe the technical competences that trainees acquire during their vocational training. In addition, the trade unions see their role as representing the interests of trainees in the training companies.

In contrast, the governance structures for the dual study programme do not provide for comparable involvement of the trade unions. For example, the programme content is determined by the cooperation partners, the higher education institutions and the company partners. However, the trade unions see themselves as representing the interests of dual students in the companies, and carry out surveys and formulate corresponding demands to improve the situation of dual students.

Another significant systematic difference is the legal basis of dual VET compared to dual study programmes. Dual VET has its legal basis in the Vocational Training Act, whereas there is nothing comparable for dual study programmes. The general higher education law of the federal states applies here. The Vocational Training Act contains, for example, regulations on the suitability of the training company, the remuneration of trainees, the structure of the training contract between the company and the apprentice, and so on. The national training regulations that apply to VET occupations are also developed on this legal basis. The Vocational Training Act therefore plays a particularly important role in the quality assurance of dual VET.

These structural differences form the background for criticism of dual study programmes, particularly from trade unions (DGB-Jugend, 2023a, 2023b). For example, the unions call for legal requirements regarding the amount of practical training, company quality assurance and a minimum remuneration for dual students. Higher education institutions and companies are also called upon to do much more to harmonise learning content and to take their quality assurance obligations seriously, including regular checks to ensure that theory and practice are well coordinated (DGB-Jugend, 2023a). Essentially, the trade unions demand compliance with the quality standards from the Vocational Training Act also for dual study programmes.

### Interlocking and Quality Assurance

The dovetailing of vocational and academic learning content at the core of the dual study programmes makes their organisation particularly challenging. The higher education institutions must ensure the academic quality of the programme, while at the same time meeting the demands of the company partners for practical orientation. If there is a lack of close harmonisation and coordination, students would not be able to take full advantage of both components (Nickel *et al.*, 2022). In addition, theory and practice not only represent different types of knowledge, but the knowledge is imparted within the framework of their own institutional culture, whether higher education institution or company partner. The issue of quality assurance is therefore of particular importance (Stifterverband, 2015; Wissenschaftsrat, 2013).

The German Council of Science and Humanities demands that the higher education institution learning location should have a minimum time scope of 50% and that the practical phases should be designed in a learning-oriented manner (Wissenschaftsrat, 2013). It sees the overall responsibility for the quality of dual study programmes as lying with the higher education institutions. As part of the accreditation process that every degree programme in Germany has to undergo, the quality of the company as a place of learning must also be ensured by the higher education institution. However, this approach also faces critical scrutiny, with suggestions that it de facto subordinates company-based learning to the principles of academia (Weiß, 2016).

A survey of dual study programme students revealed that students' assessment of quality criteria varies greatly depending on the sector (DGB-Jugend, 2023a). The top ranks are held by sectors that have comparatively longer experience with dual study programmes and in which larger companies are often found. Dual study programme students from the manufacturing industry in particular gave above-average ratings. At the lower end of the scale are two sectors in the social professions, health and social services and education and teaching, which were rated below average in the survey. Dual study programmes have not been around for long in these two sectors, which are also under high cost pressure and suffer from a pronounced shortage of skilled workers.

Various initiatives have been launched to ensure quality, such as the "Dual Study Quality Network", in which ten German higher education institutions have developed innovative measures for the quality assurance of dual study programmes (Stifterverband, 2015). Guidelines for companies have also been developed (Stifterverband, 2018). The higher education institutions, such as the DHB, also develop individual quality assurance instruments themselves. These are part of the cooperation rules for collaboration with company partners. They include, for example, cooperation agreements to define mutual rights and obligations, suitability principles for accepting new partners and harmonised quality assurance instruments for the teaching and learning formats at both learning locations (Duale Hochschule Baden-Württemberg DHBW, 2018; Gerstung and Deuer, 2021a).

### Social Aspects of the Students

The design of the dual study programme means a high workload for students. The study programme is tightly scheduled and recovery phases are rare. However, the drop-out rate for dual study programmes is generally below 5% and is therefore significantly lower than for conventional study programmes.

Nevertheless, it is recommended that companies should be made aware of the particular burden that students are confronted with doubts and thoughts of dropping out. As a result, there have been calls for the expansion of relevant counselling services (Bundesministerium für Bildung und Forschung, 2022).

An important reason for students to take up a dual study programme is the financing model. It provides for the payment of a remuneration and, in many cases, the payment of tuition fees and other services or benefits. However, the financial benefits vary greatly across the different subject areas. They are highest in the fields of law, economics and social sciences as well as engineering, and lowest in linguistics and cultural studies. The trade unions in particular therefore see potential for improvement. They point out that for 80% of students, the company and university are not in the same geographical area and 25% of students have two places of residence. Commuting or running two households would result in considerable additional costs (DGB-Jugend, 2023b).

The majority of students want the company to hire dual students after they have completed their studies, and this is an important element in the attractiveness of the dual study programme. Seventy-five per cent actually receive a permanent offer of employment, while a quarter only receive an offer for a fixed-term follow-up contract (DGB-Jugend, 2023b). A survey of graduates from 2017 shows that around two-thirds of graduates actually start their career in the training company. The others start with a part-time position or combine their first job with a part-time or dual master's degree programme. Around a third leave the training company to study either full time or part time/dual in another company or to establish themselves elsewhere (Krone *et al.*, 2019).

In some cases, it is noted that dual study programmes attract the highest-achieving young people in particular. On the other hand, it is argued that it is particularly attractive to those whose parents have not studied, and thus dual study programmes contribute to widening access to university. Both statements contain empirical evidence. A study from 2023 shows that the dual study programme, like the other degree programmes at universities of applied sciences, does indeed have a high proportion of students whose parents have not studied (Christoph *et al.*, 2023). Within the group of students whose parents did not attend university, dual study programs are particularly attractive to high-achieving individuals who have directly obtained their higher education entrance qualification. This may be due in part to the requirement of securing a training contract with a partnering company, which is a prerequisite for admission to a dual study program (Gerloff and Reinhard, 2019). Because companies have a say in the selection of candidates, highly motivated and high-performing applicants are more likely to be admitted (Gerloff and Reinhard, 2019).

## The Swiss Approach

Dual study programmes also developed at universities of applied sciences[8] in recent years in Austria (Tritscher-Archan and Schmid, 2016). Like Germany,

Austria has a comparatively strong VET sector at secondary level, including apprenticeship training comparable to dual VET in Germany. Nevertheless, dual study programmes developed much later in Austria. One of the main reasons for this was the lack of large companies in particular, the core drivers of dual study programmes (Hippach-Schneider and Schneider, 2016). Interestingly a similar development cannot be observed in Switzerland; in fact Germany and Switzerland in particular have almost opposing strategies. These education systems, which are very similar in the area of vocational education and training at secondary level, reveal remarkably different approaches at tertiary level (Hippach-Schneider and Schneider, 2018).

In Switzerland, a clear separation of vocational tertiary education and higher education is favoured. A convergence of the various elements of the tertiary education system is even seen as a threat to the performance of the tertiary education system (Schweizerischer Wissenschafts- und Innovationsrat, 2014) [Swiss Science and Innovation Council]. The focus is on strengthening the differentiation between vocational tertiary education and higher education by emphasising the key distinguishing features.

The vocational baccalaureate (Berufsmaturität) plays an important role in combining vocational and academic education. Originally introduced in the 1990s, the Berufsmaturität was directly linked to the upgrading of higher vocational education institutions[9] to universities of applied sciences. After completing initial VET in conjunction with a specific baccalaureate examination, the vocational baccalaureate provides access to a bachelor's programme at a university of applied sciences. The universities of applied sciences offer practice-oriented degree programmes as well as application-oriented research and development and were specifically designed in the mid-1990s as an academic further education option for graduates of VET. This means that universities of applied sciences in Switzerland have a completely different role in the education system from that found in Germany. While in Germany they are an application-oriented form of higher education, with almost the same admission requirements as universities, whereas universities of applied sciences in Switzerland are clearly focussed on those with a VET qualification at secondary level.

The link between vocational and academic education in Switzerland may thus be viewed as consecutive: initial VET remains untouched. This provides a useful contrast with forms of dual study programmes in Germany, where initial VET is combined with academic content in the university sector.

## Conclusion

The dual study programme is characterised by a particularly high level of participation by companies through the practical phases; they are co-designers of the study programmes and in some cases also members of the university committees that decide on the strategic development of the dual study programmes. But not only that, they were the drivers and initiators of dual study programmes in Germany. The initiative for the dual study programme did not come from the world of education, but from the world of business. This gave rise to a form of higher education study programme that can certainly be described as a successful model, even if, as explained earlier, there are aspects that could and should be improved, such as the coordination of the two learning sites and the respective organisation of the study plans.

The great heterogeneity of the dual study programme, which is not least due to the regulatory responsibility of the 16 federal states, has led to considerations as to whether there is a need for – or even the legal possibility of – enacting uniform federal regulations. The trade unions, for example, are pushing for greater legislation of dual studies, similar to the Vocational Training Act for dual training in secondary education. As part of the amendment of the Vocational Training Act in 2019, the German Bundestag passed a formal resolution calling for a corresponding research study to be conducted. The resulting study developed numerous recommendations for improving the quality and organisation of dual study programmes. However, it does not include the trade union demand for greater legislation. Even if a need for further development of the legal framework and the need to close some regulatory gaps is observed by some, the study actually indicates legal overregulation (Nickel *et al.*, 2022). It is also noted that the dual study programmes must be able to orientate themselves strongly to the individual circumstances of the respective locations and the possibilities of the cooperation partners involved. Overall, the stakeholders surveyed also see little need to improve the legal framework. Only 38.6% of those responsible at universities and only 13% of companies see a need for action. It remains to be seen whether and how further discussion will develop.

Finally, another development should be highlighted: study-integrated VET programmes have recently been introduced in Germany. As training-integrated dual study programmes, these are intended to result in a double qualification. However, while students on a training-integrated dual study programme decide on the dual qualification before they start their studies, apprentices enrolled on study-integrated VET programmes can decide between vocational qualification, bachelor's degree or double qualification at a later date. Since 2020, the federal state of Hamburg has had its own Hamburg University of Cooperative Education (BHH). The students here are also apprentices with a training and study contract in a company. For the students, this means three places of learning: company, university and vocational school, similar to the training-integrated dual study programmes. These programmes are offered in four business administration courses and computer science. A large pilot project is currently underway in the largest federal state of North Rhine-Westphalia, which is also trialling study-integrated training programmes.[10]

A further hybrid programme profile combining vocational and academic education has thus emerged in addition to the dual study programmes. It remains to be seen how the now numerous different formats and concepts will fare in the future. Regardless, Germany continues to rely on these forms of practice-based higher education programmes to secure the skilled labour it needs.

**Notes**

1 Compared to universities, universities of applied sciences are characterised by a particular application orientation and a stronger focus on the requirements of professional practice.
2 In Germany, the tertiary sector essentially comprises the various types of higher education institutions and, to a limited extent, institutions outside the higher education sector. This also includes the vocational academies.
3 Example of the DHBW module handbook for the Engineering department, Mechanical Engineering degree programme www.dhbw.de/fileadmin/user/public/SP/KA/Maschinenbau/Allgemeiner_Maschinenbau.pdf [Accessed 9 February 2024].
4 The students were also surveyed at the same time, as were the lecturers.
5 The data refer to the training- and practice-integrated degree programmes.
6 www.demografie-portal.de/DE/Fakten/ausbildung-studium-anfaenger.html [Accessed 19 February 2024].
7 www.bibb.de/en/463.php [Accessed 19 February 2024].
8 Universities of applied sciences have existed in Austria since 1994, making it a relatively young higher education sector. However, in the winter semester 2021, around 25% of all first-year students started their studies at a university of applied sciences; www.bmbwf.gv.at/Themen/HS-Uni/Hochschulsystem/Fachhochschulen.html [Accessed 19 February 2024].
9 For example Höhere Technische Lehranstalt, Höhere Wirtschafts- und Verwaltungsfachschule.
10 https://sia-nrw.de/ [Accessed 18 February 2024].

**References**

Autorengruppe Bildungsberichterstattung (2022) *Bildung in Deutschland 2022: Ein indikatorengestützter Bericht mit einer Analyse zum Bildungspersonal* [Online]. Available at https://www.bildungsbericht.de/de/bildungsberichte-seit-2006/bildungsbericht-2022/pdf-dateien-2022/bildungsbericht-2022.pdf [Accessed 13 October 2022].
Baethge, M. and Wolter, A. (2015) 'The German skill formation model in transition: From dual system of VET to higher education?', *Journal for Labour Market Research*, vol. 48, no. 2, pp. 97–122.
Bauer-Hailer, U. and Wezel, H.-U. (2008) *Die Berufsakademie: eine baden-württembergische Erfolgsgeschichte*, Statistisches Monatsheft Baden-Württemberg [Online]. Available at https://www.statistik-bw.de/Service/Veroeff/Monatshefte/PDF/Beitrag08_09_04.pdf [Accessed 14 January 2024].
Brünner, K., Chvosta, A. and Oertel, S. (2016) 'Die Institutionalisierung dualer Studiengänge: Hintergründe, Verlauf und Entwicklung', in Fasshauer, U. and Severing, E. (eds) *Verzahnung beruflicher und akademischer Bildung: duale Studiengänge in Theorie und Praxis* [Online], Bielefeld, W. Bertelsmann Verlag, pp. 63–80. Available at www.bibb.de/dienst/publikationen/de/7940 [Accessed 6 February 2024].
Bundesinstitut für Berufsbildung (2023) *AusbildungPlus – Duales Studium in Zahlen 2022* [Online]. Available at https://www.bibb.de/dokumente/pdf/AiZ_Duales_Studium_2022_bf.pdf [Accessed 19 January 2024].

Bundesministerium für Bildung und Forschung (2022) *Duales Studium: Umsetzungsmodelle und Entwicklungsbedarfe: Zentrale Ergebnisse der Studie* [Online]. Available at https://www.bmbf.de/SharedDocs/Publikationen/de/bmbf/4/677798_Duales_Studium_Kurzbericht.pdf?__blob=publicationFile&amp%3Bv=10 [Accessed 19 January 2024].

Christoph, B., Patzina, A. and Toussaint, C. (2023, 15) *Soziale Ungleichheit in den Bildungsentscheidungen nach dem Abitur: Kinder von Eltern ohne Hochschulabschluss nehmen eher ein duales Studium auf*, IAB-Kurzbericht.

Deloitte and Stifterverband (2015) *Ergebnisse der Unternehmensbefragung Duales Studium: Erschließung neuer Bildungs-und Karrierewege* [Online]. Available at http://www.stifterverband.de/pdf/duales_studium_unternehmensbefragung.pdf [Accessed 15 February 2024].

DGB-Jugend (2023a) *Qualitätsreport Duales Studium* [Online]. Available at https://jugend.dgb.de/ueber-uns/meldungen/studium/++co++34bb137a-5871-11ee-b351-001a4a16011a [Accessed 19 February 2024].

DGB-Jugend (2023b) *Report Duale Studierende – zur aktuellen Lage in einem hybriden Ausbildungsformat: Schwerpunkt: Betriebliche Praxisphasen* [Online]. Available at https://jugend.dgb.de/ueber-uns/meldungen/studium/++co++34bb137a-5871-11ee-b351-001a4a16011a [Accessed 19 February 2024].

Duale Hochschule Baden-Württemberg DHBW (2018) *Qualitätshandbuch* [Online]. Available at https://www.dhbw.de/fileadmin/user_upload/Dokumente/Qualitaetsmanagement/DHBW_Qualitaetshandbuch.pdf [Accessed 9 February 2024].

Ertl, H. (2020) 'Dual study programmes in Germany: Blurring the boundaries between higher education and vocational training?', *Oxford Review of Education*, vol. 46, no. 1, pp. 79–95.

Gerloff, A. and Reinhard, K. (2019) 'Work-integrated leading dual study programs', *International Journal of Work-Integrated Learning*, vol. 20, no. 2, pp. 161–169 [Online]. Available at https://files.eric.ed.gov/fulltext/EJ1226179.pdf [Accessed 18 January 2024].

Gerstung, V. and Deuer, E. (2021a) *Ein Markenzeichen auf dem Prüfstand: Die Perspektive der dualen Partner auf die Theorie-Praxis-Verzahnung im dualen Studium*, Hochschulforschung an der DHBW 11 [Online]. Available at https://www.dhbw.de/fileadmin/user_upload/Dokumente/Schrifterzeugnisse/Gerstung_Deuer_2021_Markenzeichen_auf_dem_Pruefstand_Teil3_Forschungsbericht_11_2021.pdf [Accessed 9 February 2024].

Gerstung, V. and Deuer, E. (2021b) 'Theorie-Praxis-Verzahnung im dualen Studium: Ein konzeptioneller Forschungsbeitrag', *Zeitschrift für Hochschulentwicklung*, vol. 16, no. 2, pp. 195–213 [Online]. https://doi.org/10.3217/zfhe-16–02/14 [Accessed 6 February 2024].

Hessisches Ministerium für Wirtschaft, Energie, Verkehr und Wohnen (2020) *Duales Studium Hessen: Beste Aussichten für Unternehmen* [Online]. Available at https://wirtschaft.hessen.de/sites/wirtschaft.hessen.de/files/2023-02/duales_studium_beste_aussichten_fuer_unternehmen_0.pdf [Accessed 9 February 2024].

Hippach-Schneider, U. and Schneider, V. (eds) (2016) *Tertiary vocational education in Europe – examples from six education systems* [Online], Bonn. Available at https://www.bibb.de/dienst/publikationen/en/8155 [Accessed 19 February 2024].

Hippach-Schneider, U. and Schneider, V. (2018) 'Eine Gefahr für die Leistungsfähigkeit der tertiären Bildung? Bildungspolitische Unterschiede zwischen Deutschland und der Schweiz', *Berufs-und Wirtschaftpädagogik-Online*, no. 34 [Online]. Available at http://www.bwpat.de/ausgabe34/hippach-schneider_schneider_bwpat34.pdf [Accessed 19 March 2024].

Konegen-Grenier, C. and Winde, M. (2017) *Bildungsinvestitionen der Wirtschaft 2015*, Stifterverband der Deutschen Wissenschaft e.V. and Institut der Deutschen Wirtschaft.

Krone, S., Nieding, I. and Ratermann-Busse, M. (2019) *Dual studieren – und dann?: Eine empirische Studie zum Übergangsprozess Studium-Beruf dualer Studienabsolvent/inn/en* [Online], Düsseldorf, Hans-Böckler-Stiftung. Available at http://hdl.handle.net/10419/194584.

Nickel, S., Pfeiffer, I., Fischer, A., Hüsch, M., Kiepenheuer-Drechsler, B., Lauterbach, N., Reum, N., Thiele, A.-L. and Ulrich, S. (2022) *Duales Studium: Umsetzungsmodelle und Entwicklungsbedarfe*, Bielefeld, wbv Media GmbH.

Schweizerischer Wissenschafts- und Innovationsrat (2014) *Die Tertiärstufe des Schweizer Bildungssystems: Bericht und Empfehlungen des Schweizerischen Wissenschafts- und Innovationsrates SWIR; vom Rat verabschiedet am 11. November 2014*, SWIR Schrift.

Stifterverband (2015) *Qualitätsentwicklung im dualen Studium: Ein Handbuch für die Praxis* [Online]. Available at https://www.bibb.de/dokumente/pdf/Stifterverband_Handbuch_Qualitaetstentwicklung_im_dualen_Studium.pdf [Accessed 15 February 2024].

Stifterverband (2018) *Erfolgsmodell Duales Studium: Leitfaden für Unternehmen* [Online]. Available at https://www.stifterverband.org/medien/erfolgsmodell-duales-studium [Accessed 15 February 2024].

Tritscher-Archan, S. and Schmid, K. (2016) 'Vocational education and training on EQF-levels 5 to 7 in Austria', in Hippach-Schneider, U. and Schneider, V. (eds) *Tertiary vocational education in Europe – examples from six education systems* [Online], Bonn, pp. 181–212. Available at www.bibb.de/dienst/publikationen/en/8155 [Accessed 19 February 2024].

Weiß, R. (2016) 'Duale Studiengänge – Verzahnung beruflicher und akademischer Bildung', in Fasshauer, U. and Severing, E. (eds) *Verzahnung beruflicher und akademischer Bildung: duale Studiengänge in Theorie und Praxis* [Online], Bielefeld, W. Bertelsmann Verlag, pp. 21–39. Available at www.bibb.de/dienst/publikationen/de/7940 [Accessed 6 February 2024].

Wissenschaftsrat (1993) *10 Thesen zur Hochschulpolitik* [Online]. Available at https://www.wissenschaftsrat.de/download/archiv/1001-93.pdf?__blob=publicationFile&v=1 [Accessed 14 February 2024].

Wissenschaftsrat (2013) *Empfehlungen zur Entwicklung des dualen Studiums: Positionspapier*, Wissenschaftsrat.

Woisch, A. and Mentges, H. (2018) *Wer nimmt ein duales Studium auf? Ergebnisse einer Befragung von Studienberechtigten des Schulabschlussjahrgangs 2015* [Online]. Available at https://www.dzhw.eu/publikationen/pub_show?pub_id=5393&pub_type=kbr [Accessed 5 February 2024].

Wolter, A. (2016) 'Der Ort des dualen Studiums zwischen beruflicher und akademischer Bildung: Mythen und Realitäten', in Fasshauer, U. and Severing, E. (eds) *Verzahnung beruflicher und akademischer Bildung: duale Studiengänge in Theorie und Praxis* [Online], Bielefeld, W. Bertelsmann Verlag, pp. 39–60. Available at www.bibb.de/dienst/publikationen/de/7940 [Accessed 6 February 2024].

Chapter 5

# GUSS at 5

## A Retrospective of Work-Based Learning Within an In-House Student-delivered Software Service

*Nader Al Haffar, Sayan Bandyopadhyay, Len Lukowski, Nihanth Manyam, Ahmad Salman, Derek Somerville, Tim Storer, Stella Eva Tsiapali and Tess Vaughan*

### Introduction

The Glasgow University Software Service (GUSS) was created in the summer of 2019. Prior to the service being established, the School of Computing Science within the university regularly received enquiries regarding the availability of services to support software development projects. These enquiries came from several sources, such as other research and business units within the university, local charities, small to medium-sized (typically not technology) enterprises, start-ups and scale-ups.

For many enquiries, the scale of envisaged software development was too small for the clients to secure the necessary capacity to realise the project. Typically, these projects might require around 200 hours of person time to complete. Recruiting software engineers is in any case difficult, and roles that require a flexible skillset for short periods of often part-time work are unattractive, particularly for experienced engineers, for whom more attractive prospects are available. Similarly, software development agencies are less interested in small-scale projects, since they do not require a proportionately lower time investment in terms of scoping, estimating, negotiating and/or bidding as compared to larger projects.

Unfortunately, with a research and teaching focus, the school lacked the capacity to respond to enquiries for routine software development work. The enquiries often focused on innovation work but lacked the need for lower technology readiness level (TRL) computing science research capacity, or if they did were unlikely to align with the necessarily narrow and focused interests of academic researchers. In some cases, enquiries could be diverted to a dissertation project course, such as our Student Team Project (Simpson and Storer 2017). Although some of these projects have been very successful, they can often lead to unsatisfactory long-term outcomes for the clients, since the

DOI: 10.4324/9781003496779-5

students working on the projects are themselves learning about group-based software engineering and lack the experience of managing a client and technical development effort.

Some solutions for small-scale software development do exist in the marketplace. Individual software engineers will advertise their availability for contract work (Akhmetshin *et al.* 2018), sometimes through services such as Freelancer (Taylor and Joshi 2019; "Freelancer Service Website" 2024). However, many potential clients within the university lack the knowledge to determine whether potential contractors have the correct skillset or the experience to manage a software project, risking the same outcomes as for dissertation projects. In any case, procuring such services from within a large organisation such as the university, subject to budgeting and contracting rules, is difficult.

To address this need, the Glasgow University Software Service (GUSS) was created in the summer of 2019 to utilise the talent of student software engineers to provide affordable software development services for small- to medium-scale software development projects, typically of less than 1000 hours of person-effort. At the outset, the founders of the service agreed three related objectives:

- Provide real-world work experience for students in the school.
- Enable research impact across the university.
- Support local social enterprises, charities, SMEs and start-ups in the first stages of their journey.

These three objectives are interlinked and have the potential to provide added value to one another. Students who work on projects that enable impact for other academic units are exposed to cutting-edge research across a number of different disciplines and learn about how software can be used to create solutions in these domains. This therefore widens their range of experiences whilst at university, as well as their perceptions of post-graduation career options, into roles such as research software engineering (Cosden *et al.* 2022). Similarly, students who work on projects for local start-ups are exposed to an entrepreneurial environment. Indeed, several of our student software engineers (SSEs) have proceeded into direct employment with start-ups we have contracted with post-graduation.

Hosting the service within an academic unit under the oversight of an academic director ensures that the service is sympathetic to the particular needs of researchers, who contend with uncertainty in the requirements for their work. A supplementary benefit of this arrangement is that there is opportunity to recognise when particular enquiries from within the university or externally may benefit from specialist computing science research expertise. The service can therefore act as a gateway into the wider school, enabling interdisciplinary research collaborations to form.

GUSS has now been operating within the university for five years. The service has evolved considerably during that time. In this chapter, we outline how the service operates today and reflect on the service from the perspective of the core team and (most importantly) the student software engineers themselves. The participants in the retrospectives are also the co-authors of this chapter. Together, we therefore provide the first substantive reflective analysis of the successes and challenges experienced by a university-based, student-staffed software service.

The rest of this chapter is organised as follows. The second section outlines the history of the development of GUSS and explains the nature of the work undertaken and how the service operates. The third section describes the method followed for eliciting reflections on the work-based learning undertaken in GUSS, using a series of retrospectives amongst the co-authors. The fourth section presents the results and key findings from our analysis of the data gathered from the retrospectives. The fifth section reviews the existing literature on student-delivered software services. Finally, the sixth section summarises the paper and key findings in relation to the related literature and identifies future work for the service in terms of enhancing the work-based learning experience.

## GUSS at 5 – A Historical Sketch

The potential for professionally led student-delivered software service to deliver on small- to medium-scale software projects had been discussed for several years within the school. During the summer of 2019, a decision was made to put these ideas into practice. Since then, the purpose and model envisaged at the outset has largely remained the same. The service would consider enquiries for development work to be undertaken provided there was a viable means of funding, and students would be employed as software engineers working under the supervision of a project manager who would have responsibility for managing both the software team and the client.

Several practical obstacles had to be resolved to realise this. First, the service would need a means of collecting funding from other parts of the university. This was achieved by the creation of a budget code within the School of Computing Science, allowing funding to be journalled to the service internally from other budget codes or for funding to be allocated to the service following an invoice being issued to an external client. Second, the service needed a means of employing SSEs and ensuring that they would be compensated. The school's HR point of contact helped with the development of a job description for a fractional-hours grade 4 software engineer. The service also needed an engineering manager to lead on the organisation of the service and manage the first projects. Initially, the school provided seed funding for an internship stipend for the service's engineering manager, allowing him to work with Tim Storer throughout the summer. A formal job description was then created in the autumn and a role advertised, to which Omar Tufayl was subsequently appointed.

With these practical difficulties resolved, the service could begin advertising for potential clients in earnest. This was done using internal university communications and some direct contact with business development managers in other academic units. This resulted in the first projects for GUSS in the autumn of 2019. One of the earliest web applications built by GUSS was designed to host a data set of "re-municipalisation" case studies curated by the Adam Smith Business School (Trans-national Institute 2024).

Since that first project, GUSS has worked on a wide range of software-related projects. As well as undertaking development work, the service also offers consultancy and training. For example, the service has performed reviews on behalf of clients seeking to transfer code bases between providers and conducted feasibility studies of applications of large language models to different tasks. Similarly, the service also provides training on basic programming skills as optional courses for students in social sciences. The technologies employed have also been wide ranging. Where feasible, low-code content management tools such as WordPress are used for website hosting. If necessary, more flexible frameworks, such as React and Django for web development of custom solutions, have been used. Although web applications are a substantial area of work, the service has also developed mobile applications and analytical software utilising data science technologies.

Most SSEs are recruited from the undergraduate population, typically at the end of their third of four or five years of study, although SSEs can be recruited from earlier years in the undergraduate programme, where the candidate's skills and experience warrant it. This enables students to work for GUSS over a minimum of two summers, including for a short period post-graduation. In addition, GUSS will also recruit from the post-graduate taught (PGT) and post-graduate research (PGR) student populations. PGT students often bring significant experience into GUSS, having worked in the software industry prior to returning to study. Similarly, PGR students often bring specialist capabilities to the service centred on their research experience and will typically be available within the service for longer periods of time.

Each SSE works up to 10 hours per week during term time. SSEs are employed on flexible hours contracts, with each completing a timesheet at the end of each month. This provides flexibility when allocating them from a pool of those available to projects as and when they arise, although efforts are made to minimise the number of "unallocated" SSEs to ensure they are occupied. Equally, the flexibility allows students to withdraw or pause their work on projects at short notice, for example when they have upcoming coursework deadlines. Hours can also be increased during holiday periods, subject to availability of projects. To supplement the software engineering skillset of the SSEs the service also recruits user experience (UX) designers, who are also students on design courses.

Given the size of many GUSS projects, individual teams are typically small, consisting of two to four SSEs. A software project manager has responsibility for the overall conduct of GUSS's projects, with each manager typically managing several projects simultaneously. The project manager is responsible for negotiating requirements with the customer and for supervising and directing work by SSEs. Teams follow an agile model of software development, working in weekly sprints within an overall project backlog of tasks. The project manager identifies work to be done on a weekly basis in discussion with the software team and the client. Contemporary software practices are advocated wherever possible, with a particular emphasis on early and subsequently continuous delivery to clients. This enables early feedback on work, whilst also providing the client with immediate value.

The service also employs a finance administrator who controls the process for issuing quotes and invoices to customers, as well as processing the timesheets of SSEs and mapping them to relevant projects. Funding for projects comes from a variety of sources, including general university funds, costed work on research grants, Scottish Funding Council Innovation Vouchers and, more recently, the university's impact acceleration account. As a consequence, the service has grown substantially over the last five years and now has (as of summer 2024) a core management team of an engineering manager, an assistant service manager, a project manager and a part-time adjunct project manager (who is also an alumnus of the service and full-time software engineer in a local organisation). The service currently employs two UX designers and 34 SSEs. The service has 20 active projects and has completed over 50. Turnover has grown to approximately £300,000 per year, with the largest project to date involving a team of 10 SSEs.

**Research Design**

Retrospectives are a common process improvement technique used within agile software development teams (Cockburn 1998). The technique features significantly within the Scrum software development method (Schwaber and Beedle 2001) and has been used by GUSS previously at the close of individual projects. The aim is to reflect on current ways of working, including both successes and failures, and seek opportunities for improvement in a structured manner.

Retrospectives can be conducted in person or online (Khanna and Wang 2022) and are often managed by the facilitator to ensure that everyone has an opportunity to contribute. In general, the method has several phases. First, an icebreaker activity is used to encourage discussion and ensure that everyone is comfortable participating in the process. Second, a data-gathering phase is used to generate topics for discussion. A common approach for data gathering is to ask participants to populate a "board", either a physical whiteboard or a web application, with items of interest to them written onto sticky notes. To focus data gathering, the board is often organised according to a number of sub-themes. For example, the Sailboat board is divided into Sun (things that made the participants feel good), Wind (things that drove the project forward), Anchor (things that held the participants back) and Reef (future risks). Participants populate the board independently completing as many topics as they wish. Once this process is complete, the participants collectively group the items into topics. Note that a topic can collate items from several themes into a topic, sometimes indicating disagreement. The participants then choose topics to prioritise for further discussion, exploring thinking in more depth and identifying possible actions.

The co-authors of this chapter participated in three retrospectives, facilitated by one (Somerville) who is not a member of the GUSS team. The first retrospective was conducted within the core management team. This focused on eliciting this group's thinking about the successes and obstacles within GUSS, using the Island of Golocans template (D'Souza 2024) to facilitate this – sweet fruits (what went well), hidden gold (shout out to the team), message in a bottle (action points) and pirates on the shoal (what didn't go well). The second retrospective was also within the core team, but used the Sailboat template (Torstensson 2024) and focused on the strategic challenges and opportunities of the model that GUSS has adopted. The final retrospective was conducted with a group of SSEs and focused on their experiences of working within the service, including what they have learned about software engineering and how they think the support offered by the service could be improved due to struggles they've experienced.

The retrospectives were all conducted online by the facilitator and were recorded for subsequent analysis. Each retrospective lasted between 60 and 90 minutes. The facilitator then documented the major topics that were discussed in each of the retrospectives in the next section (Results).

## Results

This section presents the key themes identified in the retrospectives with the core team and the students. We combine the results from the first two retrospectives in which the core team participated as there was some overlap in themes. However, we present the results from the third retrospective with the SSEs separately to convey the different perspectives.

### *GUSS Manager Retrospectives*

These retrospectives focused on both the perceived successes of the service, particularly in terms of outcomes for clients and impacts on students, and the challenges for recruiting and training student software engineers.

*Recruitment and Turnover*

As described earlier, SSEs are recruited from several different student populations and have to be onboarded through the university's recruitment system. The participants described this process of working with the university's human resources (HR) as "straightforward", particularly when recruiting internally, as HR permits GUSS to conduct its own process for this. However, obstacles and challenges remain. For example, the issue of ensuring continuity of process between successive contacts in HR was raised, as these members of staff progress in their careers. A wiki, or similar, should be considered to allow the lessons learnt to be shared with the next HR coordinator.

Despite this supportive process, the participants acknowledged the pressure of continually hiring and onboarding new developers. The service prefers to onboard new recruits at the beginning of the summer, as this allows time for training and for the new SSEs to become familiar with the service's workflows without the "distraction" of their studies, as well as getting to know the project managers. However, more experienced SSEs tend to leave the service at the end of their final exams before the start of the summer, reducing the opportunities for new SSEs to learn from them. SSEs will sometimes leave the service after a short notice period and in some cases only work for a few weeks due to the unanticipated pressures of both working for GUSS and their coursework. The GUSS team report that they emphasise to SSEs that their coursework should take priority, and they are encouraged to inform the project manager if they need to pause their work on a project, even if this is at short notice.

However, the service's very responsiveness and the turnover in SSEs means that there is often a need for multiple recruitment rounds during the academic year. The approach can be a challenge to project planning, with the flexibility towards students and responsiveness towards clients creating the potential for disruption to projects. This can be exacerbated by the tendency for students to work on coursework close to deadlines. The risk is explained to clients and most were found to be sympathetic to the risks, although the participants have noticed that internal clients tend to be more receptive to this message than external clients are.

GUSS has addressed this by modifying the interview process to include a question on time management with increased workload. This is intended to both assess how well organised candidates are and encourage them to explicitly consider the consequences of accepting a role. The service puts more effort into maintaining documentation on software projects than might be the case elsewhere due to the greater turnover of staff. One practice used in GUSS is to record a handover or record the final meeting on a project for future SSEs. Some exit interviews have been carried out, although this isn't systematic and departing SSEs tend not to complete the exit surveys they are sent. A suggestion was made to have the completion of the form be paid for explicitly, signalling its importance. In addition, the service has been more prepared to turn down potential external projects where there was perceived to be a lack of understanding of the nature of student-delivered software projects.

A final issue raised under this category was the method for compensating SSEs. The participants were well aware that some of the SSEs perform far more strongly than others do and take on strong leadership roles. The service had attempted to find ways to reward this initiative through the creation of a senior SSE role. However, difficulties had emerged in creating a selection process that was demonstrably fair, as did complications of costing software projects with different grades of SSE involved.

There were concerns about requiring SSEs to complete timesheets that must be approved by two members of the core team. If any part of this process missed the relevant deadline, the payment is delayed to the next end of month. There was concern that the resource constraints within the university meant that it adopted a too strict policy on the deadlines, although some flexibility was noted. One suggestion was to assign the approval to multiple parties, but only requiring two of a level or group to approve.

### Working With Customers

Software projects are often complex and challenging, even at a small scale, where there is a customer with real needs. Given this, it was felt that the GUSS team do not congratulate themselves on the work they do and have an efficient and flexible working model, responding quickly to enquiries for work continuously throughout the year. The responsiveness is perceived as one of the service's key strengths, enabling GUSS to start work on projects within a short time frame by agreeing a budget and then allocating SSEs from a pool of those available for work. One participant describing the culture as "let's get stuff done". This has led to some "amazing" feedback on projects from customers in a wide variety of domains. The expansion of the project management team and the inclusion of a dedicated member of staff for finance and timesheets has helped to give greater stability and assisted with the need to mediate data entry in the university's and the service's tracking systems.

On the whole, there was a feeling that the service had been successful in building a strong internal and external reputation for cost effective delivery. One issue covered in both core team retrospectives was the lack of formal marketing for the service, with a lot of work being referred by word of mouth. Previously, this had not been an issue as the volume of work received this way kept the service at capacity. However, there have recently been a number of onboarded students who couldn't be allocated to projects recently, and the enquiry process can sometimes be a bottleneck for new projects. Several solutions were proposed. For example, it was felt the GUSS team should put together a portfolio of success stories for SSEs and projects. In addition, the enquiry process could be streamlined with the creation of recorded videos that explain how the service works and a more complex enquiry form to help with triage. This would help with clients who have constrained budgets, since scopes could be narrowed more quickly.

Similarly, the service has received very strong feedback on its alumni. Several external service clients have gone on to recruit SSEs directly into their organisations post-graduation. One scale-up owner (not a client) had noted the maturity of the GUSS alumni compared to other graduates, identifying their "real empathy" for the customer. The participants recognised this description in the SSEs, who were characterised as organised and punctual. One participant felt there are some "exceptional" software engineers, "leaning towards very capable" software engineers. During meetings with customers, the SSEs were considered to "come across well" and "with the exception of a few instances they are very professional". There is no coaching given to the SSEs prior to the meetings and feedback is given on demand after the meetings if required. This professionalism was manifested when SSEs needed to liaise with other colleagues in the university, such as IT services, where they were able to demonstrate their negotiating skills to achieve desired outcomes. One participant did note that it helped for SSEs to use their corporate rather than student accounts when communicating with other colleagues.

The participants noted that some SSEs "can be shy" and are reluctant to double check details in client meetings, sometimes waiting for the next meeting before highlighting issues. This is part of the learning process, and allowance should be made for SSEs to learn from their mistakes. The participants felt that most of the SSEs learned to speak up about uncertainties after a few weeks. However, there were a few cases where SSEs needed extra guidance or "weren't able to improve as the projects progressed". One suggestion made was to encourage newer SSEs to explain their understanding to the project team after requirements have been gathered in meetings with clients.

A key factor was felt to be managing the expectations of clients from the outset of a project and ensuring that the scope is reasonable for the budget available. One example given was of an external client expecting a fully developed web application for a budget of £7,500. Several participants noted that it could be difficult to track how much time has been spent on individual projects, given the variety of work being undertaken. Some SSEs only work on one project, but others work on several, so it can be time consuming to audit. This can lead on some occasions to projects running over, leading to unexpected costs for the service or a need for the client to make further investment.

The service has tried to adopt an iterative approach to delivery, whereby *something* of value is delivered as early as possible to the client, however minimal the functionality. This is intended to mitigate the risk of a project having no deliverable should budgets be exhausted before work is completed. The emphasis is therefore on setting up the infrastructure for delivery first and then working on features. The service has worked on creating templates for infrastructure to ease this process. Similarly, one participant noted that the SSEs have a reluctance to commit their work to the project repository if they are uncertain it is acceptable, "I was not sure what was wanted so I did nothing".

They felt this reflected a "coursework" mindset from their academic studies, when work is rarely submitted as "in progress". There was an ongoing need to encourage SSEs to get past this mindset and recognise that "wrong early" is better, as it "gets the conversation happening".

A final concern when dealing with customers was ensuring that maintenance period commitments are both clearly defined and enforced in agreements. Generally the service continues to support clients for a considerable time after the agreed end of the maintenance period. This is sometimes due to a lack of clarity regarding when the maintenance period should end, but is also due to a desire to keep previous customers satisfied. One suggestion was to develop template emails to be sent to customers that explicitly move the project into a maintenance mode and set dates for the period to end. Another option might be to allow former SSEs to "take projects with them" when they leave, enabling them to continue the relationship with the customer directly.

*Agile Practices and Technical Skills*

The service has attempted to follow agile software practices since its inception, although this has not always been successful. For example, retrospectives are not held systematically within projects, which could be used to identify challenges and highlight and share methods to address these issues amongst SSEs, as well as helping improve the general GUSS process and improving specific workflows. The participants felt the GUSS team should consider linting, testing, code review and quality assurance in projects. The team should adopt feature branching and draft merge requests for all projects systematically, rather than within selected projects. Consideration should be given to creating a more methodical process for bringing on SSEs.

A lack of awareness of secure development practices amongst SSEs was highlighted by one participant, and a similar concern was raised regarding UX. The service had deliberately hired UX designers as an explicit role to mitigate these gaps, as well as require SSEs to undergo security practices awareness training. One further consideration was to hire a technical lead as a core member of the project team. A job description has been created, but it has not yet been implemented due to budget constraints. A technical team lead would help maintain standards of software engineering processes for projects.

*Peer Learning*

Peer learning (Sadler and Good 2006) enables students gain a clearer understanding about their own performance through comparison and feedback from other students. The participants in the retrospective felt that team meetings often have SSEs with a variety of skills, and this same process is used for learning. The participants reported that peer learning was important in the service and explored ways this could be strengthened. One participant felt that SSEs tend to "pick up some of those things informally and organically" and that "we are not doing it explicitly as part of a formal program of investing in someone". The participants had seen how much some developers grow and learn in GUSS, one noting that their mindset changed from academic coursework thinking, and one saying "I have seen devs in GUSS progress much faster compared to others overall".

The participants did however report that new recruits often appreciate being paired with a more experienced SSE who can answer questions and with whom they can build a closer relationship. Some SSEs can appear to experience "imposter syndrome" and can be reluctant to ask questions to the wider team. This is eased when they know they are assigned a fellow SSE to help them. More experienced SSEs will give an in-depth knowledge on the technical stack of a project, provide familiarisation with the business and customer and help share the working practices of GUSS. The need for this pairing is felt to be more important for external projects and larger projects. As a consequence, the core team felt that most SSEs improve significantly during their time in GUSS. One participant stated, "devs are flexible as they are still in learning stage".

One suggestion made was to hold frequent "brown bags" meetings as a means of sharing knowledge about projects and technology stacks. These are held during lunch hours and include presentations on both the business domain and the technical aspects of recently completed projects. The participants agree this was a positive idea for the future. One option suggested was having pizza and presentations every three to six months.

Another way to share knowledge and avoid having a *key person dependency* is to enforce code reviews (Sadowski *et al.* 2018). A code review entails a second engineer on a project reviewing a *merge request* of changes to the code base. This has benefits for enhancing the quality of code in terms of readability and maintainability, but can enhance knowledge sharing across a project. One of the participants had tried introducing code reviews into a project they managed, but found that the SSEs often didn't see the value of the practice, since they had limited experience of long-term collaborative ownership of code. They thought it was difficult to justify in small-scale software development.

## Student Software Engineer Retrospective

Student software engineers were encouraged to use this retrospective to reflect on their challenges and learning within GUSS. The SSEs provided a varied account of what has helped them improve from university and their learning on the GUSS projects. This section covers the different themes described by the SSE participants in the third retrospective.

### Prior Learning

The SSEs described a variety of sources of prior learning that were useful for them once they started working with the service. All students in the school are introduced to Git during their second and third years at the university, as well as associated change management processes. These were reported as being useful for GUSS. One SSE mentioned that the courses they had taken on machine learning was also beneficial for the project they worked on with GUSS.

There was value in seeing immediate application of classroom concepts being applied in new practice. Another felt there was "tangible results from putting learned material into practice". One participant noted that it is helpful that projects tend to use the same frameworks as taught in courses. Django and Python were given as examples. This was felt to be less of a barrier to start a project.

*Learning From Being a GUSS SSE*

Several participants described the reward of working on real-world projects that created impact for the university and external partners. One participant felt that the "core ideology" of the service "was sound" seeking to create mutual benefit for the SSEs and the clients through software development projects. Another reported that a lecturer had recommended they apply to GUSS, which had improved their confidence in their abilities.

In one case, a participant was working on a project that focused on improving student well-being and engagement. The SSE highlighted the reward of working on projects that demonstrated the university's value of student well-being. In addition, they noted the rewards of working on projects outside the university. This would manifest itself in interactions with clients; one participant described the reward of seeing progress being made on projects and getting feedback from clients.

One difficulty identified by the participants was determining suitable projects for new starts. The skillsets of SSEs can vary considerably when they begin working for the service, so finding the right combination of projects that both exploit their existing skills that they are comfortable to work on and support them in learning new ones is a difficult balance.

Similar to the core team, the SSEs recognised the benefits of learning to work with fellow SSEs with different skills and knowledge. One described this as a "two-way street". They learned a lot from others about the projects and how to approach problems; they also had periods acting as a mentor to share experience and skills with others. Learning and improving mentoring skills will help with recruitment and the skills needed when the SSEs move into new roles as team leads and senior software engineers. The participants reported that the GUSS team structure is not hierarchical and you get to "meet everyone". It was felt the handover and pairing during this time is important. This was felt to "build confidence and enthusiasm" for newcomers. This was felt to be important in the first few weeks of joining a project.

In contrast to the perceptions of the core team, the SSEs felt they made extensive use of code reviews, one saying "lots of times". This was perhaps influenced by different code bases and different sizes of project. The participants said they had learnt from code reviews from looking at others' work and their comments. This has confirmed the right approach for them to solve problems, one saying that it has given "a bit of dynamicism to how I approach these kinds of problems". GUSS was considered to have projects with clean and easy to maintain code. Although on one project an SSE felt the code was not well organised, such as when someone changes "something here and everything else breaks".

Finally, of course, they recognised the monetary incentive gives the SSE a sense of market value and helps incentivise them to apply for roles. One participant commented that the income from GUSS helped with the financial stress of being at university. One participant raised the concern that the existence of GUSS is not well known within employer organisations, and they would like the "brand" to have better recognition so that more people are informed about what the GUSS team can do for the university and companies. This would benefit the SSEs after they leave GUSS and are seeking employment.

*Experiences of Project Management*

Interestingly, a difference was noticed between the organisation of internal university and external projects. Internal projects more closely followed the agile practices taught at university and gave SSEs the opportunity to practice these. The external projects were felt to be organised more specifically to the project, "just figuring out as you go and wait". This was felt to be an additional experience. One SSE highlighted that they worked on a smaller project with very few developers and the way they worked may have been a challenge if the external project and team had been bigger, but "in this case worked well".

Participants reported that working for GUSS helped them learn to become better organised and structure their time better. They perceived this would make them more effective software engineers in the future. One participant commented that the changing and evolving projects helped their learning to become a "proper software engineer". Another stated that the specialised knowledge they had acquired would help them apply for jobs in the future. In general, the SSEs valued the interactions with experienced peers and managers that can help a software engineer move forward faster.

Not all experiences of project management were positive. One SSE described a project where they would have been "cautious" about raising concerns and the team had not routinely conducted retrospectives. One suggestion from this was for the service to have better processes for SSEs to raise concerns with others in the core team, such as an anonymous feedback mechanism.

Some of the participants who had worked on a larger project for the service reported their unhappiness with the amount of "bureaucracy" they became involved in. This included the need to speak to a large number of different clients about requirements, support the development of data privacy impact assessments and support the preparation of presentations to secure further funding. They found this "frustrating", because they didn't have the legitimacy as junior software engineers to get these tasks completed. Enquiries were often unanswered and they lacked a means of escalating requests to get action. This reflects the core team's concerns about ensuring that SSEs are seen as having legitimacy with colleagues within the wider university.

They were uncertain whether these "operational tasks" were part of their roles as software engineers and were uncertain as to "who's doing exactly what, and are they best equipped". Overall, they felt this experience meant that they were distracted from engineering tasks, which impacted on their ability to deliver the project. As a consequence, the service should consider how to better reorganise large projects as they scale. Additional resources for project management, for example explicitly separate roles for product owner and scrum master, should be considered once projects reach a certain scale.

There was unhappiness reported concerning the larger project due to the scale of funding and associated uncertainties that were involved. The project experienced periods of uncertainty as to future funding, which inevitably affected the morale of the project team as a whole. The project was felt to be close to fruition, but would get "stuck" due to this uncertainty. Many of the tasks and pressures described by the SSEs are inevitable consequences of the increased administration that surrounds larger projects with greater demands for accountability. However, how the service organises work at this much larger scale needs to be reconsidered to ensure that the SSEs feel fully supported and are aware of the different circumstances of large-scale development.

**Related Work**

We are aware of several student-staffed software services operated in other academic institutions. For example, the University of Aberdeen operates the Aberdeen Software Factory (Scharlau 2015); Bowling Green State University operated the Agile Software Factory, from 2008 until at least 2017 (Sims 2008; Green and Chao 2017); and Radford University reported on the operation of a Small Projects Clearing House in 2007 Chase et al. (2007).

There is relatively little scholarship on the operation of student-staffed software services. Where it is available, some of the findings contrast with our own. For example, Green and Chao (2017) provided a short report on the accomplishments and achievements of the Agile Software Factory at Bowling Green State University. Similarly, Chase et al. (2007) describes the experiences of operating their clearing house. Both Chase et al. (2007) and Green and Chao (2017) note similar challenges with regard to securing funding for projects, whereas the experience for the GUSS team has been one of managing the flow of projects through the enquiries pipeline.

Both Green and Chao (2017) and Chase et al. (2007) note the challenges of turnover of SSEs, with Green and Chao (2017) reporting on an explicit transitioning programme and Chase et al. (2007) describing the extent to which their service works to maintain documentation. GUSS has adopted some of both of these measures, although we are wary of creating extensive documentation that becomes outdated. The service has in addition experimented with recruiting software developers for longer periods of time, from either the postgraduate research community or earlier in the undergraduate programme.

Finally, Green and Chao (2017) note some of the risks of working with the software industry and external clients. This has been a challenge for GUSS, and the extra risks and responsibilities are recognised. However, the service continues to see its role in facilitating start-up creation within the local economy, as well as working with non-digital SMEs.

The operational model of GUSS and the student-staffed services that we were able to identify bears some similarities to team-based software engineering project courses (Tomayko 1998; Bruegge *et al.* 2015). For example, team-based courses will often require students to work on real-world projects, for real-world customers, and contemporary software engineering methods such as modern version control, continuous integration, automated testing, code reviews and infrastructure-as-code are either strongly encouraged or mandated. Indeed, several authors, such as Siqueira *et al.* (2008), refer to the Software Factory model as applying to team-based courses. However, the model identified in the introduction to this chapter has important differences. In particular, the service ensures that students are in a professional, fully compensated role when working on projects. In addition, the incorporation of a professional software project manager on every project provides for supervision, direction and mentoring without relying on the direct guidance of academic staff.

## Conclusion

This chapter has described the origins of the Glasgow University Software Service and reported an analysis of three retrospectives conducted with the core management team and a cohort of student software engineers (SSEs). As far as we can determine this chapter is the first full reflective study of a professional student-delivered software service in the literature. The retrospectives review the successes and challenges experienced by the GUSS team over the first five years of its existence. The analysis shows that the service has had considerable success in delivering software systems that enable research impact across the university and successfully supported external partners in the early stages of their entrepreneurial journeys. As a consequence, the service has also demonstrably enhanced the work-based learning of the more than one hundred SSEs who have passed through its employment, a view shared by the core management team, the SSEs who participated in the retrospective and future employers.

Nevertheless, the analysis has revealed a number of challenges and limitations to how the service operates that need to be addressed. The service continues to experience disruption to project progress due to both the pressures and constraints of assessments on SSEs and turnover of staff. Whilst some mitigations have been identified, such as employing students who will be in the university for longer periods, other possibilities should be considered, such as altering the start dates for new SSEs and experimenting with alternative handover documentation and processes. Longer-term organisational memory could be further enhanced by the appointment of a permanent technical lead for the service, within the core management team.

Similarly, the SSEs reported negative experiences of project management and bureaucracy when participating in one of the service's larger projects, with the perception that they were spending too much time on presentations and reports rather than software development. On the one hand, this may itself be useful learning, since students will likely have similar experiences when they progress in their careers. However, this value to be learning must be made explicit for the SSEs and there is a need to ensure they are properly supported when negotiating unfamiliar administrative processes and structures.

The service is now established within the university, as the core management team continues to grow and evolve more formal processes. The service will need to continue to evolve in supporting students on small- to medium-scale projects. In particular, the impact of AI on knowledge work, particularly for inexperienced engineers, is not well understood. Further work in the future will be required to understand how these tools can be incorporated into small-scale projects to enhance productivity and deliver greater impact.

## Acknowledgements

The authors would like to thank Jill Dykes and Omar Tufayl, two early members of the GUSS team for their extensive work in creating the service, although they did not contribute to the paper. The authors would like to thank Andrew Blair for reviewing an early draft of this chapter.

## References

Akhmetshin, Elvir Munirovich, Kseniya Evgenievna Kovalenko, Julia Eduardovna Mueller, Almaz Khamitovich Khakimov, Alexei Valerievich Yumashev, and Albina Dzhavdatovna Khairullina. 2018. "Freelancing as a Type of Entrepreneurship: Advantages, Disadvantages and Development Prospects." *Journal of Entrepreneurship Education* 21 (Special Issue 2): 1–10.

Bruegge, Bernd, Stephan Krusche, and Lukas Alperowitz. 2015. "Software Engineering Project Courses with Industrial Clients." *ACM Transactions on Computing Education* 15 (4): 1–31. Article No. 17.

Chase, Joseph D., Ed Oakes, and Sean Ramsey. 2007. "Using Live Projects without Pain: The Development of the Small Project Support Center at Radford University." In *Proceedings of the 38th SIGCSE Technical Symposium on Computer Science Education, SIGCSE 2007, Covington, Kentucky, USA, March 7–11, 2007*, edited by Ingrid Russell, Susan M. Haller, J. D. Dougherty, and Susan H. Rodger, 469–473. ACM.

Cockburn, Alistair. 1998. *Surviving Object-Oriented Projects*. Pearson Education.

Cosden, Ian A., Kenton McHenry, and Daniel S. Katz. 2022. "Research Software Engineers: Career Entry Points and Training Gaps." *Computing in Science and Engineering* 24 (6): 14–21.

D'Souza, Clyde. 2024. "Island of Golocans Retrospective Template." [Online] https://miro.com/miroverse/retrospective-in-the-island-of-golocans/.

"Freelancer Service Website." 2024. [Online] www.freelancer.com.

Green, Robert C., II, and Joseph T. Chao. 2017. "Ten Years of the Agile Software Factory for Software Engineering Education and Training." In *30th IEEE Conference on Software Engineering Education and Training, CSEE&t 2017, Savannah, GA, USA, November 7–9, 2017*, edited by Hironori Washizaki, and Nancy Mead, 182–186. IEEE.

Khanna, Dron, and Xiaofeng Wang. 2022. "Are Your Online Agile Retrospectives Psychologically Safe? The Usage of Online Tools." In *Agile Processes in Software Engineering and Extreme Programming – 23rd International Conference on Agile Software Development, XP 2022, Copenhagen, Denmark, June 13–17, 2022, Proceedings, Lecture Notes in Business Information Processing*, edited by Viktoria Stray, Klaas-Jan Stol, Maria Paasivaara, and Philippe Kruchten, 445: 35–51. Springer.

Sadler, Philip M., and Eddie Good. 2006. "The Impact of Self- and Peer-Grading on Student Learning." *Educational Assessment* 11: 1–31.

Sadowski, Caitlin, Emma Söderberg, Luke Church, Michal Sipko, and Alberto Bacchelli. 2018. "Modern Code Review: A Case Study at Google." In *Proceedings of the 40th International Conference on Software Engineering: Software Engineering in Practice, ICSE (SEIP) 2018, Gothenburg, Sweden, May 27 – June 03, 2018*, edited by Frances Paulisch, and Jan Bosch, 181–190. ACM.

Scharlau, Bruce. 2015. "Aberdeen Software Factory." [Online] www.abdn.ac.uk/ncs/departments/computing-science/aberdeen-software-factory-338.php.

Schwaber, Ken, and Mike Beedle. 2001. *Agile Software Development with SCRUM*. Prentice Hall.

Simpson, Robbie, and Tim Storer. 2017. "Experimenting with Realism in Software Engineering Team Projects: An Experience Report." In *30th IEEE Conference on Software Engineering Education and Training, CSEE&t 2017, Savannah, GA, USA, November 7–9, 2017*, edited by Hironori Washizaki, and Nancy Mead, 87–96. IEEE.

Sims, Chris. 2008. "Bowling Green Students Build Agile Software for Non-Profit Clients." [Online] www.infoq.com/news/2008/12/Agile-Software-Factory/.

Siqueira, Fábio Levy, Gabriela Maria Cabel Barbarán, and Jorge Luís Risco Becerra. 2008. "A Software Factory for Education in Software Engineering." In *Proceedings 21st Conference on Software Engineering Education and Training, CSEET 2008, 14–17 April 2008, Charleston, South Carolina, USA*, edited by Hossein Saiedian, and Laurie A. Williams, 215–222. IEEE Computer Society.

Taylor, Joseph, and K. D. Joshi. 2019. "Joining the Crowd: The Career Anchors of Information Technology Workers Participating in Crowdsourcing." *Information Systems Journal* 29 (3): 641–673.

Tomayko, James E. 1998. "Forging a Discipline: An Outline History of Software Engineering Education." *Annals Software Engineering* 6: 3–18.

Torstensson, Johanna. 2024. "Sailboat Retrospective." [Online] https://miro.com/miroverse/sailboat-retrospective/.

Trans-national Institute. 2024. "Public Futures. Global Database on the de-Privatisation and Creation of Public Services." [Online] publicfutures.org (CC BY 4.0).

Chapter 6

# Bringing the Real World Into the Classroom Through Team-Based Live Brief Projects

Jonathan Jackson, Nicholas Day and Kevin Maher

## Introduction

Attending university for better employment prospects and increased lifetime earnings is an established narrative that continues to be conveyed to today's students. Unfortunately, expensive tuition fee loans against a backdrop of increased living costs (in response to COVID-19, Brexit, and global conflicts) have contributed to a challenging climate with some students having to choose between attending their lectures or shift work (Johnson, 2023).

Despite students overcoming challenges with mental health, resilience, and maintaining a sense of belonging in a post-pandemic society (Jones and Bell, 2024), the difficulties do not stop after graduation. As well as wanting to employ graduates who have achieved a good degree (typically 2:1 or above), many employers look for meaningful experience that has helped graduates develop competencies relevant to the workplace.

Some employers have been reported to be critical of students who had been recruited shortly after graduation with commonly cited issues around their lack of work readiness; having spent most of their formative time in the classroom, they lack the context of the workplace and often are not able to apply their theoretical understanding of a subject domain to "real" problems in industry (Bethel, 2017).

Meanwhile, a globalised economy has seen a shift in focus away from manufacturing towards an information-based society. New media and advancements in communication technologies are facilitating significant revisions to our ways of working (Kennedy *et al.*, 2001). This, in turn, has necessitated a re-evaluation of the skills and competencies that university graduates should possess to be suitably prepared for employment and life in general (Tynan and Lee, 2009). Oliver (2015) has further described employability as being more than simply preparing for a job but rather "about empowering learners as critical reflective citizens".

Higher education plays a key role in providing courses and meaningful student experiences that produce work-ready graduates who can take responsibility for their own continuing learning and development while adapting to a world where change is the new constant.

Positive steps were made when the UK Government introduced degree and higher-level apprenticeships in 2014 (Mulkeen et al., 2017), which has seen organisations hire apprentices into respectably paid employment while supporting them in their studies on a fully funded degree programme (James Relly and Laczik, 2022; Smith et al., 2021; Cerdin and Peretti, 2020). Being situated in the workplace allows apprentices to learn the interpersonal and self-management skills which employers look for in graduates, in addition to subject specific skills via the projects and content taught as part of the degree programme.

Unfortunately, the availability of degree apprenticeships is limited, and traditional full-time or part-time degree education remains the dominant means of attaining a degree in the UK. Even so, there are various approaches which can close the gap between academia and industry (Beckman et al., 1997) regardless of the delivery model and whether students are in employment.

One such approach is the use of live briefs and the involvement of external stakeholders to support authentic team-based learning experiences. This chapter explores the benefits of live briefs combined with team-based learning (TBL), social and emotional learning (SEL), and student-staff-stakeholder partnerships in developing student employability.

In the context of this chapter, a "student" may refer to any learner at undergraduate or postgraduate level participating in higher education as a full-time student, part-time student, or apprentice. It is hoped that this chapter can help academic teams engage with the concept of live briefs and provide some practical foundations upon which to build new learning experiences with a student-centred focus on employability.

## Live Briefs

Live brief projects can be described as a type of "experiential learning where students are supported through their university to work on a real world project involving a client or user" (Rochon, 2022, p. 10) and can afford transformative experiential learning (Sara, 2011; Wink, 2005). With an appropriate live brief which balances stakeholder expectations and pressure on students, a "real" work situation can help students build their confidence and workplace readiness (Chance et al., 2018, p. 18).

Schonell and Macklin (2019, p. 3) describe live brief projects (or "live case studies") as "experiential and highly authentic forms of learning that are fully embedded or integrated in academic units or courses", which sets them apart from other initiatives such as work placements or internships. They offer "substantial pedagogical advantages" compared to theoretical case studies, exemplified by the work of Baaken et al. (2015). Boz et al. (2021) define live briefs as a type of work-integrated learning (WIL) and an approach to engaging and assessing students "by using current, real-world activities devised and presented by professional partners in collaboration with academic staff".

Live briefs can be negotiated between students and stakeholders instead of being driven solely by the academic (Sara, 2011), although there are differing degrees of flexibility here depending on the specificity of the brief. Some stakeholders may come with a very specific requirement or problem to be solved, whereas others may bring a nebulous idea which requires exploration and refinement as part of a student's learning experience.

External stakeholder involvement can result in students "producing something that is of value to the external collaborator, which might range from ideas, feasibility reports, or research" while also encouraging students to work within a community "for the benefit of another" (Sara, 2011, p. 2).

The practicalities of running a module which utilises a live brief mean that the academic's role is to facilitate the learning experience through appropriate scaffolding, expertise, and coaching (Schonell and Macklin, 2019, p. 3), while acting as a collaborator or partner in the learning process (Sara, 2011, p. 15), which is discussed in more depth later in this chapter.

Due to the level of involvement typically required by the academic(s) running a live brief learning experience, the approach can be difficult to scale beyond relatively small cohorts, but this is not to say it is impossible. Certain published examples demonstrate an ability to scale live brief projects across an institution with appropriate planning and resourcing. For example, Porubän and Bačíková (2016) outline how they were able to involve 45 inter-university teams in a single year to tackle live industry projects.

The existing literature on live brief projects demonstrates the variability and flexibility of the approach, as evidenced by a sample presented in Table 6.1.

As with any undertaking that is worthwhile, there are inherent challenges depending on the context. Examples include working effectively with stakeholders, sourcing live briefs, institutional buy-in, time limitations, and lack of resources (Dollinger and Brown, 2019, p. 6), and these are discussed in more detail later in this chapter.

## Learning and Work

As was established in the introduction to this chapter, there is demand from employers for work-ready graduates that can transition smoothly into employment and become productive employees in a short time frame. In other words, employers would like graduates to have the "ability to transfer the theoretical foundations into applied problems found in the workplace" (Bethel, 2017, p. 1) and so they should.

But it is important to distinguish between the terms "work" and "workplace" as well as "employability" and "employment". In addition, there can be ambiguity over the differences between work-related learning (WRL), work-based learning (WBL), workplace learning (WPL), and work-integrated

Table 6.1 Published examples of live briefs being utilised in higher education institutions

| Country | Students | Size of teams | Level | Mode | Subject context | Notes and references |
|---|---|---|---|---|---|---|
| Poland | 296 | 4 | P | ? | Informatics/Software | Included inter-university teams (Porubän and Bačiková, 2016) |
| USA | unknown | 3–5 | U + P | F2F | Human-Computer Interaction | Involved cross-disciplinary and inter-level teams (Bethel, 2017) |
| Germany | 63 | up to 17 | U/P | O + F2F | Marketing | Included large inter-university teams (Baaken et al., 2015) |
| USA, Canada, UK, Australia | 6000+ | ~5 | U/P | O | Various | Experiential learning software vendor perspective (James et al., 2020) |
| Australia | 100+ | 3–8 | U/P | O + F2F | Business and Management | (Schonell and Macklin, 2019) |
| Ireland | 48 | 6 | P | F2F | Marketing | (Freeman et al., 2020) |
| USA | 4+ | 4 | U + P | F2F | Engineering/Manufacturing | (Perrin et al., 2008) |
| UK | ~30 | ~5 | U | F2F | Architecture/IT Consultancy | (Sara, 2011) |

U + P = individual teams included both undergraduate (U) and postgraduate (P) students
U/P = undergraduate (U) and postgraduate (P) students were not mixed
O + F2F = individual teams included both online (O) and face-to-face (F2F) students

learning (WIL), as outlined by Fergusson and van der Laan (2021). They define "work" to include the "innate human expression of effort . . . given to tasks that contribute to the overall social and economic welfare of communities and environments from which personal meaning and benefit are derived", and they go on to define workplaces or "work environments" as workspaces or domains of practice within which this work occurs. In short, meaningful work is by no means restricted solely to activities carried out as part of employment.

While WRL, WBL, WPL, and WIL sometimes appear to be used interchangeably in some literature, work-related learning can be viewed as an umbrella term which describes any kind of learning that is related to work in some way, not limited by place or employment status (see Table 6.2). In simple terms, WRL can be effectively implemented by using live brief projects which sit "between the binaries of theory and practice, university and community . . . and ideas about what it is to be a student, and what it is to be a professional" (Sara, 2011, p. 2).

The live brief approach to project-based learning can apply to WPL but is more commonly aligned with WBL and WIL, where there is less of a focus on a specific workplace and more of a focus on the work carried out.

WBL relates to learning taking place in a work environment or context but not necessarily a workplace (Fergusson and van der Laan, 2021). Ball and Manwaring (2010) highlight that professionals use their work context "as a key component of their learning to participate in higher education programs deliberately planned to integrate learning and practice". WBL is commonly employed in degree apprenticeship programmes, for example, where learners are employed while studying on a funded programme which is designed to enhance and acknowledge learning that takes place as part of their employment (Crawford-Lee and Moorwood, 2019).

Table 6.2 Summary of pedagogical terms which incorporate "work" and "learning"

| Initialism | Term | Description |
| --- | --- | --- |
| WRL | Work-Related Learning | An umbrella term taken to mean any learning related to work |
| WBL | Work-Based Learning | "Seeks to integrate learning, generally through higher education, into the work environment" |
| WPL | Workplace Learning | Almost always the same as WBL, but with an emphasis on a specific workplace |
| WIL | Work-Integrated Learning | "Emphasises learning experiences of work via placements, practicums and internships and their integration into the university curriculum" |

Source: Fergusson and van der Laan, 2021

WPL has a focus on the situational context or location of the work being carried out for learning, and is described by Kyndt *et al.* (2016, p. 2) as "the development of knowledge, skills and attitudes necessary for improving the quality and progress of work in situations at or near the workplace".

WIL aims to give students practical experience which is directly related to the subject of their studies in order to improve their transition from university to work (Fergusson and van der Laan, 2021). This helps students develop their employability while engaging with an "embedded industry-informed curriculum" which may include work-based placements or field trips (Dollinger and Brown, 2019). A WIL curriculum will be designed to provide opportunities for students to be connected with employers, providing value to those employers in the process (Drewery *et al.*, 2020).

As highlighted by Boz *et al.* (2021, p. 12), many conceptualisations for WIL exist but live briefs afford "the intentional integration of theory . . . with the practice of work" (Dollinger and Brown, 2019, p. 90) and can, as a result, lead to an authentic learning experience (Herrington and Oliver, 2000). Authenticity of learning and assessment is discussed in greater depth later in this chapter, but Oliver (2015) concisely states that effective assessment in relation to employability relies on the two key principles of "authenticity" and "proximity". Authentic tasks resemble "those required in professional life" and proximity means "the setting resembles professional contexts". Adhering to these principles should "increase student's ability to cope with challenges in the real world" (Daun *et al.*, 2016, p. 10), but it is worth noting the limitations of the term "real world" and how conflating it with the "world of work" can be counterproductive (McArthur, 2023, p. 86).

## What Is Employability?

While it may seem axiomatic that employability is tightly linked to the demands of employers, it is important to avoid constricting the definition to the detriment of students' personal growth and benefits to society. Employability should indeed lead to increased opportunities for employment, but there is more to the term than just "training for a job" (Oliver, 2015, p. 4) or getting a job. Thinking beyond the conventional dictionary definitions of employability, Oliver (2015) refers to employability as "a process of learning for life" and builds on the definition presented by Yorke (2006) by proposing the following:

> Employability means that students and graduates can discern, acquire, adapt and continually enhance the skills, understandings and personal attributes that make them more likely to find and create meaningful paid and unpaid work that benefits themselves, the workforce, the community and the economy.
>
> (Oliver, 2015, p. 4)

Clarke (2018) identifies six dimensions to employability, demonstrating its multifaceted nature: "human capital, social capital, individual attributes, individual behaviours, perceived employability and labour market factors".

Even though there are intrinsic difficulties in measuring employability as a graduate attribute, particularly as its definition can vary, it is nevertheless widely held to be of importance to those both inside and outside of higher education (Dollinger and Brown, 2019). The involvement of employers in the educational process can enhance employability through collaboration, "closing the gap between academia and industry" by working together on education and training goals in partnership (Beckman *et al.*, 1997, p. 1).

Degree apprenticeships in the UK are a prime example of employers and higher education working hand in hand, catalysed by the apprenticeship levy introduced by the UK Government in 2017 (HM Revenue and Customs, 2023). Apprenticeships can provide opportunities for transformational personal development as well as alleviating the digital skills gap (Carolina Feijao *et al.*, 2021; Jackson, 2023; Taylor-Smith *et al.*, 2019). Apprentices are, by definition, already employed as part of their apprenticeship, but this does not mean that employability is any less important for them, as indicated by the wider definitions of employability already discussed.

Fletcher-Brown *et al.* (2015) coined the term "employagility" to highlight the need for graduate agility by engaging in life-long skills development which can enhance their "potential to contribute to local and wider economies". A positive attitude towards life-long learning is certainly a valuable aspect of employability, along with other "higher-order skills which support other skills" (Taylor-Smith *et al.*, 2019, p. 2) such as the ability to work effectively in teams, stronger communication skills, emotional intelligence, and learning how to learn.

Some students engaging in live brief project work feel the experience helps them prepare "for going into a practice" and develop a "sense of professionalism" (Sara, 2011, p. 10). Working towards a common goal as part of a live brief can enhance inter-student relationships as part of team-working, potentially widening students' networks through exposure to industry contacts and, in some cases, students studying at different levels, as outlined by Perrin *et al.* (2008). Emotional intelligence (Goleman, 2020) further supports team-working and effective communication. It can be fostered through reflective practice, as part of experiential learning in combination with approaches such as SEL, which is discussed later in this chapter.

According to Knight and Yorke (2006), equipping students with a solid grasp of metacognition is also a key aspect of employability. Shaw (2005) also affirms that reflection and interpretation are more important than memorisation or drilling. Students can be guided to reflect in order to develop self-awareness and a comprehension of how they learn, reflecting "on, in and for action" (Oliver, 2015, p. 4), and well-designed reflective questions can "facilitate a transfer from the concrete experience to the reflective observation mode of experiential learning" (James *et al.*, 2020, p. 642).

Live brief projects can offer a channel through which students can develop all these higher-order skills through immersion in authentic learning experiences that are supported by partners working in collaboration with academic institutions. In fact, while Perrin *et al.* (2008) talk about a "corporate-academic relationship" in the context of live projects, this can be taken a step further if framed as a three-way partnership in learning between students, academic staff, and project stakeholders.

## Student-Staff-Stakeholder Partnerships

Harrington *et al.* (2014) define a partnership as a relationship where "all participants are actively engaged in and stand to gain from the process of learning and working together". It is a way of doing things, rather than a product, and must be viewed as highly contextual and dependent on many factors (Harrington *et al.*, 2014, p. 14). As with any healthy relationship, the parties involved in a partnership should be able to demonstrate commitment to the principles of respect, reciprocity, and responsibility (Cook-Sather *et al.*, 2014).

This section explores the three bi-directional relationships that exist within a student-staff-stakeholder partnership, as visualised in Figure 6.1.

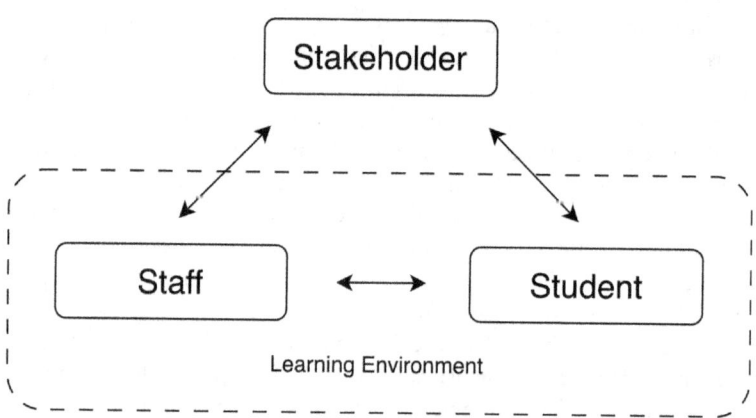

*Figure 6.1* Student-staff-stakeholder partnership visualised with an external stakeholder.

## Staff-Stakeholder Partnerships

Sara (2011) presents criteria that should be taken into consideration when selecting suitable external stakeholders for a live brief learning experience, such as engaging clients who are motivated and enthusiastic but also open to new ideas; identifying projects which have a public service element rather than purely commercial; identifying projects related to students' future professions. It is often the responsibility of academic staff to select stakeholders with suitable motivations, and it needs to be made clear that students are not simply a source of cheap labour; a live brief project is an educational experience which should be beneficial to both parties. It is important for academic staff to effectively manage and communicate with stakeholders in order to maintain a physically, intellectually, and emotionally safe learning environment for students (Thompson and Wheeler, 2008).

Strong communication is needed in order to manage expectations, and Perrin et al. (2008) have noted that persistence is required when trying to cultivate opportunities to collaborate with external stakeholders. Different stakeholders will be able to offer varying degrees of engagement with students, so academic staff can act on behalf of stakeholders if they can represent their needs effectively. The pressure on stakeholders to interact directly with multiple student teams can be eased by academic staff acting as a conduit through which student communication can be filtered and aggregated. In more extreme examples, academic staff can take the place of stakeholders entirely (Daun et al., 2016), but this can have a detrimental effect on the authenticity of the learning for employability (Oliver, 2015; McArthur, 2023).

## Student-Staff Partnerships

In the transformative model of pedagogy, students and teachers can be seen as partners in the learning process (Wink, 2005), but it is still important for academic staff to be able to demonstrate authentic leadership, which is a significant contributing factor to students' psychological safety within the learning environment (Soares and Lopes, 2020).

Hagenauer et al. (2023) refer to the impact of positive "teacher-student relationships" (TSRs) on factors such as motivation and wellbeing (Eloff et al., 2023; Leenknecht et al., 2023), underlining the importance of student-staff partnerships in a learning environment when working on a live brief.

In the context of co-creation in or of the curriculum (Bovill and Woolmer, 2019), Jarvis et al. (2013) conclude that student-staff partnerships have a significant impact on learning enhancement and employability. Live briefs can provide an opportunity for academic staff and students to work closely together in collaboration to co-create deliverables, strengthening the sense of partnership which can positively influence students' engagement with the learning process.

Bovill and Woolmer (2019) highlight that the "teacher's attitude, motivations and outlook are critical to co-creation" and academic staff have a responsibility to clearly establish the terms of a student-staff partnership to avoid confusing or alienating students.

### Student-Stakeholder Partnerships

Feedback from industry stakeholders as part of a well-managed student-stakeholder partnership can help students reflect meaningfully on their own professional development and practice which would otherwise be difficult to do as novices and without "reference points from professional practice" (James et al., 2020, p. 639).

Potential employers acting as a stakeholder for a live brief project can guide and influence their future workforce for the benefit of their own recruitment needs or they could be motivated from a corporate social responsibility (CSR) perspective. As noted earlier, academic staff need to ensure that stakeholders' motivations do not conflict with the interests of students.

Even if external stakeholders are not potential employers, students can still benefit from an authentic work context that helps them build confidence through an increased sense of independence by working with a real client, which they will likely not have experienced before (Chance et al., 2018, p. 18).

### Pedagogical Underpinnings

While some pedagogical theories have already been mentioned in this chapter, more detail related to the pedagogical underpinnings of live brief project work will be presented in this section along with the applicability of specific theories to a live brief context.

*Transformative pedagogy* is described by Wink (2005) as the most effective type of learning compared with transmission and generative pedagogy as it positions teachers and students as partners in learning, transforming knowledge into new ideas. Live briefs enable students to create new knowledge through this transformative approach by providing opportunities for theory and practice to collide.

The concept of creation is also key to *Bloom's Revised Taxonomy* (Anderson and Krathwohl, 2001) in which creation sits at the top of the pyramid of learning. Creation does not have to be an individual act, but can be a collaborative process, as underlined by *social constructivism* (Dewey, 1938; Driscoll, 2000; Mcleod, 2024) which posits that knowledge is constructed through social interactions and collaboration. *Team-based learning* makes this explicit by ensuring that assignments are designed to "promote both learning and team development" (Michaelsen and Sweet, 2008, p. 8) and a richer learning experience due to the complexities inherent in team work (James et al., 2020).

Working with live briefs to provide a real-world context is a good example of *active learning* (Barnes, 1989; Bonwell and Eison, 1991), which has the goal of deepening learning by engaging students "in actively processing information by reconstructing that information in such new and personally meaningful ways" (King, 1993) and enabling them to "perform their understanding, not just tell us about it" (Biggs, 2003). Providing a variety of methods available to engage with materials and activities contributes towards *active blended learning* (Palmer et al., 2017), which can support more flexible synchronous and asynchronous learning suited to the diverse learning needs of students.

*Problem-based learning* (*PBL*) is an example of active learning and focuses on critical reasoning and knowledge construction through problem-solving (Grabinger and Dunlap, 2002) while helping students transition from lower-order thinking to higher-order thinking within an applied context (Biggs and Tang, 2011). PBL is a broad term that can encompass working on problems of any size, whereas *project-based learning* (*PjBL*) is typically larger in scope and complexity and lends itself more directly to real-world contexts and collaborative learning, instilling valuable transferable skills relevant to employability (Chen and Yang, 2019). While all PjBL inevitably includes some form of PBL, not all PBL is PjBL.

*Experiential learning*, as defined by Kolb and Kolb (2009), "results from synergetic transactions between the person and the environment" and follows the experiential learning cycle which is designed to enhance the learning gained from experiences by encouraging active experimentation to apply new knowledge. As well as collective and individual reflection being an important part of experiential learning (Gibbs, 1988), feedback is also an essential element (James et al., 2020, p. 637) which can come from peers, tutors, and project stakeholders (Bethel, 2017, p. 3).

Linking pedagogy back to employability, *authentic assessment* plays a key role in giving students the opportunity to "engage in the construction of meaning" and autonomously "perform real-world tasks that demonstrate meaningful application of essential knowledge and skills" (Mueller, 2005) while developing a clear sense of ownership over their own learning (Freeman et al., 2020, p. 7). While the authenticity of an assessment may often be judged based on how close it aligns with professional activities (Oliver, 2015), a deeper appreciation of authenticity will enable assessments to be designed which enable students to "find their place in society and be recognised for their contribution to that society" by carrying out tasks that matter (McArthur, 2023, p. 96). In short, "the real world" is much more expansive than simply "the world of work", and appropriate live briefs can offer opportunities to engage students emotionality through *social and emotional learning*, helping them to manage their emotions and develop qualities such as empathy (CASEL, n.d.) and emotional intelligence (Goleman, 2020). As the next section shows, live briefs with a significant social focus can be of significant pedagogical value.

## Examples of Live Briefs

This section outlines the live brief projects run at Buckinghamshire New University (BNU) as part of a "Digital Innovation" module (previously known as "Enterprise Systems Development") which is taken by final-year software engineering and computing undergraduate students as well as final-year apprentices on the Digital and Technology Solutions Professional degree apprenticeship (IfATE, 2015).

Live briefs were adopted for this module as part of a two-year Higher Education Funding Council for England (HEFCE)-funded research project which started in 2016 (Rochon, 2022; Chance et al., 2018). Over an eight-year period, 11 discrete live brief projects were tackled by 12 cohorts of students (see Table 6.3). Each project lasted three to four months, which equated to the duration of a 15-week semester.

As part of a retrospective thematic classification exercise, four main categories of live brief were identified, and most of the live briefs sat within more than one category: social, health, commercial, and education. The following sub-sections describe a selection of these live briefs.

### *Social*

Projects deemed to fit within the Social category involved a significant focus on having a positive human impact (Oades et al., 2011). The first live brief project that was adopted as part of the original HEFCE-funded research project was a Heritage Trail web application and map developed for Wycombe District Council (P1). The aim of the project was to create a location-sensitive, interactive digital map which would guide users around points of interest connected to the First World War in the Wycombe area and present information in various formats (text, images, video). The project's intent was to engage local people with the history of their area and their community. Student teams were able to engage with the stakeholders throughout the project and benefited from an in-person tour of the local area. Funding was available through the local council and associated lottery funding, part of which was used to remunerate the winning student team for their continued work on their prototype after the taught module had finished. The final project was then launched and hosted for a five-year period by a local IT provider.

Approximately seven years after this first project, another interactive digital map project formed the basis of a live brief which involved the development of a Food Poverty Map for Buckinghamshire (P11). This project involved researching ways to alleviate food and hygiene poverty through digital mapping technology and the main stakeholder was BNU's Head of Civic Engagement, even though there were external stakeholders who had an interest in the project such as local charities and Buckinghamshire Council. There were many

Table 6.3 Example live briefs deployed in final-year "Digital Innovation" module at BNU between 2016 and 2023

| # | Project title | Categories | Themes | Stakeholders | Student type |
|---|---|---|---|---|---|
| P1 | Wycombe District Council World War I Heritage Trail Map | Social; Education | Local history; Community education | Local authority | U |
| P2 | Safe Places Administrative Portal | Social; Health | Community support; Mental health | Local authority; Community interest company (CIC) | U |
| P3 | 360-degree Virtual Property Tours for Estate Agents | Commercial | Business optimisation; Property market | Module tutor | U |
| P4 | Property Data Mapping Tool | Commercial | Geographic information systems (GIS); Housing and planning | Local entrepreneur | U |
| P5 | Signly Meet | Social; Commercial | British Sign Language (BSL); Accessibility | Startup founder | A |
| P6 | Apprenticeship Learning Tracker | Commercial; Education | Vocational education | Module tutor | U |
| P7 | Embedded Trigger Warnings for a Media Streaming Service | Social; Commercial | Digital accessibility; Mental health | Digital accessibility manager | A |
| P8 | MediLingo: Medical Terminology Learning App | Commercial; Education | Educational technology; Healthcare education | Extra-departmental academic | U |
| P9 | Reflecta: reflection for learning and wellbeing | Commercial; Education; Health | Wellbeing; Reflective learning; Privacy | Extra-departmental academic | A |
| P10 | Digital Communication Solutions for Private Healthcare Providers | Commercial; Health | Digital healthcare | General practitioner (GP) | U |
| P11 | Food Poverty Mapping Project | Social; Health | Civic engagement; Food poverty | Head of Civic Engagement within university | A/U |

A = Apprentice (part time)
U = Undergraduate (full time)

opportunities to embed SEL with this live brief due to its focus on supporting vulnerable people, and even though there was no immediate funding available, there was strong institutional buy-in due to BNU already being involved in initiatives relating to food poverty in the local area prior to the project becoming a live brief for students to work on.

### Health

One live brief in the health category related to healthcare provider communication (P10) and was brought to the module by an entrepreneurial general practitioner (GP) who had prior links to the university and the module tutor. The focus was on exploring how digital technology could be used to enhance communication between private healthcare clinics and their patients. As part of his engagement with the student group, the GP gave an overview of the problem in an initial class visit and provided feedback on student presentations near the end of the module. Several students became emotionally invested in the project as it related to easing the extreme pressure on healthcare professionals across the UK. Further positive impact was realised when one student started working for the GP on a freelance basis prior to graduation, giving them a platform upon which to build their own web development business after graduation.

### Commercial

Signly Meet (P5) was a live brief presented by a startup founder who had previously engaged with the module tutor over a mutual interest in British Sign Language (BSL). While there were potentially commercial elements to the project, there was a strong social element relating to inclusivity and accessibility for deaf individuals. Students were tasked with designing and building a prototype for an online booking system which could be used by organisations (e.g., banks) to book BSL interpreters in order to fulfil their obligations to make reasonable adjustments in line with the Equality Act of 2010. While the project did not end up being developed into a live system, the apprentices still benefited from the learning experience while gaining insights into important societal issues outside of their immediate workplace context.

### Education

Two examples of projects with an educational focus were MediLingo (P8) and Reflecta (P9), both of which came from extra-departmental academics within BNU and had research-based underpinnings (McAllister *et al.*, 2023; McAllister *et al.*, 2023; Rochon, 2023a, 2023b). The MediLingo live brief asked students to design an app to support nursing students in learning and retaining medical terminology, while the module tutor was able to act as a lead consultant on the project. MediLingo subsequently developed into an early-stage university spin-out (MediLingo, n.d.) and Reflecta gained funding to develop a working platform suitable for public launch (Reflecta, n.d.). These two examples demonstrate the potential for fostering educational innovation while benefiting the learning experience of students through authentic project work.

It is important to note that many of the live briefs listed in Table 6.3 had commercial potential, which naturally raises the question of intellectual property and other ethical considerations, which are discussed later in this chapter.

## Sourcing Live Briefs

Building relationships with industry partners for the purposes of developing live briefs can be daunting for academics who have not done it before (Bethel, 2017, p. 2), but there are less intimidating intermediary steps that can be taken which still result in pedagogical benefits.

For example, the use of realistic industry-oriented case studies can have a positive effect on student motivation and comprehension of theoretical material (Daun *et al.*, 2014, p. 2) while reducing the gap between theoretical concepts and their application in industry (Beckman *et al.*, 1997; Shaw, 2005). Even without the direct input from external stakeholders, compelling case studies can still be curated from existing sources or developed with relative ease by leveraging generative AI and large language models, which are discussed in more detail later in this chapter.

It is also important to note that stakeholders do not always need to be from "industry", nor do they necessarily need to be "external" in order to contribute to a highly authentic and meaningful learning experience. External stakeholders such as local authorities, charities, and social enterprises are likely to represent non-commercial interests which can lead to live briefs that focus on societal issues such as community support, accessibility, wellbeing, mental health, educational enrichment, and healthcare. Stakeholders internal to an educational institution such as academics working on research projects can also be a source of compelling live briefs, as evidenced by projects P8 and P9 listed in Table 6.3.

There are many potential sources of live briefs, some of which may be harder than others to engage with depending on various contextual factors such as an academic's workload and previous experience working with external stakeholders. Table 6.4 outlines various possible sources of live briefs which can be considered by academic staff or teams looking to develop a live brief initiative.

*Table 6.4* Potential sources of live brief classified by degree of externality

| Live brief source | Description | Degree of externality |
| --- | --- | --- |
| Module tutor | The academic staff member leading the module itself may present a live brief from their own experience and act as the stakeholder throughout the learning experience. | Internal |
| Intra-departmental academics | Academics within the same department as the module tutor who may be working on active research projects. | Internal |
| Extra-departmental academics | Academics working within the wider university community (e.g., P8 and P9 from Table 6.3). | Internal |
| Research, Enterprise, or Innovation departments | Teams dedicated to engaging with innovation projects or schemes such as knowledge transfer partnerships (KTPs) may be able to provide support with live briefs or make introductions to external stakeholders. | Internal |
| Civic engagement or community outreach departments | A potential source of projects with a focus on local community, wellbeing, or positive social impact. | Internal |
| Students' Union | Potentially well placed to propose live briefs that could more directly appeal to students. | Internal/ External |
| Apprentice employers | Employers already engaging with the educational institution in the form of apprenticeship training (e.g., P7 from Table 6.3). | External |
| Local employers | SME or larger enterprise employers who have previously recruited graduates and are motivated to enhance employability. | External |
| Charities | Third-sector organisations may be able to offer compelling live briefs which focus on societal benefits. | External |
| Local authorities | Public sector organisations keen to enrich students' civic engagement through appropriate live briefs (e.g., P1 and P2 from Table 6.3). | External |

## Leveraging Generative AI

There is a significant amount of research being published on understanding the potential applications of generative AI (GenAI) within higher education as well as the perceptions of students and staff towards GenAI (Chan and Hu, 2023; Prather *et al.*, 2023; Smolansky *et al.*, 2023). It is a generally held view that GenAI necessitates a shift towards more authentic assessment and live briefs are well suited to this. Conversely, live brief learning experiences can, in fact, be enhanced with GenAI in several ways which are outlined in this section.

Firstly, if a stakeholder is not available, large language model (LLM) tools such as ChatGPT or Microsoft Copilot can be used to generate the basis of a simulated live brief with direction from an academic staff member. As with any application of GenAI, it is important for a human to remain "in the loop" to refine the generated output and apply prompt engineering techniques where needed (Cain, 2024).

Taking this a step further, once a simulated live brief has been formulated, an LLM can be instructed to behave as the stakeholder of the live brief by utilising a technique Reynolds and McDonell (2021) refer to as "task specification by memetic proxy". While this won't provide the same level of authenticity for students as working with a real stakeholder, a module tutor can simulate stakeholder interactions using this approach to gain real-time feedback. Seeding an LLM task specification with instructions such as "behave like a difficult client" or "regularly change your mind" can lead to many teachable moments on how to communicate and negotiate effectively.

An example LLM prompt utilising task specification by memetic proxy:

> Imagine you are the client for this project, and your goal is to provide guidance and requirements to the team. You may not have in-depth knowledge of digital technology or app development, but you have a clear vision of what you want the app to achieve for your target audience. Your role is to provide feedback, suggest features, and steer the direction of the project based on your expertise in the subject matter. Give short answers unless I ask for more information. You will often not be sure what you want so you can ask the team for advice if you are not sure. Behave like a difficult client (but don't be rude). Here is an overview of the live brief: [live brief overview]

Due to the probabilistic nature of LLMs, generated outputs will vary and experimentation with different contextually appropriate prompts is recommended. It is also vital to maintain an ethics-first approach when using GenAI (Stahl et al., 2023) and to ensure the wider ethical factors associated with live briefs are considered, as discussed in the following section.

## Ethical Considerations

Ethical factors such as the risk of marginalisation, conflicts of interest, whether students are paid for their work, and intellectual property (IP) must be considered when embarking on live brief project work.

If students do not have a choice of live brief and it relies heavily on cultural or background-specific knowledge, for example, there may be a risk of student marginalisation or alienation. Academic staff need to be aware of ways in which they may unwittingly "create barriers to student engagement" (Mann, 2001) through selection of a live brief.

Conflicts of interest may occur if a stakeholder's motivations do not align with the interests of students and a sense of partnership is lost (Cook-Sather et al., 2014; Harrington et al., 2014). Live briefs with a strong commercial focus may pose a higher risk, particularly if the stakeholder(s) are primarily concerned with profiting from the work carried out by students with no expectation of remuneration. Baaken et al. (2015, p. 5) outline one approach where commercial live brief projects have a cost which is paid to the university by the client and disbursed accordingly.

In relation to this, the perceived exploitation of free labour and student concerns over "working for free" (Sara, 2011, p. 10) can be tackled in various ways. In some cases, students may be remunerated for their work, as was the case in some projects listed in Table 6.3 (P1 and P2) where funding was available, and a winning team was able to complete a final deliverable with academic and professional supervision after the taught module had finished. Alternatively, live briefs with a strong social or charitable focus can negate concerns over exploitative gain, as the purpose of these projects is to have a positive social impact rather than to generate commercial revenue.

Potential IP issues can be avoided where remuneration is involved, and the ownership of deliverables is transferred between parties as a result. The applicability of this approach will typically depend on whether the project deliverables (e.g., software, a research report) have the potential for commercialisation, and it is, of course, important to ensure compliance with any institutional IP policies.

## Challenges

In addition to ethical factors, there are other challenges to consider when adopting live briefs within a team-based learning context. The following list draws on work from Sara (2011), Dollinger and Brown (2019), Daun et al. (2016), Baaken et al. (2015), and Williams et al. (1991):

1. Academic time and workload.
2. Effort required to find suitable projects.
3. Project scopes that align with academic timeframes.
4. Resistance from academic colleagues.
5. Resistance from students.
6. The free-rider effect.
7. Unpredictability of outcomes.
8. Lack of institutional buy-in.
9. Lack of resources.

Many of these challenges may be intertwined, and while some may be difficult to address, many can be mitigated through adjusting the approach being taken. As was highlighted by the literature summarised in

Table 6.1, there is no one correct approach to using live briefs within higher education.

Academic time and workload (1) may seem an immovable obstacle in terms of not being able to get more time, but starting off simple and taking "small steps towards co-creating the curriculum" with students can be a sustainable approach (Cook-Sather *et al.*, 2014). If the effort required to find suitable projects (2 and 3) seems overwhelming, smaller steps such as sourcing case studies or simulating stakeholder interactions through GenAI may be appropriate.

Resistance from academic colleagues (4) or students (5) can be softened through authentic leadership (Soares and Lopes, 2020) and transparency in communication. Scaffolding enough of a structure to help students engage with the live brief process can mitigate disengagement (Dollinger and Brown, 2019, p. 93) and also help academics feel more confident in guiding the learning experience and dealing with a certain level of unpredictability (7). Adopting a clearly communicated student-staff partnership approach to learning can help reduce student anxiety by making them feel supported and remind them that the focus of assessments will be on "knowledge discovery rather than optimal solutions" as suggested by Daun *et al.* (2016).

Williams *et al.* (1991) talk about the "free-rider effect" (6) within student groups which can be a cause of student resistance and anxiety, but adopting an "appropriate award structure that . . . allows an individual accountability for each student" can be a way to mitigate this, examples of which may include peer evaluation forms, interaction logs, and academic staff interventions based on progress reports.

While institutional buy-in (8) and a high level of resources (9) may be required for some work-related learning initiatives such as industry placements (Dollinger and Brown, 2019, p. 92) and live briefs at scale (Boz *et al.*, 2021; James *et al.*, 2020), starting off small and maintaining a relatively straightforward approach can reduce the need for wider institutional buy-in without losing the benefits of authentic experiential learning.

## Conclusion

While there are indeed challenges in adopting live briefs in higher education, the pedagogical benefits are numerous and the positive impact on employability is significant. It is also vital to emphasise that "the real world" is much more expansive than simply "the world of work" and employability is about much more than just employment.

There are already many academic teams engaging with external stakeholders on live brief projects, demonstrating both the viability of this approach and the benefits to their students, regardless of their mode of study. It is hoped that more institutions will leverage the benefits of wider, subject-agnostic, and cross-disciplinary applications of student-staff-stakeholder partnerships in higher education using live briefs.

## References

Anderson, L. W. and Krathwohl, D. R. (eds.) (2001) *A Taxonomy for Learning, Teaching, and Assessing: A Revision of Bloom's Taxonomy of Educational Objectives*, Complete ed., New York, Longman.

Baaken, T., Kiel, B. and Kliewe, T. (2015) 'Real world projects with companies supporting competence development in higher education', *International Journal of Higher Education*, vol. 4, no. 3, p. 129 [Online]. https://doi.org/10.5430/ijhe.v4n3p129.

Ball, I. and Manwaring, G. (2010) 'Making it work', in *A Guidebook Exploring Work Based Learning*, Scotland, QAA [Online]. Available at https://core.ac.uk/download/pdf/4151189.pdf (Accessed 7 March 2024).

Barnes, D. R. (1989) *Active Learning*, Leeds University TVEI Support Project.

Beckman, K., Coulter, N., Khajenoori, S. and Mead, N. R. (1997) 'Collaborations: Closing the industry-academia gap', *IEEE Software*, vol. 14, no. 6, pp. 49–57 [Online]. https://doi.org/10.1109/52.636668.

Bethel, C. L. (2017) 'Improving student engagement and learning outcomes through the use of industry-sponsored projects in human-computer interaction curriculum', *2017 15th International Conference on Emerging eLearning Technologies and Applications (ICETA)*, pp. 1–6 [Online]. https://doi.org/10.1109/ICETA.2017.8102468 (Accessed 28 February 2024).

Biggs, J. (2003) *Aligning Teaching for Constructing Learning*, Advance HE [Online]. Available at www.advance-he.ac.uk/knowledge-hub/aligning-teaching-constructing-learning (Accessed 30 May 2024).

Biggs, J. and Tang, C. (2011) *Teaching for Quality Learning at University: What the Student Does*, 4th ed., Maidenhead, England New York, NY, Open University Press.

Bonwell, C. C. and Eison, J. A. (1991) *Active Learning: Creating Excitement in the Classroom. 1991 ASHE-ERIC Higher Education Reports*, Washington, DC, ERIC Clearinghouse on Higher Education, The George Washington University [Online]. Available at https://eric.ed.gov/?id=ED336049 (Accessed 24 February 2024).

Bovill, C. and Woolmer, C. (2019) 'How conceptualisations of curriculum in higher education influence student-staff co-creation in and of the curriculum', *Higher Education*, vol. 78, no. 3, pp. 407–422 [Online]. https://doi.org/10.1007/s10734-018-0349-8.

Boz, M., Acevedo, B., Middleton, A., Scruton, A., Hawkins, C., Outteridge, J. and Kite, L. (2021) 'Work-integrated learning as an inclusive pedagogy for employability: The case of Live Briefs at Anglia Ruskin University', in *Employability: Breaking the Mould. A Case Study Compendium*, Advance HE, p. 12.

Cain, W. (2024) 'Prompting change: Exploring prompt engineering in large language model AI and its potential to transform education', *TechTrends*, vol. 68, no. 1, pp. 47–57 [Online]. https://doi.org/10.1007/s11528-023-00896-0.

CASEL (n.d.) *Fundamentals of SEL* [Online]. Available at https://casel.org/fundamentals-of-sel/ (Accessed 24 February 2024).

Cerdin, J.-L. and Peretti, J.-M. (2020) *The Success of Apprenticeships: Views of Stakeholders on Training and Learning*, John Wiley & Sons.

Chan, C. K. Y. and Hu, W. (2023) 'Students' voices on generative AI: Perceptions, benefits, and challenges in higher education', *International Journal of Educational Technology in Higher Education*, vol. 20, no. 1, p. 43 [Online]. https://doi.org/10.1186/s41239-023-00411-8.

Chance, H., Mather, R., Rochon, R. and Jones, R. E. (2018) *Traversing Digital-Creative Perspectives: Preparing Design and Technology Students for Interdisciplinary Work*, Report, Buckinghamshire New University [Online]. Available at https://bnu.repository.guildhe.ac.uk/id/eprint/18097/ (Accessed 24 February 2024).

Chen, C.-H. and Yang, Y.-C. (2019) 'Revisiting the effects of project-based learning on students' academic achievement: A meta-analysis investigating moderators', *Educational Research Review*, vol. 26, pp. 71–81 [Online]. https://doi.org/10.1016/j.edurev.2018.11.001.

Clarke, M. (2018) 'Rethinking graduate employability: The role of capital, individual attributes and context', *Studies in Higher Education*, vol. 43, no. 11, pp. 1923–1937 [Online]. https://doi.org/10.1080/03075079.2017.1294152.

Cook-Sather, A., Bovill, C. and Felten, P. (2014) *Engaging Students as Partners in Learning and Teaching: A Guide for Faculty*, 1st ed., San Francisco, Jossey-Bass.

Crawford-Lee, M. and Moorwood, S. (2019) 'Degree apprenticeships: Delivering quality and social mobility?', *Higher Education, Skills and Work-Based Learning*, Emerald Publishing Limited, vol. 9, no. 2, pp. 134–140 [Online]. https://doi.org/10.1108/HESWBL-05-2019-123.

Daun, M., Salmon, A., Tenbergen, B., Weyer, T. and Pohl, K. (2014) 'Industrial case studies in graduate requirements engineering courses: The impact on student motivation', *IEEE 27th Conference on Software Engineering Education and Training – (CSEE&T)* [Online]. https://doi.org/10.1109/CSEET.2014.6816775.

Daun, M., Salmon, A., Weyer, T., Pohl, K. and Tenbergen, B. (2016) 'Project-Based Learning with Examples from Industry in University Courses: An Experience Report from an Undergraduate Requirements Engineering Course', *2016 IEEE 29th International Conference on Software Engineering Education and Training (CSEET)*, pp. 184–193 [Online]. https://doi.org/10.1109/CSEET.2016.15 (Accessed 28 February 2024).

Dewey, J. (1938) *Experience and Education*, New York, Macmillan Company.

Dollinger, M. and Brown, J. (2019) 'An institutional framework to guide the comparison of work-integrated learning', *Journal of Teaching and Learning for Graduate Employability*, vol. 10, no. 1, pp. 88–100 [Online]. https://doi.org/10.21153/jtlge2019vol10no1art780.

Drewery, D., Pretti, T. J. and Church, D. (2020) 'Contributions of work-integrated learning programs to organizational talent pipelines: Insights from talent managers', *International Journal of Work-Integrated Learning*, vol. 21, no. 3, pp. 275–288.

Driscoll, M. P. (2000) *Psychology of Learning for Instruction*, 2nd ed., Boston, Allyn and Bacon [Online]. Available at http://books.google.com/books?id=fTydAAAAMAAJ (Accessed 10 May 2024).

Eloff, I., O'Neil, S. and Kanengoni, H. (2023) 'Students' well-being in tertiary environments: Insights into the (unrecognised) role of lecturers', *Teaching in Higher Education*, Routledge, vol. 28, no. 7, pp. 1777–1797 [Online]. https://doi.org/10.1080/13562517.2021.1931836.

Feijao, C., Flanagan, I., van Stolk, C. and Gunashekar, S. (2021) *The Global Digital Skills Gap: Current Trends and Future Directions*, RAND Corporation [Online]. https://doi.org/10.7249/RRA1533-1 (Accessed 24 February 2024).

Fergusson, L. and van der Laan, L. (2021) 'Work + learning: Unpacking the agglomerated use of pedagogical terms', *Journal of Work-Applied Management*, Emerald Publishing Limited, vol. 13, no. 2, pp. 302–314 [Online]. https://doi.org/10.1108/JWAM-12-2020-0053.

Fletcher-Brown, J., Knibbs, K. and Middleton, K. (2015) 'Developing "employagility": The 3Es case for live-client learning', *Higher Education, Skills and Work-Based Learning*, vol. 5, no. 2, pp. 181–195 [Online]. https://doi.org/10.1108/HESWBL-05-2014-0011.

Freeman, O., Hand, R. and Kennedy, A. (2020) 'Breaking down Silos through authentic assessment: A live case analysis', *6th International Conference on Higher Education Advances (HEAd'20)*, Universitat Politècnica de València [Online]. https://doi.org/10.4995/HEAd20.2020.11150 (Accessed 28 February 2024).

Gibbs, G. (1988) *Learning by Doing: A Guide to Teaching and Learning Methods*, Oxford, Further Education Unit, Oxford Polytechnic.

Goleman, D. (2020) *Emotional Intelligence*, 25th Anniversary ed., London, Bloomsbury Publishing.

Grabinger, S. and Dunlap, J. C. (2002) 'Problem-based learning as an example of active learning and student engagement', in Yakhno, T. (ed), *Advances in Information Systems, Lecture Notes in Computer Science*, Berlin, Heidelberg, Springer, pp. 375–384 [Online]. https://doi.org/10.1007/3-540-36077-8_39.

Hagenauer, G., Muehlbacher, F. and Ivanova, M. (2023) '"It's where learning and teaching begins – is this relationship" – insights on the teacher-student relationship at university from the teachers' perspective', *Higher Education*, vol. 85, no. 4, pp. 819–835 [Online]. https://doi.org/10.1007/s10734-022-00867-z.

Harrington, K., Flint, A. and Healey, M. (2014) *Engagement through Partnership: Students as Partners in Learning and Teaching in Higher Education* [Online]. Available at https://repository.londonmet.ac.uk/5176/ (Accessed 24 February 2024).

Herrington, J. and Oliver, R. (2000) 'An instructional design framework for authentic learning environments', *Educational Technology Research and Development*, vol. 48, no. 3, pp. 23–48 [Online]. https://doi.org/10.1007/BF02319856.

HM Revenue & Customs (2023) *Pay Apprenticeship Levy* [Online]. Available at www.gov.uk/guidance/pay-apprenticeship-levy (Accessed 9 March 2024).

IfATE (2015) *Digital and Technology Solutions Professional (Integrated Degree)* [Online]. Available at www.instituteforapprenticeships.org/apprenticeship-standards/digital-and-technology-solutions-professional-integrated-degree-v1-1 (Accessed 9 March 2024).

Jackson, J. (2023) 'Upskilling a new generation of digital technologists', *ITNOW*, vol. 65, no. 4, pp. 50–51 [Online]. https://doi.org/10.1093/itnow/bwad132.

James, N., Humez, A. and Laufenberg, P. (2020) 'Using technology to structure and scaffold real world experiential learning in distance education', *TechTrends*, vol. 64, no. 4, pp. 636–645 [Online]. https://doi.org/10.1007/s11528-020-00515-2.

James Relly, S. and Laczik, A. (2022) 'Apprenticeship, employer engagement and vocational formation: A process of collaboration', *Journal of Education and Work*, Routledge, vol. 35, no. 1, pp. 1–15 [Online]. https://doi.org/10.1080/13639080.2021.1983524.

Jarvis, J., Dickerson, C. and Stockwell, L. (2013) 'Staff-student partnership in practice in higher education: The impact on learning and teaching', *Procedia – Social and Behavioral Sciences, 6th International Conference on University Learning and Teaching (InCULT 2012)*, vol. 90, pp. 220–225 [Online]. https://doi.org/10.1016/j.sbspro.2013.07.085.

Johnson, K. (2023) 'Cost of living: "I skip university lectures to do paid work instead"', *BBC News*, 6th March [Online]. Available at www.bbc.com/news/newsbeat-64816948 (Accessed 6 March 2024).

Jones, C. S. and Bell, H. (2024) 'Under increasing pressure in the wake of COVID-19: A systematic literature review of the factors affecting UK undergraduates with consideration of engagement, belonging, alienation and resilience', *Perspectives: Policy and Practice in Higher Education*, Routledge, vol. 0, no. 0, pp. 1–11 [Online]. https://doi.org/10.1080/13603108.2024.2317316.

Kennedy, E. J., Lawton, L. and Walker, E. (2001) 'The case for using live cases: Shifting the paradigm in marketing education', *Journal of Marketing Education*, SAGE Publications Inc, vol. 23, no. 2, pp. 145–151 [Online]. https://doi.org/10.1177/0273475301232008.

King, A. (1993) 'From Sage on the stage to guide on the side', in *College Teaching*, Taylor & Francis Group [Online]. Available at www.tandfonline.com/doi/abs/10.1080/87567555.1993.9926781 (Accessed 24 February 2024).

Knight, P. T. and Yorke, M. (2006) 'Employability: Judging and communicating achievements', in *Learning & Employability*, vol. 2, Higher Education Academy [Online]. Available at www.advance-he.ac.uk/knowledge-hub/employability-judging-and-communicating-achievements (Accessed 9 March 2024).

Kolb, A. Y. and Kolb, D. A. (2009) 'Experiential learning theory: A dynamic, holistic approach to management learning, education and development', in *The SAGE Handbook of Management Learning, Education and Development*, London, SAGE Publications Ltd, pp. 42–68 [Online]. https://doi.org/10.4135/9780857021038 (Accessed 10 May 2024).

Kyndt, E., Vermeire, E. and Cabus, S. (2016) 'Informal workplace learning among nurses: Organisational learning conditions and personal characteristics that predict learning outcomes', *Journal of Workplace Learning*, Emerald Group Publishing Limited, vol. 28, no. 7, pp. 435–450 [Online]. https://doi.org/10.1108/JWL-06-2015-0052.

Leenknecht, M. J. M., Snijders, I., Wijnia, L., Rikers, R. M. J. P. and Loyens, S. M. M. (2023) 'Building relationships in higher education to support students' motivation', *Teaching in Higher Education*, Routledge, vol. 28, no. 3, pp. 632–653 [Online]. https://doi.org/10.1080/13562517.2020.1839748.

Mann, S. J. (2001) 'Alternative perspectives on the student experience: Alienation and engagement', *Studies in Higher Education*, Routledge, vol. 26, no. 1, pp. 7–19 [Online]. https://doi.org/10.1080/03075070020030689.

McAllister, N., Tavener-Smith, T. and Jackson, J. (2023) *mLearning with MediLingo: Decoding Medical Terminology Like a Language for Nursing Students*, South Kensington, Imperial College London [Online]. Available at www.imperial.ac.uk/medicine/study/clinical-academic-training-office/non-medical-opportunities/nwl-research-symposium/ (Accessed 13 March 2024).

McAllister, N., Tavener-Smith, T. and Williams, J. (2023) 'Decoding medical terminology: Implementing digital teaching innovations to support nursing students' academic and clinical practice', *Teaching and Learning in Nursing*, vol. 18, no. 1, pp. 84–90 [Online]. https://doi.org/10.1016/j.teln.2022.09.006.

McArthur, J. (2023) 'Rethinking authentic assessment: Work, well-being, and society', *Higher Education*, vol. 85, no. 1, pp. 85–101 [Online]. https://doi.org/10.1007/s10734-022-00822-y.

Mcleod, S. (2024) *Constructivism Learning Theory & Philosophy of Education* [Online]. Available at www.simplypsychology.org/constructivism.html (Accessed 24 February 2024).

MediLingo (n.d.) *Learn Medical Terminology with MediLingo* [Online]. Available at https://medilingo.co.uk/ (Accessed 13 March 2024).

Michaelsen, L. K. and Sweet, M. (2008) 'The essential elements of team-based learning', *New Directions for Teaching and Learning*, vol. 2008, no. 116, pp. 7–27 [Online]. https://doi.org/10.1002/tl.330.

Mueller, J. (2005) 'The authentic assessment toolbox: Enhancing student learning through online faculty development', *Journal of Online Learning and Teaching* [Online]. Available at https://repository.stkipjb.ac.id/index.php/lecturer/article/download/2335/1949 (Accessed 29 February 2024).

Mulkeen, J., Abdou, H. A., Leigh, J. and Ward, P. (2017) 'Degree and higher level apprenticeships: An empirical investigation of stakeholder perceptions of challenges and opportunities', *Studies in Higher Education*, Routledge, vol. 44, no. 2, pp. 333–346 [Online]. https://doi.org/10.1080/03075079.2017.1365357.

Oades, L. G., Robinson, P., Green, S. and Spence, G. B. (2011) 'Towards a positive university', *The Journal of Positive Psychology*, vol. 6, no. 6, pp. 432–439 [Online]. https://doi.org/10.1080/17439760.2011.634828.

Oliver, B. (2015) 'Redefining graduate employability and work-integrated learning: Proposals for effective higher education in disrupted economies', *Journal of Teaching and Learning for Graduate Employability*, Deakin University, vol. 6, no. 1, pp. 56–65 [Online]. https://doi.org/10.3316/informit.174658230609829.

Palmer, E., Lomer, S. and Bashliyska, I. (2017) *Overcoming Barriers to Student Engagement with Active Blended Learning: Interim Report*, University of Northampton [Online]. Available at https://research.manchester.ac.uk/en/publications/overcoming-barriers-to-student-engagement-with-active-blended-lea (Accessed 24 February 2024).

Perrin, B., Thompson, A., Agarabi, C. and Maier-Speredelozzi, V. (2008) 'Integrating graduate and undergraduate education with real world projects', *2008 38th Annual Frontiers in Education Conference*, pp. F4F-20–F4F-25 [Online]. https://doi.org/10.1109/FIE.2008.4720681 (Accessed 28 February 2024).

Porubän, J. and Bačíková, M. (2016) 'Live IT projects at a university in large-scale', *2016 International Conference on Emerging eLearning Technologies and Applications (ICETA)*, pp. 275–281 [Online]. https://doi.org/10.1109/ICETA.2016.7802044 (Accessed 28 February 2024).

Prather, J., Denny, P., Leinonen, J., Becker, B. A., Albluwi, I., Craig, M., Keuning, H., Kiesler, N., Kohn, T., Luxton-Reilly, A., MacNeil, S., Petersen, A., Pettit, R., Reeves, B. N. and Savelka, J. (2023) 'The robots are here: Navigating the generative AI revolution in computing education', *Proceedings of the 2023 Working Group Reports on Innovation and Technology in Computer Science Education*, ITiCSE-WGR '23, New York, NY, USA, Association for Computing Machinery, pp. 108–159 [Online]. https://doi.org/10.1145/3623762.3633499 (Accessed 18 March 2024).

Reflecta (n.d.) *Reflecta: Reflection for Learning and Wellbeing* [Online]. Available at https://reflectaproject.com/ (Accessed 13 March 2024).

Reynolds, L. and McDonell, K. (2021) 'Prompt programming for large language models: Beyond the few-shot paradigm', in *Extended Abstracts of the 2021 CHI Conference on Human Factors in Computing Systems, CHI EA '21*, New York, NY, USA, Association for Computing Machinery, pp. 1–7 [Online]. https://doi.org/10.1145/3411763.3451760 (Accessed 11 February 2024).

Rochon, R. (2022) 'Live brief projects in higher education: A contextualized examination of student and staff perceptions of experiential learning', doctoral, Buckinghamshire New University [Online]. Available at https://bnu.repository.guildhe.ac.uk/id/eprint/18506/ (Accessed 24 February 2024).

Rochon, R. (2023a) *Think about yourSELF: Reflection as a Tool for Both Learning and Wellbeing*, Keele University [Online]. Available at www.advance-he.ac.uk/programmes-events/conferences/teaching-learning-2023#Programmes (Accessed 13 March 2024).

Rochon, R. (2023b) *Evaluating SELF: A New Model of Reflection for Learning and Promoting Wellbeing*, Manchester [Online]. Available at www.advance-he.ac.uk/Mental-Wellbeing-23 (Accessed 13 March 2024).

Sara, R. (2011) 'Learning from life – exploring the potential of live projects in higher education', *Journal for Education in the Built Environment*, vol. 6, no. 2, pp. 8–25 [Online]. https://doi.org/10.11120/jebe.2011.06020008.

Schonell, S. and Macklin, R. (2019) 'Work integrated learning initiatives: Live case studies as a mainstream WIL assessment', *Studies in Higher Education*, vol. 44, no. 7, pp. 1197–1208 [Online]. https://doi.org/10.1080/03075079.2018.1425986.

Shaw, M. (2005) 'Software engineering for the 21st century: A basis for rethinking the curriculum', *Technical Report CMU-ISRI-05-108* [Online]. Available at http://reports-archive.adm.cs.cmu.edu/anon/anon/home/ftp/usr/ftp/isri2005/CMU-ISRI-05-108.pdf (Accessed 29 February 2024).

Smith, S., Caddell, M., Taylor-Smith, E., Smith, C. and Varey, A. (2021) 'Degree apprenticeships – a win-win model? A comparison of policy aims with the expectations and experiences of apprentices', *Journal of Vocational Education & Training*, Routledge, vol. 73, no. 4, pp. 505–525 [Online]. https://doi.org/10.1080/13636820.2020.1744690.

Smolansky, A., Cram, A., Raduescu, C., Zeivots, S., Huber, E. and Kizilcec, R. F. (2023) 'Educator and student perspectives on the impact of generative AI on assessments in higher education', *Proceedings of the Tenth ACM Conference on Learning @ Scale, L@S '23*, New York, NY, USA, Association for Computing Machinery, pp. 378–382 [Online]. https://doi.org/10.1145/3573051.3596191 (Accessed 18 March 2024).

Soares, A. E. and Lopes, M. P. (2020) 'Are your students safe to learn? The role of lecturer's authentic leadership in the creation of psychologically safe environments and their impact on academic performance', *Active Learning in Higher Education*, vol. 21, no. 1, pp. 65–78 [Online]. https://doi.org/10.1177/1469787417742023.

Stahl, B. C., Schroeder, D. and Rodrigues, R. (2023) *Ethics of Artificial Intelligence: Case Studies and Options for Addressing Ethical Challenges*, Springer Nature [Online]. https://doi.org/10.1007/978-3-031-17040-9 (Accessed 11 February 2024).

Taylor-Smith, E., Smith, S., Fabian, K., Berg, T., Meharg, D. and Varey, A. (2019) 'Bridging the digital skills gap: Are computing degree apprenticeships the answer?', *Proceedings of the 2019 ACM Conference on Innovation and Technology in Computer Science Education, ITiCSE '19*, New York, NY, USA, Association for Computing Machinery, pp. 126–132 [Online]. https://doi.org/10.1145/3304221.3319744 (Accessed 24 February 2024).

Thompson, N. E. and Wheeler, J. P. (2008) 'Learning environment: Creating and implementing a safe, supportive learning environment', *Journal of Family Consumer Sciences Education*, vol. 26, no. 2, pp. 33–43.

Tynan, B. and Lee, M. J. W. (2009) 'Tales of adventure and change: Academic staff members' future visions of higher education and their professional development needs', in Richter, J. (ed), *On the Horizon*, Emerald Group Publishing Limited, vol. 17, no. 2, pp. 98–108 [Online]. https://doi.org/10.1108/10748120910965485.

Williams, D. L., Beard, J. D. and Rymer, J. (1991) 'Team projects: Achieving their full potential', *Journal of Marketing Education*, SAGE Publications Inc, vol. 13, no. 2, pp. 45–53 [Online]. https://doi.org/10.1177/027347539101300208.

Wink, J. (2005) *Critical Pedagogy: Notes from the Real World*, 3rd ed., Boston, Pearson/Allyn & Bacon.

Yorke, M. (2006) *Employability in Higher Education: What It is, What It is Not*, York: Higher Education Academy.

Chapter 7

# Moving From Industry-Sponsored Academic Projects to Supporting Student Learning in Industry

Rebecca Bates, Ron Ulseth, Cody Mann and Lin Chase

## Introduction

Integrated Engineering at Minnesota State University, Mankato, has offered work-based learning opportunities through co-op positions for over a decade. The award-winning, project-based learning model integrates the development of professional, design and technical skills through industry-sponsored projects and originally with limited (semester-long) work-based experiences. In our programs, students earn a bachelor's degree in engineering by completing lower-division courses at two-year institutions and then entering our upper-division program. Building on the project-based degree that requires four upper-division, semester-long project experiences, we now offer a formalized work-based program. Program evaluation showed that senior students learned well in co-ops after "in house" skill development. In our new approach, an intensive, one-semester academy prepares students to apply their knowledge to engineering projects, acquire new knowledge efficiently, and build professional skills. The project-based model has now been extended to computer science. Because of the growing demand for software engineers with different lower-division preparation, we are extending our offerings to include a bachelor's degree in software engineering that has similar work-based experience to the integrated engineering model. This chapter includes more detail about the intensive coaching and faculty support that allows students to rapidly develop their engineering skills *in situ* and prepares them for sustainable careers.

## The Project-Based Model

Iron Range Engineering (IRE), the project-based learning (PBL) model, was initially motivated by the dissatisfaction of a group of engineering faculty members with their own engineering education and that of their students (Ulseth et al., 2011a). The dissatisfaction stemmed from a large gap between the skills and knowledge needed to perform well as engineers as compared to the skills and knowledge acquired by graduation. Further, there was an observed lack of

DOI: 10.4324/9781003496779-7

knowledge transfer from the learning in traditionally taught technical courses to either application or even to follow-on technical courses.

The gap areas recognized at the time were particularly in professional and design domains (Sheppard *et al.*, 2009). Students in a traditional curriculum were simply not spending adequate coursework time in these areas. In upper division courses, design was taught, per the Accreditation Board for Engineering and Technology (ABET) accreditation expectations, as a two-semester final year capstone experience while professionalism might show up in an ethics course tailored to engineers. The initial design of the PBL curriculum expanded to have 12 credits of professionalism and 12 credits of design, three credits per semester for each of the final four semesters. With regard to the technical curriculum, a philosophy of prioritizing conceptual knowledge over calculational knowledge was adopted (Ulseth *et al.*, 2011b). These three learning domains, design, professionalism, and technical, are combined in the PBL curriculum to provide relevant and meaningful experiences that supports knowledge retention in all areas.

### *Design Curriculum*

Early in the development of IRE, the founders became aware of the Aalborg University (Denmark) PBL model that is delivered to a student body of ~20,000 students. In place since the 1970s, the entire university experience is centred on team-based, open-ended, semester-long projects where technical learning supports the completion of the project (Kolmos *et al.*, 2004). The founders visited Aalborg in fall 2008 and found much inspiration for the creation of the IRE model. It can definitely be stated that the IRE model was an adaptation of the Aalborg model. Projects were one semester in duration. They were complex design problems that came directly from industry and were not re-scoped by professors. Students applied an iterative engineering design approach that led them from scoping at the start to design evaluation and delivery to the client at the end. Each project team had a project mentor with engineering experience to guide from the side as the team navigated their project (Ulseth *et al.*, 2011a).

### *Professionalism Curriculum*

Professional learning happened *in situ* in the projects where teams had to form, struggle, and learn to become productive (Johnson and Ulseth, 2017). Written and spoken communication skills were acquired and sharpened as the design team submitted extensive technical documents and gave regular design review presentations. This aligned with the Aalborg model. However, in addition, a series of workshops, learning journal entries, metacognitive analyses (Marra *et al.*, 2018), and a variety of other professional learning opportunities were added to the experience each semester for the IRE students. Students assembled and presented professionalism best works portfolios to further demonstrate their learning and development (Spence *et al.*, 2022).

### Technical Curriculum

In a traditional course, which is typically three-semester credits, the professors lecture during class time, the students do large (sometimes very large) problem sets from the chapters in the text, and there are two to three high-stakes, problem-oriented exams. From the beginning of IRE, the technical courses were one credit and characterized by flipped classroom mini-lectures (~10 minutes), discussion during class time, small problem sets, verbal exams where students discuss their understanding of engineering principles, and a large "deep learning activity" where the students apply their knowledge contextually. All students took 16 of these "core" courses as well as 16 more elective courses where they could dive deeper, expanding their knowledge in any of these areas or beyond. Where possible, the technical learning was aligned with the needs of the project, either fundamental knowledge which was needed to understand the problem or advanced knowledge that emerged during the completion of the design work (Ulseth *et al.*, 2011c).

After three years of successful graduates in Minnesota's Iron Range, a rural area where mining is the dominant industry, the model was extended to a location in the metropolitan area of Minneapolis and St. Paul, Minnesota, and

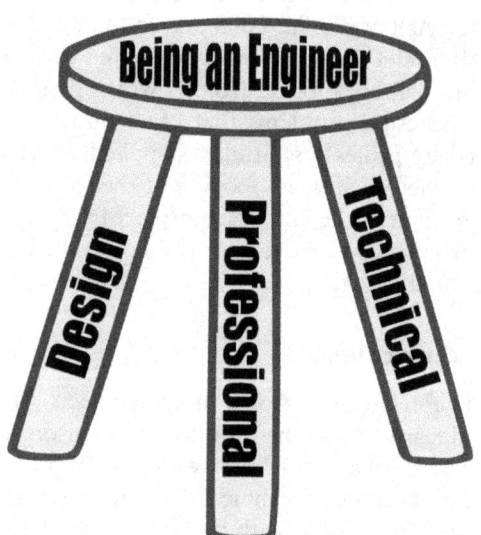

*Figure 7.1* The three legs of the stool, showing how engineering needs balanced support from the three domains of engineering.

Source: (Pluskwik, 2019; Johnson et al., 2022)

named Twin Cities Engineering (TCE). Goals of the extension included providing access for community college graduates to the project-based approach in an additional geographic area and testing the efficacy of the model under different resource conditions to show viability of the IRE model. The replication of the IRE model was successful, with graduates working in a broad range of engineering roles in the metro area and beyond.

Additional learning opportunities within the project-based context now include certificates in project-based engineering and integrated technology and design. The first provides exchange students and students in other engineering majors the opportunity to embed in an industry-sponsored project team and gain similar experiences related to technical, design, and professional learning. The second provides opportunities for students in non-engineering majors to work with engineering teams and provide input related to their courses of study including technical communication, media interaction, management, finance, and entrepreneurship. This also provides opportunities for IRE and TCE students to work in interdisciplinary teams that go beyond the engineering disciplines.

In one of the early years of the project-based model, a last semester student requested to do her project in industry on a paid co-op work placement rather than on campus with a student team. Unlike a traditional co-op where students pause their progression to graduation for a co-op, this student wanted to continue full-time studies while working full time. While initially a big challenge, the program found a way for the student to succeed in both ventures. With this student and many more who followed over the next few years, there was a noticeable increase in their motivation, identity development, and capability development when on co-op as compared to on-campus on-project teams (Johnson, 2016).

Also adopted from Aalborg University (Kolmos *et al.*, 2008a), the project-based model included the role of the project supervisor first known as a project mentor and then as the project facilitator. The facilitator guides the student development as they learn engineering design, acquire teaming skills, and communicate with industry clients (Kolmos *et al.*, 2008b). Facilitation in the IRE and TCE contexts included engineers who had practiced in industry bringing their years of expertise to the student experience while carrying out the aforementioned roles (Johnson, 2016).

In both instances of the IRE model, student engineers develop a strong sense of community and collaborative learning. Project teams consist of vertically integrated teams with members potentially coming from each of the four upper-division semesters, promoting leadership development and organic transfer of knowledge and program culture. Studies of belonging showed that students learning in this model had a stronger sense of belonging than in more traditional programs (Wilson *et al.*, 2015). Cohorts of students develop good interpersonal relationships and value how they can balance skills and knowledge with their peers. This development of relationships and structure for learning across the three legs of the stool (Figure 7.1) is supported and nurtured by engineering faculty and facilitators who have open-door policies and are accessible to students.

## The Practice-Based Model

A combination of factors led to the development of the practice-based model that is now available. Among them were the prior successful experiences the program had with students learning while on co-op placement and the successful guidance provided by the facilitators with engineering experience. Other factors including student demographics, enrolment trends, economic considerations for the program and in the Iron Range region led to a desire for the development of what was initially called IRE v2.0.

In 2016, the founders of Charles Sturt University (CSU) engineering program (Australia) visited IRE to capture best practices they might implement in their new program. The CSU model had students starting right after high school as opposed to the IRE model where students already had two years of community college experience before entry. In the CSU model, students spent 1.5 years on campus in an Aalborg-like PBL model before going on four years of co-op placement while completing their engineering curriculum in parallel. At the end of the 5.5 years, students graduated with a master's degree in civil engineering.

This model was a large inspiration to the IRE leaders. They foresaw a transformation of IRE from project based to practice based. A grant to study work-based learning and develop a pilot version was obtained and the work was undertaken. A new model (see Figure 7.2) was created (Bates *et al.*, 2020; Ulseth *et al.*, 2021).

The new "Bell model" was a combination of the old IRE model and the CSU model. In this model, students would complete their community college (first two years of a four-year bachelor's degree) and then transfer into

*Figure 7.2* Graphic description of IRE Bell model.
Source: (Bates *et al.*, 2020; Ulseth *et al.*, 2021)

a one semester "boot camp" (called the Bell Academy) where they would spend ~50 hours per week learning engineering design while doing an IRE industry project, begin taking their upper-division technical courses, become professionally adept and ready to thrive in an industry setting, and polish their job-search skills while interviewing for and obtaining their first co-op. After the Bell Academy, students would enter 24 months of practice-based learning, working in engineering positions acquiring design, professional, and technical skills. Students spend their time during the work day getting paid for their work and then approximately 15 hours outside of work each week documenting their design and professional learning, taking evening technical classes, visiting with their program learning coach (mentor), and being evaluated on their learning. The curriculum of the new model is identical to the old model. The number of semesters increased from four to five and the modality for learning switched from purely project based to a combination of practice based and project based.

The pilot began in fall 2019. In 2022, it became obvious to program leadership that the new model experience for students was preferred in the IRE context to the project-based model which had still been running in parallel during the pilot. As the new model better met the enrolment, demographic, resource, and economic needs of the regions, the old model was discontinued in this location. Now all IRE students take part in the Bell model of practice-based learning (Johnson *et al.*, 2022).

## Program Features

Unique features distinguish the new program co-op experience from a traditional engineering co-op. These features result in a steep development trajectory enabling the students to earn full college credit towards their baccalaureate degree. Features include the training experience before the co-op placement, technical credit learning from engaged professors during co-op placements, frequent support and feedback from facilitators, peer team support for professional and technical learning, a substantial development through reflection during all aspects of the program, and a one-week face-to-face examination period after each year of co-op completion (Ulseth *et al.*, 2021).

The model is fiscally sustainable for both students and the institution. Differential tuition is charged to enable the program to operate on minimal external funding (~ $14,000 USD per semester for five semesters). Students earn a co-op salary for the last two years of their education (more than $25/hour, which translates to ~ $50,000 per year).

The student body of this program is made up of community college graduates from around the entire United States. These students transfer to the institution from community colleges everywhere to attend the Bell Academy in person in northeastern Minnesota, or virtually from anywhere. For their next two-years, students work in co-op placements anywhere in the world. They are expected to return to the institution for a one-week exam and professional development symposium following each year of co-op placement (Johnson and Ulseth, 2021). The enrolment is driven by a desired intake of 25–45 students every six months. At full capacity, this will result in about 175 students in the program at the five different stages.

### Program Operation

The learning model uses strategies for student development that emerged from the over ten years of operation at IRE. These strategies include models for professional development, self-directed learning development, structured reflection, technical competence development, facilitation, culture management, leadership, innovation, design learning, and inclusivity (Rogalsky *et al.*, 2020).

The program has three distinct faculties. (1) The "professors" (PhD-level engineers) create, facilitate, and support the self-directed learning of technical competencies and give verbal exams to students while the students are in the Bell Academy, while on co-op placement, and when they return for exams at the end of each year. (2) The "facilitators" (engineers hired from engineering practice to this role) mentor students in their professional and engineering design development during the Bell Academy and in their co-ops through frequent encouraging feedback on the students' reflection journals and development plans. Feedback is both in writing and face to face electronically. Learning coaches also liaise with company supervisors and facilitate peer-to-peer support teams. (3) The on-ground academic team consisting of some professors, some facilitators, and a support staff deliver the Bell Academy.

### Facilitation

IRE continues to seek best practices to support the development of students in their career field (Christensen *et al.*, 2023; Johnson *et al.*, 2018; Ulseth, 2016). Expectations of students in the program are to develop in the necessary professional, design, and technical learning realms that allow them to thrive on the job in industry (Christensen *et al.*, 2023). Intensive student preparation to thrive in their industry positions is highlighted in the first semester of the program. After the Bell Academy semester, students enter their co-op semesters in a hybrid learning format. This unique hybrid learning includes evening classroom instruction while also applying acquired knowledge and furthering their learning in the workplace. It has been discovered that student motivation to learn in this unique work-based learning format is directly tied to the role of the mentors in the program (Christensen *et al.*, 2023; Johnson *et al.*, 2018). There is a clear need for mentoring in a hybrid model where students require support in both onsite and online learning (Andersen and West, 2020; Christensen *et al.*, 2023; Johnson *et al.*, 2018).

Within the IRE program, a facilitator is an engineer with experience working in an engineering industry who has returned to work in the field of education to support and mentor students in their learning (Johnson *et al.*, 2018). Each student engineer is assigned a program facilitator to serve as a learning coach with whom to work one-on-one. Conversations between the facilitator and student take place on a weekly basis in the Bell Academy to discuss the progress of short-term and long-term goals in relation to personal, technical, design, and professional realms. These meetings serve as a space for supporting planning and strategy development that is meaningful and relevant to the student's learning. The facilitators are mentors for the students in all aspects of their educational experience at IRE. The relationships continue post-academy throughout the co-op years.

As part of their mentorship from a facilitator, each student is regularly assigned opportunities to reflect on their experiences via learning journal reflections. The reflection topics vary, but student engineers regularly write about a prompted past experience or area of development, assessing their progress and looking forward to what can be improved. Since the facilitators are in charge of assessing these written reflections, the learning journals serve as a guide for open dialogue between the facilitator and student engineer and a way to enhance student capacity for monitoring progress (Christensen *et al.*, 2023).

Mentorship has existed for many years in education, and the benefits to students are substantial. Some examples of these benefits are that mentoring can increase student engagement, enhance the recruiting efforts of a diverse population of students, increase identity formation, increase retention of students, and create an inclusive culture (The National Academies Press, 2019). As defined in the book titled *The Science of Effective Mentorship in STEMM*, "mentorship is a professional, working alliance in which individuals work together over time to support the personal and professional growth, development, and success of the relational partners through the provision of career and psychosocial support" (The National Academies Press, 2019). Mentorship can take many structures, which can include formal versus informal, one-on-one versus group, traditional versus peer, and so on (The National Academies Press, 2019).

While traditional mentorship and peer mentorship are generally well studied, facilitators do not necessarily fit into either of those categories. This type of mentorship, which is mentorship combined with life and career coaching, is unique within the engineering profession to help with the student's transition from the classroom to the workplace. This mentoring occurs outside the traditional classroom setting. Students live and work in various parts of the country during their industry experience while they are still full-time students with IRE, which comes with a novel level of remote mentorship. Communication happens through email, texts, phone calls, and video calls, and may occur one-on-one or in facilitator-led peer group sessions.

### Career Development

The process of equipping students with the skills and resources necessary to secure interviews and job offers for their co-op placements is known as "career development" within the IRE program (Rogalsky *et al.*, 2020). Throughout their time in the Bell Academy, students dedicate approximately five hours per week to engaging in various career development activities. These activities include crafting a polished résumé, seeking input from professors and facilitators, and incorporating the received feedback to enhance the quality of their job search documents. This iterative process persists not only throughout the duration of the Bell Academy semester but also spans across all four semesters of their co-op experience (Rogalsky and Ulseth, 2021).

Similarly, students undergo a structured process to enhance their interview skills and gain valuable practical experience. Within the Bell Academy, students actively participate in three to four networking events and two to three career fairs, both in virtual and physical settings. Students on co-op regularly return for virtual networking and career fairs.

Moreover, beyond receiving guidance from program staff, students engage in a peer-to-peer feedback loop where they evaluate and provide constructive criticism to their fellow students on various aspects such as resume building, human resources practices, communication skills, and interview techniques.

### Experiences for International Students

In the United States, international students can generally work full time for no more than a year before graduation and still maintain their ability to work for up to three years post-graduation under an extension of their student visas, without needing industry sponsorship to remain in the United States. This makes it a challenge to participate in a practice-based program that calls for two years of full-time work. Options for international students start with full-time co-op experience for about 11.5 months after the Bell Academy. For the remainder of their academic time, student engineers have three options. The first is to work in the engineering industry in any place in the world they are legally eligible to work. The second is to work on an in-house, client-sponsored project in the traditional PBL model with other students in a similar situation or to work as a project lead on a Bell Academy project. As a project lead, students gain valuable leadership and project management experience. The third option is a blend of the two, where the student can work up to 20 hours per week at a paid co-op position and then serve proportionally on an in-house project. In all cases, students maintain their connections with their facilitator/learning coach.

### Building a Culture of Community

Being a student engineer is not easy. A strong community of diverse learners, including faculty and facilitators, supports retention and persistence. In the traditional PBL models used at IRE and TCE, proximity and project challenges supported the development of community. Moving to a program where students would work individually in industry without close peers or easy access to faculty and facilitators required intentional planning. The first tactic takes advantage of the Bell Academy for proximity. Students live in a communal dorm, have assigned project work rooms, and student-life activities occur multiple times per week. Activities may be a brief snack break, a yoga class, a movie, a pizza lunch, or a more intensive weekend hiking/camping trip. At the end of the Bell Academy, students who are a year and two years out return for their exam and professional development week. Along with shared learning and networking activities, graduation ceremonies are publicly celebrated. New students develop relationships with peers who are a few steps ahead of them and have a vision of how their own graduation may be celebrated before heading off to their first co-op position.

While on co-op, students attend a seminar that meets synchronously every one to two weeks. Some seminar sessions meet as individual cohorts and some meet with mixed cohorts. Seminars address program timelines, provide opportunities for learning about professional skills (as opposed to the technical and design learning happening in other settings), and support work completion. Students also have meetings of student chapters of professional societies. These times provide formal opportunities for students to maintain connections and relationships with their peers.

The program needs to balance the demands of a full-time job as well as the work of technical learning with these additional commitments. School commitments are significant since students also have regular meetings with facilitators and smaller peer groups and attend synchronous and asynchronous evening classes. The benefit of having multiple connection opportunities for each student during any week is a reduced sense of isolation as (usually) the youngest person on the job, development of an engineering identity that connects to the range of learning each student experiences, and a safety net that can support students when they are in a challenging time, whether because of work, school, or their personal life.

### Connections to Other Work-Based Models

One of the key things that sets IRE apart from other work-based models is the strong connection between engineering work in industry and the curriculum. However, other models still play an important role in student development by providing experiences in professional contexts. Two examples at the same institution, Minnesota State University, Mankato, are Project Maverick and Bureau 507. Both are associated with the Department of Computer Information Science.

Maverick Software is a consulting firm that uses student developers to meet industry needs (www.mavericksoftware.com/). Along with an office located at Minnesota State Mankato, the firm has had offices on other university campuses. Project Maverick, the extension of Maverick Software located on the Mankato campus, is set up as a consulting firm for Thomson Reuters, a publishing company based in Minneapolis, MN, and one of the first major clients of Maverick Software. Operating on the Mankato campus since 2006, Project Maverick hires students majoring in computer science, computer engineering, information technology, and management information systems to address projects specific to the publishing company (Minnesota State University, Mankato, 2019; Brandt, 2020). Undergraduate students are hired to work on campus up to 20 hours per week during the school year and full time during the summer, with an on-campus manager who coordinates training, supervises the student workers, and assigns tasks or groups within the Thomson Reuters context. Funding is structured through renewable grants from the company to the university and students are paid through university student payroll. The manager is an employee of Maverick Software and there is a faculty member who serves as the primary point of contact with the university.

Students are typically hired during their second (of four) academic years and many maintain their positions until graduation. Graduates are frequently hired into positions with the companies sponsoring their projects upon graduation. Benefits to the companies include a pool of trained and engaged workers who can easily step into entry-level positions with very little training needed, especially since student workers are often embedded into work teams with the company and attend regular meetings with industry teams. Clients of Maverick Software save on average $50,000–$75,000 per new hire on training and onboarding costs.

Student interns are treated as part of the team that they are working with, attending all stand-up meetings and sprints when possible and meeting high performance expectations. They work independently and with teams that contain a range of industry roles. Teams may or may not include other student interns. Because of the long-term relationship with Thomson Reuters, the company understands the nature of the academic year and school schedules, allowing for flexibility to attend classes, prepare for exams, and prioritize schoolwork. This helps students successfully manage and meet competing expectations, making the transition into full-time work a positive experience for students. Examples of student projects include software testing and development for a wide range of applications.

The focus of this Project Maverick is on software development, in contrast to the work of Bureau 507, also known as B507. B507 is a student-run, faculty-mentored consulting group that addresses "creative" projects such as innovative websites, animations, videos, logs, print design, and user experience. B507 was modelled after a similar successful program at HAN University in the Netherlands (https://b302.nl). The HAN Talent B302 program calls itself a "creative media mob". HAN University is an exchange partner with MSU. MSU exchange students had positive experiences working with B302 while on semesters abroad at HAN in the Netherlands. B507, a version of the creative media mob in Minnesota, was motivated by the opportunity to create similar interdisciplinary experiences for MSU students at home as well as to provide creative experiences for HAN exchange students. Students who work on projects come from majors like information technology, technical communication, graphic design, and management.

Multiple successful projects came from the teams associated with B507 with the crucial distinction from within-major capstone projects of interdisciplinary teams that purposefully draw expertise from multiple majors. Some of these can be seen at www.b507.us. While engineering accreditation guidelines value interdisciplinary teamwork, the disciplines represented are often just different engineering disciplines. A highlight of this endeavour is the breadth of majors affiliated with the creative teams. Student opportunities with B507 were reduced during the pandemic as both student and faculty capacity for extracurricular activity diminished and businesses refocused resources on pandemic responses. The infrastructure remains and students are currently hired on a project-by-project basis. There is discussion about ways to revive the program as capacity increases.

The context of learning through working is not novel in and of itself as these examples and others in this book show. They are presented to show that there is a culture of acceptance and support for learning through formal industry partnerships and mentoring at the university that go beyond typical senior or capstone projects that often have industry sponsors. It is within this context that the models developed through IRE are expanding to other departments and programs at the university.

## New Programs

The department of Computer Information Science (CIS) has had a similar arc of program development, first with a project-based program in computer science (CS) and now moving towards a practice-based program in software engineering (SE). Public education in the United States faced significant funding challenges during the US recession of 2008. In response, the historical computer science program was eliminated, while programs in information technology and management information systems were retained. As the project-based engineering programs flourished, industry desire for graduates with computer science training with additional analysis skills and deeper math knowledge and student interest in more degree options both became apparent. College leadership asked a team of faculty from both Integrated Engineering and CIS to apply the project-based approach to rebuild the computer science program (Bates *et al.*, 2020). This combination of administrative leadership and faculty buy-in and joint program development is crucial to sustainable implementation of new programs (Allendoerfer *et al.*, 2015). The team went through several iterations of cross-disciplinary and cross-organizational planning in order to:

- Apply project-based learning in the CS upper division
- Create a program that makes participation accessible and workable for students from underrepresented populations in the science, technology, engineering, and math (STEM) fields
- Connect to both national and regional industry participants as project partners and career accelerators for our students
- Prepare our local students for this project-based approach during lower-division courses, including creating a common lower-division core curriculum to be shared by all programs requiring computing classes
- Coordinate with the regional and national two-year colleges that serve as student pathways to our program
- Focus on student inclusion and student access to degree pathways at all levels
- Provide training for faculty to make the shift to development and teaching practices used in project-based learning

The CS program began with a pilot upper-division group in fall of 2020 (two students), alongside the lower-division students who were the first to be able to declare the major as first-year students in over a decade. The first significant upper-division cohort (11 students) began in fall of 2021. Since then 30 students have graduated and entered industry or graduate school. Because the instructional cost of running a project-based program in tight collaboration with industry partners is high, the CS program is limited to admitting 50 upper division students per year (for a maximum of 100 upper division students in the CS program at any given point in time). This means that we do not have the space to accommodate every student who has already matriculated at Mankato and has declared that they want to join the project-based CS program.

During the spring 2024 semester, 17 CS projects were completed from 12 different entities, including a range of industry partners, non-profit organizations, and researchers from multiple institutions. Projects are "pitched" by partner representatives during an intensive orientation day before the semester starts and students submit a list of their top ten choices. Students carefully consider the type of client they will be working with, the subject matter learning they will do, their career goals, and their personal interests before submitting their choices. Faculty then create teams prioritizing diverse participation on teams, known skills in communication, teamwork, and leadership, and student choice. Project teams have a facilitator/coach, access to faculty subject matter experts, and a primary partner contact. Students are supported in their technical, professional, and project learning through project, seminar, and technical classes.

Although there is not a work-based or co-op component in the CS program as there is with TCE and IRE, many students participate in Project Maverick or other computing-related internships during the summers and part-time during the academic year. All students participate in career development coaching. As with IRE and TCE, coaching and practice helps students articulate how their project-based experiences can translate into successful industry experiences.

At the MN Tech Workforce Summit (mntech.org) held at Best Buy's Minneapolis headquarters on November 16, 2022, Minnesota employers (including but not limited to Best Buy, US Bank, Target, United Healthcare, Turnberry, Genesis, Thomson Reuters, and Federated Insurance) reported that they were seeking 40,801 software developers but were not able to find their needed hires. For many years, Minnesota colleges and universities have failed to provide the needed number of trained people for the software field, producing fewer than 1000 graduates per year total across all institutions (public and private) in the combined disciplines of computer science, software engineering, information technology, information systems, and other related majors. The industry leaders speaking at the Workforce Summit were emphatic about wanting well-trained software developers who are immediately ready, both technically and professionally, to contribute within weeks of being hired. One leader in a prominent role at a major company said repeatedly that given the way preparation of software professionals is currently organized it is "impossible to succeed, even for the University of Minnesota!" [sic]. The university, through the CIS department, is launching a work-based bachelor of science in software engineering (SE) program in fall 2024 that addresses these needs and issues directly and builds on the PBL structure of the CS program, while drawing from the implementation experience of IRE.

The new SE program takes the "hands-on study" approach of the project-based CS program a step further to create a work-based, practice-based program that allows students to be in paid industry positions during their last four semesters of study. This work-based approach to learning has all the "learn by doing" benefits that the CS program has, with the added important benefit that students do not have to attend classes in person or on campus for their final four semesters. Instead, they earn full-time wages to support themselves and their families while completing their degree wherever they are working, taking remote classes in the evenings and on weekends. This opens up educational and employment opportunities to a much broader population of non-traditional students, including adult students, incumbent workers, and anyone who has not historically had success with classroom learning. The SE program is built on the same lower division course requirements as those of CS. For students who pursue their first two years of study locally at Minnesota State University, Mankato, before entering either the project-based CS program or the practice-based SE program, course delivery is shared via the CIS department's core curriculum.

Constraints on the size of the software engineering program depend primarily on industry willingness to hire student engineers after the Academy semester, whereas the CS program is limited by faculty and space capacity on the university campus. Using a staffing model that includes facilitators for scaling the co-op coaching component allows the program to be flexible to both student enrolment and industry capacity.

As with the IRE practice-based model, the SE program will begin with an Academy semester located in the Twin Cities metro area, followed by four semesters where students work and learn in parallel. International students will have the same opportunity for "in-house" projects after they have maximized their legally allowable time working in industry, which may include joining a CS project team. Students will also return to the program for a one-week face-to-face period after each year of co-op completion for exams, professional development, networking, and community building.

In the future, the program model will be modified to eliminate the requirements that students (a) stop working full time during the Academy experience, and/or (b) be resident in Minnesota to participate in the program. To accomplish this, we plan to extend the model to include an Academy option that is delivered part-time over two consecutive semesters and is available entirely online. We anticipate that this option will be made available to students no later than year three of the program's life.

A motivator for all our work with project- and practice-based learning is to expand access to education and to broaden participation in engineering and computing fields. This also requires active recruitment, outreach, and reflective awareness of barriers to ensure that people we hope will learn with us actually do. We have structured our student (and family and community) outreach to start early in the timeline of the student experience. The goal is to reach students early in their academic career with experiences that give them a real and personal sense of the possibility of a STEM career and specific options for paths to follow to success. To build long-term success we need to be recruiting at the grade school and high school levels, as well as in two-year institutions. We prioritize focusing these activities in locations and with partners who serve large populations of underrepresented students.

Another critical element of long-term success is the creation and support of an actively engaged alumni community. We have seen the powerful effects of this with our Integrated Engineering programs. Students who graduate turn into mentors and employers for students who come along behind them. This is a powerful force for growth and impact. Combining this approach with a focus on communities of colour in the US will have a hugely positive and long-term impact on our diversity, equity, and inclusion efforts.

For all of our practice-based programs, we continue to explore and negotiate relationships with a variety of two-year colleges across the US. For software engineering in particular, we are working with historically black colleges and universities (HBCUs) with the aim of providing a "win-win" solution for us and partner schools. We are specifically targeting two-year HBCs and four-year HBUs which do not offer engineering programs and for whom the work-based approach to pedagogy is a good fit philosophically. The main goal is to create software engineering degree paths for our partner schools and the opportunity to provide access to a diverse student population for us. With the related goal of faculty diversity in mind, we are also including discussions about faculty exchange and co-teaching models.

To extend our goal of broad access to four-year STEM degrees, we are also introducing a bachelor of science in integrated science and technology (ISAT). This degree is a flexible, project-based major that includes foundational knowledge in at least one STEM area, humanistic knowledge to identify and respond to ethical issues in the field, and meta-knowledge to acquire life-long learning skills and better practice reflection (Kereluik *et al.*, 2013; Mishra, 2020). While many students may benefit from this major, it is also designed to allow people with certificates and degrees in technical areas (e.g., welding, carpentry, drafting) to complete a four-year degree. As the major grows, we expect to draw cohorts of students from targeted industries and to include work-based options to support the project requirements of the degree.

## Conclusion

The integrated engineering, computer science, and new software engineering majors at Minnesota State University, Mankato, allow for effective project-based and practice-based models of learning. Students stay in our work-based programs. Attrition rates (~6%) are very low compared to university averages. Students in work-based programs often are hired full time with an employer with whom they have done a co-op. Before that, our undergraduate students have been hired into formal training programs typically used to train recent graduates. Our graduates then become vetted, and invested, employees before they earn their baccalaureate degree.

We are starting to see a consistent pattern that shows that students leave their upper division work-based program in a better personal financial situation than when they started because they can work while completing their degree. Tying hands-on industry work closely with upper division education, while supporting students intensively with skills development in parallel, pays off well for both students and employers. This is very attractive for students from a broad range of backgrounds because of the economic advantages of getting into the productive (and well-paid) workforce earlier. Benefits to the university include more students with access to and interest in computing and engineering programs, a flexible approach to hiring staff since facilitators can be hired with fewer constraints than PhD faculty, strong partnerships with industry, and ease of expansion.

While new programs may want to move immediately to a work or practice-based program because of the advantages to students and employers, these programs benefited from the foundation of PBL in multiple ways that should be considered before starting. PBL approaches, even with just one academy semester, prepare students well for industry experience. Heading into industry with the ability to grapple with an ill-structured, challenging project and direct their own learning reduces the on-ramp time for any new employee. Faculty and programmatic experience with projects has supported the Bell Academy structure. The software engineering program in particular has benefited from the strong relationships with industry partners built through the computer science program. Partners were very willing to write letters of support that helped secure program start-up funds because they trust the faculty and have had positive experiences with students. We expect the success seen in IRE and TCE to continue as we implement the software engineering program.

## Acknowledgements

The authors gratefully acknowledge the long-term support of the Minnesota Department of Iron Range Resources & Rehabilitation as well as the current faculty and staff of Integrated Engineering and Computer Science who are implementing these programs: Ashley Aho, Mansi Bhavsar, Peg Burr, Darcie Christensen, Rushit Dave, Jack Elliott, Andrew Hanegmon, Jonathan Hardwick, Jennifer Karlin, Christine Kennedy, Alex Krummi, Ryne Leytem, Andy Lillesve, Arynn Lorentz, Brandy Maki, Kaitlyn Mann, Kortani Martin, Flint Million, Jodi Nelson, Luke Nyberg, Elizabeth Pluskwik, Dennis Rogalsky, Katie Scherf, Neil Schroeder, Lauren Singelmann, Emilie Siverling, Rob Sleezer, Catherine Spence, Jake Swanson, Ryan Walerius, Yuezhou Wang, and Melissa Weske.

## References

Allendoerfer, C., Bates, R., Karlin, J., Ulseth, R., & Ewert, D. (2015, June). Leading large-scale change in an engineering program. In *Paper Presented at 2015 ASEE Annual Conference & Exposition*, Seattle, Washington, 10.18260/p.24397.

Andersen, C. L., & West, R. E. (2020). Improving mentoring in higher education in undergraduate education and exploring implications for online learning. *Revista de Educación a Distancia (RED)*, 20(64).

Bates, R., Pluskwik, E., & Ulseth, R. (2020). Startup of an innovative program x3 – iron range engineering propagated. In *2020 IEEE Frontiers in Education Conference (FIE)*, Uppsala, pp. 1–4. https://doi.org/10.1109/FIE44824.2020.9274291.

Brandt, G. (2020, October 22). Real world experience: Maverick software utilizes student talent despite pandemic. *MankatoLife*. www.mankatolife.com/real-world-experience-maverick-software-utilizes-student-talent-despite-pandemic/.

Christensen, D., Singelmann, L., Mann, C., Johnson, B., & Ulseth, R. (2023). The Bell Academy: A bridge semester where engineering students transform into student engineers who thrive in industry placements. In *Paper Presented at the 2023 SEFI Conference*.

Johnson, B. (2016). *Study of Professional Competency Development in a Project-Based Learning (PBL) Curriculum* (Doctoral dissertation, Aalborg University).

Johnson, B., & Ulseth, R. (2017). The iron range engineering model in PBL in engineering education: International perspectives on curriculum change. In S. Sheppard, K. Macatangay, A. Colby, & W. Sullivan (Eds.), *Educating Engineers: Designing for the Future of the Field*. Rotterdam: Sense Publishers.

Johnson, B., & Ulseth, R. (2021, August). Design-based research for PBL curriculum development. In *Paper Presented at Pan PBL 2021*, Aalborg, DK.

Johnson, B., Ulseth, R., & Raich, M. (2022). A multi-decade response to the call for change. In *Paper Presented at the 129th Annual Conference & Exposition of the American Society for Engineering Education*, Minneapolis, MN.

Johnson, B., Ulseth, R., & Wang, Y. (2018). Applying design based research to new work-integrated PBL model (the iron range engineering Bell program). In *Paper Presented at the 7th International Research Symposium on PBL*.

Kereluik, K., Mishra, P., Fahnoe, C., & Terry, L. (2013). What knowledge is of most worth: Teacher knowledge for 21st century learning. *Journal of Digital Learning in Teacher Education, 29*(4), 127–140.

Kolmos, A., Du, X., Dahms, M., & Qvist, P. (2008a). Staff development for change to problem based learning. *International Journal of Engineering Education, 24*(4), 772–782.

Kolmos, A., Du, X., Holgaard, J. E., & Jensen, L. P. (2008b). *Facilitation in a PBL Environment*. UCPBL UNESCO Chair in Problem Based Learning. Retrieved from June 2, 2024, https://vbn.aau.dk/en/publications/facilitation-in-a-pbl-environment.

Kolmos, A., Fink, F., & Krogh, L. (2004). *The Aalborg PBL Model*. Aalborg, DK: Aalborg University Press.

Marra, R., Plumb, C., Hacker, D., & Ulseth, R. (2018, June). Developing metacognitive skills in an undergraduate problem-based learning in engineering: Early results. In *Poster Presented at ASEE 2018*, Salt Lake City, Utah.

Minnesota State University, Mankato. (2019, September 30). *Minnesota State Mankato Signs 5-year, $2.88 Million Contract with Maverick Software Consulting*. [Press release] www.mnsu.edu/about-the-university/news-and-events/project-maverick-5-year-contract/

Mishra, P. (2020). *Designing the Futures of STEM Education*. https://learningfutures.education.asu.edu/2020/07/27/designing-the-futures-of-stem-education/.

The National Academies Press. (2019). The science of effective mentorship in STEMM. In *The Science of Effective Mentorship in STEMM*. Taylor and Francis. https://doi.org/10.17226/25568

Pluskwik, E. (2019, June 17). Iron range engineering – an overview of design and open-ended problem solving activities in an interdisciplinary, project-based learning program. In *Paper Presented at the 126th Annual Conference & Exposition of the American Society for Engineering Education*, Tampa, FL.

Rogalsky, D., Johnson, B., & Ulseth, R. (2020). Design-based research: Students seeking placement in co-op educational model. In *PAPER Presented at ASEE 2020 Virtual Conference*.

Rogalsky, D., & Ulseth, R. (2021). Design-based research: Students seeking co-op in refined educational model. In *2021 ASEE Virtual Annual Conference*. http://doi.org/10.18260/1-2-36925

Sheppard, S., Macatangay, K., Colby, A., & Sullivan, W. (Eds.). (2009). *Educating Engineers: Designing for the Future of the Field*. Jossey-Bass.

Spence, C., Nyberg, L., Chasmar, J., Nelson, J., & Tsugawa, M. (2022, August). Working full time and earning an engineering degree: Wellbeing in a co-op-based engineering program. In *Paper Presented at the 2022 ASEE Annual Conference & Exposition*, Minneapolis, MN. https://peer.asee.org/41119

Ulseth, R. (2016). *Self-Directed Learning in PBL*. Aalborg Universitetsforlag. https://doi.org/10.5278/vbn.phd.engsci.00091

Ulseth, R., Ewert, D., & Johnson, B. (2011a). Work in progress – implementation of a project-based learning curriculum. In *2011 Frontiers in Education Conference (FIE)* (pp. F1F-1). Rapid City, SD: IEEE.

Ulseth, R., Froyd, J., Litzinger, T., Ewert, D., & Johnson, B. (2011b). A new model of project-based learning. In *ASEE Annual Conference and Exposition*, Vancouver.

Ulseth, R., Johnson, B., & Bates, R. (2011c). A comparison study of project-based-learning in upper-division engineering education. In *Paper Presented at the 3rd International Research Symposium on PBL*, Coventry, U.K.

Ulseth, R., Johnson, B., & Kennedy, C. (2021). *Iron Range Engineering. Advances in Engineering Education*. https://advances.asee.org/iron-range-engineering/

Wilson, D., Jones, D., Crawford, J., Kim, M. J., Bocell, F., Veilleux, N., Floyd-Smith, T., Bates, R., & Plett, M. (2015, March). Belonging and engagement among undergraduate stem students: A multi-institutional study. *Research in Higher Education*. https://doi.org/10.1007/s11162-015-9367x.

# Chapter 8

# Integrated Professional Development Pathways

## Learning-Integrated Work?

*Stan Lester*

### Introduction

Routes into professional careers have never been either homogeneous or entirely static, despite the dominance of particular models at different points in time. Learning on the job without external training dominated for much of history even if in a few professions – principally those of the legal advocate, physician, priest and academic – a university education became a prerequisite. Guilds and associations introduced formal examinations and assessments in many fields, leading to the appearance of study associations and evening classes followed by formal study-release to colleges and professional schools, culminating in what has become the 'parallel' model still widely used in craft, trade and industrial apprenticeships. In the twentieth century concerns about raising the status of professions and putting them on a more intellectual footing led to closer involvement with universities, with an ever-increasing trend towards full-time degrees followed by workplace training. Only towards the end of the century was the effectiveness of this 'sequential' approach to professional entry seriously questioned, whether from an educational or a social justice viewpoint (e.g. Schön, 1987; Milburn, 2009), and then largely only from the perspective of using alternative pedagogies and broadening access within same basic structure.

At present the sequential model still dominates, though with a trend towards more diverse professional entry-routes (Lester, 2009). Parallel pathways continue to be used, both where it is common to progress from auxiliary roles to becoming professionally qualified and for post-degree professional training. Some professions also allow more individual routes to qualifying, generally with some form of final assessment for qualified status, although these typically only account for a small fraction of entrants. An alternative that has emerged largely since the turn of the century, though with earlier roots in fields such as teaching and social work, is what has been termed the integrated model (*ibid.*; Hordern, 2014). The essential premises of this type of pathway are that academic learning and professional training are contained within a

DOI: 10.4324/9781003496779-8

single programme structure; theory and practice are closely intertwined rather than being learned in sequence or in parallel; the workplace is a site of new academically valid learning rather than only application and transfer; and the end-point is both an academic qualification and a professional recognition in whatever form is appropriate for the field concerned. These principles apply whether the occupation under consideration is a learned or regulated profession, a corporate career-path, or a field where formal professional qualifications are optional or absent.

In some respects the integrated model has been principally a theoretical construct relating to entry-routes into professions, although at least partially justifiable claims to its realisation have been made in teaching, nursing and some other health and care professions. Lester (2024) sets out a continuum between more and less integrated forms of professional development, noting that most programmes that have claims to taking an integrated approach fall short of the fully integrated end of the spectrum (see Table 8.1). This chapter explores several types of pathway that demonstrate integrated features, discusses issues and tensions in integrated programmes, and summarises factors that support integration.

## Integrated Professional Programmes

Various types of programme have claims to being considered as integrated professional development pathways according to the basic premises given earlier. As implied by Table 8.1, there is not a hard boundary between integrated and parallel entry-routes, but some programmes will lack any meaningful integration at a structural or pedagogical level, while others will sit closer to the integrated end of the spectrum. Programmes can also be considered in terms of the degree to which the learner is located principally in the institutional 'space' (after Lefevbre, 1991), as a student on an academic course that includes work attachments or placements, or the work-space, as an employee who is working towards professional recognition. A typical bachelor of education degree, effectively a full-time degree with work placements, exemplifies one end of this spectrum, and a chartered manager degree apprenticeship, taken by existing workers and with learning strongly located in the work-space, the other. A critical point that distinguishes even the most institutionally based of these programmes from other 'work-integrated learning' (WIL) degrees is that their aim is to develop an acceptable level of professional proficiency, as opposed to enhancing employability at a general level or providing an introduction to practice that leads to a post-graduation training post. Three examples are outlined next; in the first the institutional space dominates with some programmes having a more equal balance; the second is in principle equally balanced, though with variations; and in the third the main focus is on the work-space.

Table 8.1 A continuum of integration

| | Unintegrated ⟷ | Fully integrated |
|---|---|---|
| **Workplace** | Focuses on competence for immediate job, task orientation with pressure to perform<br>Learner as a subordinate trainee, expected to defer to expertise and hierarchy<br>Task-based instruction, digital technology only as used for work tasks<br>Practice is treated as atheoretical and rarely modified beyond a standard repertoire | Supports learning for wider practice, space to consolidate, reflect and investigate<br>Learner as a member of community of practice, encouraged to contribute ideas, reflect critically and question<br>Workplace pedagogy, mentoring, extensive use of digital technology to support learning<br>Practice is both informed by theory and generates new theories leading to modified practice |
| **Programme** | Separate, uncoordinated on- and off-job components<br>Standard curriculum with no recognition of previous learning, credit for workplace learning or recognition of learner context<br>Digital technology is used if at all as a substitute for face-to-face sessions and printed materials<br>Programme assessment is context-blind and separate from any workplace evaluations | Designed and enacted as a coordinated and integrated whole both structurally and in terms of relationships between theory and practice<br>Programme reflects the starting-point of the learner, is tailored to the individual context and accredits relevant learning regardless of source<br>Digital technology is used to aid learning in multiple ways using appropriate pedagogies, including in the work-space and through learning communities<br>Assessment is integrated, authentic in relation to practice, accessible and respects context |
| **Learner** | Passive – directed by instruction and teaching | Active and self-directing – supported by resources, facilitation, discussion and mentoring |
| **Partnership** | Minimal interaction, e.g. liaison to discuss progress<br>No involvement from work organisation in programme design or delivery | Active strategic and operational partnerships with extensive crossover between staff<br>Joint programme design, recruitment, delivery and assessment |

Source: Reproduced with permission from Lester (2024)

### British Teaching and Nursing Degrees

In teaching, qualified status is normally achieved through completing a teaching degree that covers the subject area to be taught as well as educational theory and practice, or by taking a teaching qualification following on from a degree in the relevant subject area. Both cover theory and practice; the current UK requirement is a minimum of 120 days on placements of increasing length and responsibility interspersed with periods of study. A more recent variation involves schools rather than university education departments taking primary responsibility for postgraduate training. Following graduation from these programmes there is no further training or certification that is needed before gaining qualified teacher status.

In the health sector there has been a worldwide trend for professions outside medicine to move from hospital-led training to a partnership model involving a university and a hospital or other healthcare setting, along with a move to qualifying at degree level. In the UK, entry to nursing had moved fully to a degree-level partnership model by 2013. Nursing degrees require an equal split between theory and practice, which should be integrated through linking study periods with placements (see for instance Nursing and Midwifery Council, 2023). Similar principles are reflected in programmes for other health and social care professions such as physiotherapy, osteopathy, podiatry and social work, though the minimum practice requirements vary. As with teaching, no further training or certification is needed before gaining registered status.

### Dual Degrees

Dual higher education emerged in Germany and Austria in response to a trend among young people for applying to universities or *Fachhochschulen* (universities of applied science) rather than entering 'dual system' apprenticeships. Dual degrees combine study at a higher education institution with paid work, normally with a single employer, with various models co-existing such as the first year entirely in the institution, alternate periods of work and study, and less commonly two or three days in work with the remaining time in the institution (Graf, 2016; Ertl, 2020). Workplace and academic learning are linked, and a minimum amount of academic credit must be based on workplace learning. At least in principle the two components need to be systematically integrated and the workplace component must provide training for an occupation rather than only for a specific job in the employing organisation (Wissenschaftsrat, 2013). Some dual degrees lead to formal vocational certification while others do not, though in principle all should prepare learners as effective contributors to the field concerned. In Germany and Austria programmes were initially concentrated in the engineering, digital and business sectors, but they have now expanded to other fields including health and education. Similar programmes have been developed elsewhere in Europe, notably in

Spain and Hungary. Some aspects of the dual approach are also reflected in cooperative degrees in North America, although these more typically provide a lead-in to practice-based training rather than bringing graduates to what can be considered as a professionally qualified level.

### Degree and Professional Apprenticeships

While there are earlier individual examples, apprenticeship-type programmes that incorporate a bachelor's or master's degree were introduced formally in the UK in 2015 (BIS, 2015) and have since appeared in Ireland, Australia and the United States among others. In principle these programmes simply extend the pre-existing parallel apprenticeship model into higher education, but there has been widespread recognition that in order to work well they need to integrate academic learning and practical training effectively (Lester and Bravenboer, 2020). Apprentices are normally fully employed in a single organisation, spend a smaller proportion of time out of the workplace than is the norm for dual degrees (a minimum of 20% is specified in the UK), and gain recognition as being ready to work at a qualified level in an occupation, with professionally qualified status where it is available often being achieved alongside the degree. Although the learner is more clearly located in the work organisation than in the models described previously, the educational institution has responsibility for the overall programme including ensuring that workplace learning covers the apprenticeship requirements. In the UK programmes are available across a wide range of sectors including teaching, nursing, medicine, engineering, digital technology, law, policing, architecture and management, and they are as popular with existing workers taking on new responsibilities or looking for career progression as with school leavers.

### Issues and Tensions in Integrated Programmes

Integrated professional development faces challenges both from a conceptual standpoint and in terms of successful implementation. From one perspective, the ability of a nominally 'full-time' degree to develop professional proficiency can be challenged. From another, there can be doubts about being able to instil sufficient theoretical knowledge and academic competence through a workplace-based programme. Part of the answer to this is in achieving genuine integration of theoretical and practical learning, but this in itself is challenging and it is easy to duplicate a theory–practice divide within an integrated structure.

### Competence and Readiness to Practise

A concern that has emerged in some integrated pathways is the extent to which the programme successfully prepares graduates to be competent and effective practitioners from day one. In sequential routes there is generally recognition that practitioners who have completed the practice-based training phase and been licensed or accredited by the relevant body are fully qualified and able to work in a more-or-less unsupervised capacity, even if further approval can be needed to act as a business principal. In teaching and nursing, where integrated routes dominate, there is a tacit assumption that graduates need to continue learning in the workplace in order to reach a proficient level. The Willis Commission (2012) for instance views newly registered nurses as being at the beginning of a process of development, and the statutory induction period for newly qualified teachers in state schools can be viewed as analogous to the final phase of practice-based training which would come before sign-off in many chartered professions. Research by Eraut and colleagues (Eraut et al., 2005) on early-career learning in engineering, nursing and accountancy indicated that graduates from (integrated) nursing programmes experienced as much transition-shock and need for learning transfer when moving to full-time work as did those from professions where standard full-time degrees were more common.

At present less evidence is available from integrated pathways that are more strongly located in the workplace, such as degree apprenticeships. Many professional bodies in the UK and Ireland accept degree and similar apprenticeships as leading to the award of fully qualified status, for instance in engineering, law, accountancy and architecture. The overall time to qualify is broadly comparable to that for sequential routes; in engineering it is potentially slightly shorter, while in architecture the minimum is currently longer. Less commonly, professions such as heritage conservation endorse apprenticeship-type routes but position qualified status at a point beyond what could reasonably be achieved on the programme. There is tentative evidence (for instance Bravenboer and Lester, 2016) that at least in some instances learners progress more quickly on integrated programmes. In nursing where different types of integrated pathway can be compared, early evidence suggests that those more strongly rooted in the workplace are more effective in building confidence and developing proficiency at an earlier stage (e.g. Cushen-Brewster et al., 2022). Again this is tentative and other factors may come into play, such as differences in age and experience when starting the programme.

### Balancing Theory and Practice

Scott et al. (2004), in their work on professional doctorates, discuss the ideas of 'colonisation' and 'reverse colonisation' between the academy and the workplace. Colonisation refers to the values of the institution being superimposed on those of the workplace or profession, so that what constitutes valid knowledge, how enquiry should be conducted and how work should be framed and discussed are seen from a principally academic perspective. Reverse colonisation describes the values of the workplace pervading those of the institution, with academic values and criteria being at least partly displaced by those of the work organisation. These perspectives are equally applicable to professional development pathways, particularly integrated routes that fit within a single programme structure. In traditional sequential routes the academic perspective dominates in the degree and the practice one in the training period. In the integrated model there are dangers either that the demands of the degree overshadow the need to develop practical proficiency or that academic aspects become marginalised by the work culture and the operational demands of the job.

Integrated professional pathways have been equated with a 'post-technocratic' approach to development (Bines, 1992; Lester, 2009), which suggests they are broadly in alignment with experiential learning principles as outlined for instance by Schön (1983, 1987), Kolb (1984), Revans (1980) and Hase and Kenyon (2000). Rather than seeing knowledge as something that is first learned and then applied, these perspectives take a cyclic or spiral perspective where knowledge both informs and is produced by practice. In some respects this provides an intellectual device for overcoming the theory/practice tension outlined earlier, and some successful integrated programmes are permeated by experiential learning principles (as opposed to using, for instance, action learning and reflective practice tools piecemeal). However, it does not form a complete solution, as professional practice generally employs knowledge that builds from an understanding of basic principles through to more complex and specific ones, along with the ability to reformulate understandings in response to different contexts. As Young and Muller (2014) among others have pointed out, there is a difference in being able to reflect from the perspective of having the relevant theoretical understanding and from that of a layperson. A challenge for integrated programmes is therefore being able to develop knowledge, theory and intellectual capability in tandem with practice, without reverting to some form of sequential or parallel model within the integrated programme 'wrapper'.

## *Nominal Rather Than Deep Integration*

An issue reported across the different types of nominally integrated programme is that the actual level of integration between workplace and academic learning can be limited, even if the programme structure appears designed to foster links between different learning spaces; as Gerstung and Deuer (2021) point out, integrating theory and practice can become confused with theory-to-practice transfer. In nursing and teaching, for instance, there is frequent reference to a 'theory–practice gap'; although this can be traced partly to a historic tendency in these fields for theory to have been taught in a way that is decoupled from practice (Korthagen, 2010), there are a number of factors that apply across integrated programmes. These include a lack of understanding of what integrated learning involves and a consequent reluctance to redesign curricula accordingly (Mordhorst and Gössling, 2020), educators' adherence to traditional teaching methods (Van Zyl, 2014), and a lack of communication or coordination between institution and workplace (Thompson *et al.*, 2015; Weiß, 2016). These factors can be exacerbated by 'restrictive' workplace environments (Fuller and Unwin, 2008) in which immediate task requirements and pressures to become a productive contributor dominate, or by work cultures that are indifferent or hostile to academic learning (Siebert and Costley, 2013; Leek, 2020).

Problems of integration can be present as much in professional apprenticeships as in more institutionally based programmes. A parallel but largely disconnected approach is still common in the former, sometimes without even basic coordination between topics covered in the workplace and in the university or college (Lester and Bravenboer, 2020). This can be compounded by narratives and assumptions that have been carried over from the British apprenticeship revival of the 1990s such as outdated dichotomies between knowledge and competence and between on- and off-job learning (Bravenboer and Lester, 2016; Minton and Lowe, 2019). In some programmes separate assessment regimes, for instance for the degree, professional recognition and achievement of the apprenticeship itself, can also add to the sense of related but disconnected strands of learning (Saraswat, 2016; Lester and Bravenboer, 2020). On the other hand there are many examples of successful programmes that demonstrate strong integration along the lines described in the next section.

## Achieving Integration: Structures, Pedagogies and Practices

Integrated professional programmes are positioned in different industry, employment and national contexts, and they also cater to a broad spectrum of learners from school leavers entering the workplace through to experienced workers aiming to progress in, or change, their careers. Programmes will vary in format and approach, and there is no single best practice model. However, experiences from a wide range of contexts do indicate principles and practices that make for successful integration. These are considered under four headings: organisations and partnerships; the work-space; design and pedagogy; and the learners themselves.

### *Organisations and Partnerships*

The need for effective partnerships between the organisations involved in integrated professional development has been discussed extensively (e.g. Willis Commission, 2012; McKnight and Birks, 2016; Hughes and Saieva, 2019; Mordhorst and Jenert, 2023). In most instances the principal relationship is between the educational institution and the work organisation, with other organisations such as professional, trade and regulatory bodies on the periphery. For any given field, relationships may be one-to-one, one institution to multiple employers, through a consortium of institutions and employers, or more rarely one large employer working with multiple institutions. Each of these has its own challenges, with particular issues when learners are located in multiple small firms (Lester *et al.*, 2016; Lillis, 2018). Partnerships need to be constructed at a strategic level, which if it is to work effectively may require changes to the cultures of the organisations involved; at the level of programme design and resourcing; and at the level of delivery and working with learners.

The centrality to integrated programmes of strategic partnerships between institutions and work organisations is generally well recognised (e.g., Lester and Bravenboer, 2020; Gerstung and Deuer, 2021), but the implications beyond the need for partnership agreements and senior manager commitment can be less appreciated. To support integrated development adequately, work organisations need to take on some of the characteristics of learning organisations in order to offer the kind of 'expansive' learning environment discussed in the next section; for those that have a high level of deference to hierarchy or expertise this can involve a potentially uncomfortable change in culture (e.g., Leek, 2020; Csizmadia *et al.*, 2022). Universities can need to move from a culture associated principally with research and knowledge transmission to one that also values engaging with and contributing to the work-space; again this can require an uncomfortable transition if it is to be accepted throughout the institution and become more than the preserve of specialist, potentially vulnerable units (Garnett, 2016; Lester and Crawford-Lee, 2023). Finally, while professional and industry bodies normally work at a step back from programme arrangements, they can exert a strong influence over the way that programmes operate and need to ensure that their regulations do not inhibit innovative structures, methods of teaching and learning and forms of assessment.

At an operational level, partnership working needs to include things such as co-developing the curriculum for the programme, recruiting learners, sharing responsibility for teaching, assessment and supporting learning, and reviewing progress (Lester *et al.*, 2016; Weiß, 2016). In at least some of these activities the learner also becomes a partner in, for instance, negotiating and reviewing individual learning goals and activities and deciding the work to be put forward for assessment (Lester and Costley, 2010; Garnett, 2020). Effective operational partnerships also involve some crossover between staff, so that employer staff become involved in teaching and assessment while academics move closer to the workplace, sometimes with a formal role connected to it; this may extend to 'practitioner-academic' roles familiar from medicine, where professionals are employed jointly by both organisations or loaned from one to the other (Forster *et al.*, 2023).

### The Work-Space

The way that the workplace – or, more broadly, the work-space – operates, the social interactions it provides and the richness of the learning opportunities it offers are all critical to effective integrated learning. 'Restrictive' workplaces (Fuller and Unwin, 2008) have already been mentioned; the converse is the 'expansive' workplace (*ibid.*), which supports development that goes beyond immediate job requirements and enables learners to become part of a community of practice. This kind of workplace typically has a culture of learning that runs throughout the organisation (or at least the relevant part of it), makes strong connections between business and learning objectives, seeks to overcome barriers to learning and encourages curiosity and questioning (Lillis, 2018; Lester, 2020). In most professional contexts it will also make effective use of digital technology, not only for work tasks but to support learning at the point of need and integrate it into everyday activity (Martin and Ertzberger, 2013; Lester and Crawford-Lee, 2023).

Billett and colleagues (Billett and Choy, 2014; Billett, 2019), building on the work of Lave and Wenger (1990), discuss the idea of workplaces having their own pedagogies or strategies for learning. These will normally include three main aspects: a structural dimension, in the sense of how work responsibilities, tasks and resources are allocated and presented in order to lead to learning and development; a practice dimension, involving approaches such as clarifying understanding, questioning, reflecting and theorising; and a social dimension, where learners can engage with co-workers in order to develop their understanding and proficiency and contribute as members of a community of practice. An effective workplace pedagogy will support cumulative development towards greater complexity and independence, incorporating tasks that are challenging, require critical reflection and engagement with theory and providing exposure to complex problems (Bravenboer, 2019). It is also good practice that learners are supported by a mentor, normally a member of the work organisation (or exceptionally an external member of the profession) who can take a more independent view than an immediate supervisor or coach; the role of the mentor can encompass providing insights into the way the workplace and the organisation operate, acting as a sounding-board, mediating between learner, supervisor and university, aiding access to resources, questioning and aiding reflection, and helping the learner become more independent (Major *et al.*, 2011; Roberts *et al.*, 2019).

### Pedagogy and Learning Design

The idea of a 'signature pedagogy' or set of underlying teaching and learning principles for work-based or work-integrated higher education has been put forward by Dalrymple *et al.* (2014) and Lester *et al.* (2016), among others.

Building on this, Lester (2024) summarises the pedagogical principles for integrated professional development as comprising:

- Learning design that sets out to integrate practice and theory, and learning in the work-space with that which takes place outside of it; recognises how the programme sits in, influences and is influenced by the work context; and provides flexibility to accommodate the needs and starting-points of individual learners, employers and workplaces or work contexts.
- Methods of teaching, facilitation and learning that are flexible and adaptable; are closely linked to work activity; and ensure the necessary ground is covered while developing independent learning and self-efficacy, practical academic skills and professional judgement.
- Methods of assessment that are valid and accessible; authentic in terms of the work context; and sufficiently robust to provide confidence in the practitioner's ability to act effectively and appropriately.

Associated with these principles is a repertoire of approaches that have proved successful in work-based and work-integrated higher education contexts. These include recognition of previous relevant learning regardless of its source; tripartite (learner, institution and employer) learning agreements that shape the programme as experienced by the individual learner; the use of easily accessible learning resources; 'flipped' or 'inverted' approaches where live sessions are used to discuss and reinforce content rather than introduce it; reflection before, during and after practice, captured where relevant through logs, records or dialogue; practice-based projects, investigations and portfolios supported by explanatory accounts or discussions; learning communities, including to link learners across different workplaces; and regular learning conversations and progress reviews, both with a tutor alone and three-way with a workplace representative (Lester and Costley, 2010; Minton and Lowe, 2019; Garnett, 2020; Rowe et al., 2020; Mordhorst and Jenert, 2023). Assessment criteria and processes, particularly those that contribute to continuation and success on the programme, also need to follow integrative principles otherwise they can negate the message provided by the remainder of the programme (Boud et al., 2023). Summative assessments in particular might be expected to focus on the larger sequences of actions and the accompanying reasoning and judgement that are needed in complex practice situations (after Eraut, 2004), providing confidence in the ability to act as a proficient, critical and ethical practitioner.

An increasingly important part of integrated learning pedagogy is the appropriate use of digital technology. Used effectively it opens up new ways of working rather than simply substituting for face-to-face teaching or paper-based resources. Lester and Crawford-Lee (2023) chart the evolution of digital approaches in apprenticeships and similar programmes during the coronavirus pandemic, from simple substitution or 'emergency remote teaching and learning' to more sophisticated use of digital pedagogies. They have particular value in integrated programmes for overcoming boundaries between the work-space and institutional space, for instance in supporting here-and-now learning at the point of need, enabling access to in-depth resources, diagnostics and learning communities in the workplace, bringing the work-space into the study arena through simulations, video links and serious games, and enabling content and interactions to take multiple forms in order to aid access and accessibility. These opportunities will only increase as digital tools become more capable, supporting a shift from an 'on- and off-job' mentality to a more fully integrated one.

## *The Learner*

Integrated pathways typically emphasise the three-way nature of the learning process, involving the educational institution, the employer and the learner, but the role of the learner generally receives the least attention. Weiß (2016) comments that learners are often left to integrate theory and practice, making their capacities to do this critical. Billett and Choy (2014) discuss the need for learners to have appropriate skills, dispositions and epistemologies of practice, allowing them to adopt an active approach to learning, to frame and make use of learning opportunities in the workplace, and to integrate different learning experiences consciously and deliberately; Stephenson (2001) adds to this self-efficacy. These capacities are to some extent self-reinforcing (Reddan, 2016), but it cannot be assumed that learners will develop them automatically. Integrated learning can present a particular culture-shock for school leavers who are used to a learning environment that is largely organised by others, but it can also be challenging for workers who are progressing from more task-oriented or procedural roles as well as for professionals whose education and training has been more formally structured (cf. Argyris and Schön, 1974). Strategies that have been successful in supporting learners to develop the skills and approaches needed for integrated learning include fostering critical reflection and workplace enquiry (e.g. Rowe *et al.*, 2020), encouraging learners to take responsibility for work and learning goals (after Ryan and Deci, 2000), and fostering a sense of identity as a self-managing professional (Trede, 2012).

## Conclusion

### *Towards Learning-Integrated Work*

Integrated professional development programmes are often described as reflecting work-based learning (WBL) or work-integrated learning (WIL) (e.g., Rowe, 2018; Berndtsson *et al.*, 2020; Konstantinou and Miller, 2020).

Work-integrated learning has been defined as "approaches and strategies that integrate theory with the practice of work within a purposefully defined curriculum" (Patrick *et al.*, 2008, p. iv), involving the use of meaningful work tasks and the active involvement of a partner or partners from the work context (Zegwaard *et al.*, 2023). It is most widely applied to organised work placements and attachments in full-time degrees, although it is also drawn on in discussions of apprenticeship-type learning. In higher education work-based learning tends to be used either to refer to work placements in a similar but looser way to WIL, or more specifically to learning undertaken in the work-space by existing workers, both counting towards academic awards; in the latter case the 'curriculum' is constructed around individual or workplace goals and is often transdisciplinary in nature rather than being located in a specific profession or academic discipline (Stephenson and Saxton, 2005; Lester and Costley, 2010). The two fields overlap, and principles from both are drawn upon in integrated professional development as has been illustrated in the previous section of this chapter. Programmes where learners are located more firmly in the institution might be regarded as demonstrating more of the characteristics of WIL, while those that have an emphasis on employment, particularly where learners already have some experience in the field concerned, can be conceptualised as sitting at least partly in a WBL paradigm (Lester, 2024).

Particularly as the integrated nature of programmes becomes more sophisticated, alternative conceptions are likely to be needed from those of WIL, with its emphasis on work being integrated into a programme of learning, and WBL, with the assumption that learning is oriented towards the specific work context. The idea of 'learning-integrated work' is useful here, in that it stresses that the learner is working in a job into which learning is integrated. This reversed emphasis is deliberate, as the work-located nature of integrated pathways needs to be recognised in order to develop meaningful integration at a pedagogic and practical level. While there will continue to be a need to protect time for learning as opposed to engagement in work tasks, conceptions need to move beyond thinking about what is on the one hand work-based, on-job and practical, and on the other institutionally based, off-job and theoretical.

## References

Argyris, C. and Schön, D. (1974) *Theory in practice: Increasing professional effectiveness.* San Francisco: Jossey-Bass.

Berndtsson, I., Dahlborg, E. and Pernbrandt, S. (2020) "Work-integrated learning as a pedagogical tool to integrate theory and practice in nursing education – an integrative literature review", *Nurse Education in Practice* 42, 102685, https://doi.org/10.1016/j.nepr.2019.102685.

Billett, S. (2019) "Securing occupational capacities through workplace experiences: Premises, conceptions and practices", in Bahl, A. and Dietzen, A. (eds.), *Work-based learning as a pathway to competence-based education*, 25–43. Bonn: UNEVOC/BIBB.

Billett, S. and Choy, S. (2014) "Integrating professional learning experiences across university and practice settings", in Billett, S., Harteis, C. and Gruber, H. (eds.),

*International handbook of research in professional and practice-based learning*, 485–512. Dordrecht: Springer.

Bines, H. (1992) "Issues in course design", in Bines, H. and Watson, D. (eds.), *Developing professional education*, 11–26. Buckingham: Open University Press.

BIS (Department for Business, Innovation and Skills) (2015) *The future of apprenticeships*. London: The Stationery Office.

Boud, D., Costley, C., Cranfield, S., Desai, J., Nikolou-Walker, E., Nottingham, P. and Wilson, D. (2023) "The pivotal role of student assessment in work-integrated learning", *Higher Education Research and Development* 42 (6), 1323–1337.

Bravenboer, D. (2019) "The creative disruption of degree apprenticeships in the UK", in Talbot, J. (ed.), *Global perspectives on work-based learning initiatives*, 57–83. Hershey, PA: IGI Global.

Bravenboer, D. and Lester, S. (2016) "Towards an integrated approach to the recognition of professional competence and academic learning", *Education + Training* 58 (4), 409–421.

Csizmadia, P., Csillag, S., Szászvári, K. and Bácsi, K. (2022) "To learn and let learn? Characteristics of the learning environment in knowledge-intensive medium-sized enterprises", *Journal of Workplace Learning* 34 (7), 661–674.

Cushen-Brewster, N., Driscoll-Evans, P., Malloy, E., Last, D., Wood, J., Vickery, H. and Wilkinson, S. (2022) "Evaluating experiences of a degree-level nursing apprenticeship", *Nursing Times* 118 (11), 1–4.

Dalrymple, R., Kemp, C. and Smith, P. (2014) "Characterising work-based learning as a triadic learning endeavour", *Journal of Further and Higher Education* 38 (1), 75–89.

Eraut, M. (2004) "Informal learning in the workplace", *Studies in Continuing Education* 26 (2), 247–273.

Eraut, M., Steadman, S., Maillardet, F., Miller, C., Ali, A., Blackman, C., Furner J. and Caballero, C. (2005) *Learning during the first three years of postgraduate employment*. Swindon: Economic and Social Research Council (Project LiNEA).

Ertl, H. (2020) "Dual study programmes in Germany: Blurring the boundaries between higher education and vocational training?", *Oxford Review of Education* 46 (1), 79–95.

Forster, A., Pilcher, N., Murray, M., Tennant, S., Craig, N. and Galbrun, L. (2023) "Construction and engineering higher education: The role of pracademics in recoupling classical experiential educational norms", in Dickinson, J. and Griffiths, T-L. (eds.), *Professional development for practitioners in academia*, 211–227. Cham: Springer.

Fuller, A. and Unwin, L. (2008) *Towards expansive apprenticeships: A commentary by the teaching and learning research programme*. London: Institute of Education.

Garnett, J. (2016) "Work-based learning: A critical challenge to the subject discipline structures and practices of higher education", *Higher Education, Skills and Work-Based Learning* 6 (3), 305–314.

Garnett, J. (2020) "Work-based learning tools to inform the implementation of degree apprenticeships for the public sector in England", *Higher Education, Skills and Work-based Learning* 10 (5), 715–725.

Gerstung, V. and Deuer, E. (2021) "Theorie-Praxis-Verzahnung im dualen Studium: Ein konzeptioneller Forschungsbeitrag", *Zeitschrift für Hochschulentwicklung* 16 (2), 195–213.

Graf. L. (2016) "The rise of work-based academic education in Austria, Germany and Switzerland", *Journal of Vocational Education & Training* 68 (1), 1–16.

Hase, S. and Kenyon, C. (2000, December) "From andragogy to heutagogy", in *UltiBASE in-site*. Melbourne: RMIT. https://webarchive.nla.gov.au/awa/20010220130000/http://ultibase.rmit.edu.au/Articles/dec00/hase2.htm, accessed November 2023.

Hordern, J. (2014) "Productive systems of professional formation", in Billett, S., Harteis, C. and Gruber, H. (eds.), *International handbook of research in professional and practice-based learning*, 163–193. Dordrecht: Springer.
Hughes, C. and Saieva, G. (2019) "Degree apprenticeships: An opportunity for all?", *Higher Education, Skills and Work Based Learning* 9 (2), 225–236.
Kolb, D. (1984) *Experiential learning*. New York: Prentice Hall.
Konstantinou, I. and Miller, E. (2020) "Investigating work-integrated learning and its relevance to skills development in degree apprenticeships", *Higher Education, Skills and Work-Based Learning* 10 (5), 767–781.
Korthagen, F. (2010) "The relationship between theory and practice in teacher education", in Peterson, P., Baker, E. and McGaw, B. (eds.), *International encyclopedia of education*, volume 7, 669–675. Oxford: Elsevier.
Lave, J. and Wenger. E. (1990) *Situated learning: Legitimate peripheral participation*. Cambridge: Cambridge University Press.
Leek, A. (2020) "Police forces as learning organisations: Learning through apprenticeships", *Higher Education, Skills and Work-Based Learning* 10 (5), 741–750.
Lefevbre, H. (1991) *The production of space*. Oxford: Blackwell.
Lester, S. (2009) "Routes to qualified status: Practices and trends among UK professional bodies", *Studies in Higher Education* 34 (2), 223–236.
Lester, S. (2020) "Creating conditions for sustainable degree apprenticeships in England", *Higher Education, Skills and Work-based Learning* 10 (5), 701–714.
Lester, S. (2024) *Beyond degree apprenticeships: Conceptualising integrated professional development*. Bolton: UVAC.
Lester, S. and Bravenboer, D. (2020) *Sustainable degree apprenticeships*. London: Middlesex University.
Lester, S., Bravenboer, D. and Webb, N. (2016) *Work-integrated degrees: Context, engagement, practice and quality*. Gloucester: Quality Assurance Agency.
Lester, S. and Costley, C. (2010) "Work-based learning at higher education level: Value, practice and critique", *Studies in Higher Education* 35 (5), 561–575.
Lester, S. and Crawford-Lee, M. (2023) "Learning from adapting to the coronavirus pandemic: Enhancing work-based higher education", *Higher Education, Skills and Work-based Learning* 13 (4), 786–799.
Lillis, F. (2018) *Best practice in work-integrated learning for degree apprenticeships*. London: Middlesex University.
Major, D., Meakin, D. and Perrin, D. (2011) "Building the capacity of higher education to deliver programmes of work-based learning", *Higher Education, Skills and Work-based Learning* 1 (2), 118–127.
Martin, F. and Ertzberger, J. (2013) "Here and now mobile learning: An experimental study on the use of mobile technology", *Computers and Education* 68, 76–85.
McKnight, S. and Birks, F. (2016) "Growing your own graduates through degree apprenticeships: A case study of collaboration between the University of Winchester and CGI", in Way, D. (ed.), *A race to the top: Achieving three million more apprenticeships by 2020*, 77–93. Winchester: Winchester University Press.
Milburn, A. (2009) *Unleashing aspiration: The final report of the panel on fair access to the professions*. London: Cabinet Office.
Minton, A. and Lowe, J. (2019) "How are universities supporting employers to facilitate effective 'on the job' learning for apprentices?", *Higher Education, Skills and Work-Based Learning* 9 (2), 200–210.
Mordhorst, L. and Gössling, B. (2020) "Dual study programmes as a design challenge: Identifying areas for improvement as a starting point for interventions", *Educational Design Research* 4 (1), no. 24. https://doi.org/10.15460/eder.4.1.1482, accessed February 2024.

Mordhorst, L. and Jenert, T. (2023) "Curricular integration of academic and vocational education: A theory-based empirical typology of dual study programmes in Germany", *Higher Education* 85, 1257–1279.

Nursing and Midwifery Council (2023) *Standards for pre-registration nursing programmes*. London: Nursing and Midwifery Council.

Patrick, C-J., Peach, D., Pocknee, C., Webb, F., Fletcher, M. and Pretto, G. (2008) *The WIL (work integrated learning) report: A national scoping study*. Brisbane: Queensland University of Technology.

Reddan, G. (2016) "The role of work-integrated learning in developing students' perceived work self-efficacy", *Asia-Pacific Journal of Cooperative Education* 17 (4), 423–436.

Revans, R. (1980) *Action learning: New techniques for management*. London: Blond and Briggs.

Roberts, A., Storm, M. and Flynn, S. (2019) "Workplace mentoring of degree apprentices: Developing principles for practice", *Higher Education, Skills and Work-based Learning* 9 (2), 211–224.

Rowe, L. (2018) "Managing degree apprenticeships through a work based learning framework: Opportunities and challenges", in Morley, D. (ed.), *Enhancing employability in higher education through workbased learning*, 51–69. Cham: Palgrave Macmillan.

Rowe, L., Moore, N. and McKie, P. (2020) "The reflective practitioner: The challenges of supporting public sector senior leaders as they engage in reflective practice", *Higher Education, Skills and Work-Based Learning* 10 (5), 783–798.

Ryan, M. and Deci, E. (2000) "Intrinsic and extrinsic motivations: Classic definitions and new directions", *Contemporary Educational Psychology* 25, 54–67.

Saraswat, A. (2016) "Higher apprenticeships and the new apprenticeship standards: Perceived potential and limitations", *Higher Education, Skills and Work-Based Learning* 6 (4), 401–416.

Schön, D. (1983) *The reflective practitioner: How professionals think in action*. New York: Jossey-Bass.

Schön, D. (1987) *Educating the reflective practitioner*. New York: Jossey-Bass.

Scott, D., Brown, A., Lunt, I. and Thorne, L. (2004) *Professional doctorates: Integrating professional and academic knowledge*. Buckingham: Society for Research into Higher Education and Open University Press.

Siebert, S. and Costley, C. (2013) "Conflicting values in reflection on professional practice", *Higher Education, Skills and Work-based Learning* 3 (3), 156–167.

Stephenson, J. (2001) "Ensuring a holistic approach to work-based learning: The capability envelope", in Boud, D. and Solomon, N. (eds.), *Work-based Learning: A new higher education?*, 86–102. Buckingham: Society for Research into Higher Education and Open University Press.

Stephenson, J. and Saxton, J. (2005) "Using the Internet to gain personalized degrees from learning through work: Some experience from Ufi", *Industry and Higher Education* 19 (3), 249–258.

Thompson, J., Speed, M., Ponomarenko, A. and Downing, C. (2015) *Evaluation of the NMC pre-registration standards: Summary report*. London: IFF Research.

Trede, F. (2012) "Role of work-integrated learning in developing professionalism and professional identity", *Asia-Pacific Journal of Cooperative Education* 13 (3), 159–167.

Van Zyl, A. (2014) *Exploring the potential theory-practice gap in the teaching methods of nurse educators*. MPhil thesis, Stellenbosch University.

Weiß, R. (2016) "Duale Studiengänge – Verzahnung beruflicher und akademischer Bildung", in Faßhauer, U. and Severing, E. (eds.), *Verzahnung beruflicher und akademischer Bildung: Duale Studiengänge in Theorie und Praxis*, 21–38. Bonn: Bundesinstitut für Berufsbildung.

Willis Commission (2012) *Quality with compassion: The future of nursing education*. London: Royal College of Nursing.

Wissenschaftsrat (2013) *Empfehlungen zur Entwicklung des dualen Studiums: Positionspapier*. Mainz: Wissenschaftsrat.

Young, M. and Muller, J. (2014) "From the sociology of professions to the sociology of professional knowledge", in Young, M. and Muller, J. (eds.), *Knowledge, expertise and the professions*, 3–17. London: Routledge.

Zegwaard, K., Pretti, J., Rowe, A. and Ferns, S. (2023) "Defining work-integrated learning", in Zegwaard, T. and Pretti, J. (eds.), *The Routledge international handbook of work-integrated learning*, 29–48. London: Routledge.

Chapter 9

# From Inception to Delivery

## The UK's First Degree Apprenticeship in Diagnostic Radiography

*Demelza Green*

### Introduction

In March 2020 the first degree apprenticeship in diagnostic radiography was launched by the University of Exeter in partnership with National Health Service (NHS) and private providers of imaging/radiology departments across England (Heales & Green, 2020). This chapter will reflect upon the experiences of the University of Exeter programme leadership and development team from programme inception through to delivery.

### Programme Inception and Drivers

It is widely recognised that there is a shortage of radiographers across the UK and a need to broaden and increase access to the profession. Within the NHS there is acute understaffing across all professions, with the NHS further recognising radiography as a 'shortage specialism' (Foster, 2021; Green *et al.*, 2022). The Society and College of Radiographers (SCoR) reported in their 2022 Diagnostic Radiography Workforce UK Census overall vacancy rates across the UK at 12.8%, which was further broken down to England 12.8%, Wales 8.5% and Scotland 7.5% (The Society and College of Radiographers, 2022). Furthermore, in addition to lack of staff it is acknowledged that the demand on radiology department services has risen exponentially with more imaging being requested, thus increasing radiographer workload (Foster, 2021; Richards, 2020).

Green *et al.* (2022, p. 1059) recognise,

> There is a need to urgently increase the numbers of radiographers entering the profession each year in order to meet service need, and the Richards Report highlights increasing use of apprenticeships, with the radiography degree apprenticeship as another route into the profession, being a means to help alleviate this shortage.

In addition to the demands on diagnostic imaging services, pre-registration radiography funding reforms that were designed to increase training places

DOI: 10.4324/9781003496779-9

have not as yet appeared to have resulted in additional radiography training places (Green *et al.*, 2022). This is partly due to placement capacity issues limiting the growth of training places available. Furthermore, NHS bursary reform in 2017 resulting in the introduction of student-paid fees to undertake the radiography degree in 2017 may have affected student application numbers, in particular affecting students from a widening participation background adversely (Green *et al.*, 2022). In the same year, the apprenticeship levy was introduced resulting in employers with more than a £3 million staffing budget, which included most NHS Trusts, paying the levy tax. This consequently led to the rapid development of level 6 degree apprenticeships in healthcare education, including diagnostic radiography.

In order for a higher education institution to develop a degree apprenticeship, an employer or group of employers needs to approach the education provider and explore potential programme and/or course developments. It is suggested that teaching institutions, including higher education institutions, need to work in conjunction with employers to ensure that there are equal opportunities to succeed within a profession regardless of location or educational background (White, 2017). It was a drive from local employer partners experiencing chronic workforce shortages that led to the development of the university's diagnostic radiography degree apprenticeship.

## The Similarities and Differences Between the Degree Apprenticeship and the 'Conventional' Undergraduate Route Into Radiography

Until the publication on the diagnostic radiography degree apprenticeship standard in 2019, the route to qualified radiography status has been through a university course. Radiography moved to a graduate entry profession in the early 1990s following discussion around the need to move from diploma level entry qualification which commenced in the mid-1970s (Price, 2009). This meant a move away from smaller hospital-based training schools into university settings and as a result only those people in a position to physically attend higher education institution campuses could apply for courses (Green *et al.*, 2022). The degree apprenticeship route to registration slightly replicates the training method utilised from the mid-1970s until the 1990s.

Both degree apprenticeship and the 'conventional' undergraduate degree are at the same academic level, with graduates of both routes on completion receiving level 6 bachelor's degree qualification. Due to both programmes requiring professional statutory approval which leads to professional registration, the same content and material needs to be embedded within the curriculum and the delivery design. However, the packaging and delivery of this specific content is unique to each route. One key consideration is that the apprentices spend a minimum of 20% of their time on academic study and approximately 80% of their learning takes place in the workplace, whereas the university-based course is more akin to approximately 75% academic and 25% placement/work based.

The degree apprenticeship runs alongside the university pre-registration course where students apply to a university and undertake discrete clinical placements; to this end the apprenticeship is significantly different, as the apprentices are mainly based in the clinical workplace and learning primarily through workplace activities alongside undertaking pure academic study in their mandated off-the-job time (Green *et al.*, 2022).

## Programme Design

Programme design was approached to truly reflect the nature of degree apprenticeship education and to be compliant with the relevant funding rules, whilst also meeting professional regulatory requirements.

It is advocated that institutions delivering apprenticeships need to work collaboratively with their partner employers in order that all students, no matter their educational background, are afforded the opportunity to succeed within their chosen profession/career (Guest *et al.*, 2003). Within radiography and other similar allied healthcare professions with professionally statutory regulated courses, professional body recognition must additionally be adhered to, therefore it was imperative that the curriculum design meet the regulatory and professional body requirements as well as the apprenticeship standard and Education and Skills Funding Agency (ESFA) requisites too.

Through a number of workshops involving existing University of Exeter undergraduate students, public and patient involvement as well as key employer partners curriculum content and modules were developed.

Due to an apprentice spending approximately 80% of their time in the workplace, one of the key considerations when devising these modules and the associated content and delivery was careful consideration of what subject matter traditionally delivered at the university could be supported in the employing departments as work-based learning activities. It was agreed that much of the applied practical skills and knowledge that until this point had been delivered at the university, by university academic staff, could be delivered in the workplace.

The employer partners were also keen, however, that this content was supported by university academic staff and that the 'burden' of teaching was not put onto radiography staff who were already under clinical-related pressures. To this end many of the applied work-based learning activities were designed to be supported by university-led webinars or online discussion forums.

It was also agreed upon that each module would run for the duration of the academic year instead of per term or semester. On reflection this was a positive move as it has led to work-based learning modules being more flexible, thus allowing employer partners the comfort of alleviating crunch areas when there are multiple learners from different routes or programmes in their respective department. This allowed for creative rostering whilst still ensuring every learner, regardless of the programme they were registered on, to gain the required experience(s).

The final programme design model consisted of four 30-credit modules per year, two of which were purely academic and two were work-based learning (Table 9.1). Breaking this down into time allocation across the week, it was recommended that during on-the-job time (equating to approximately 80%), roughly two days a week were spent focusing on the module practice placement foundations and two days on the other work-based module practice placement. This left the final day (20%) of the apprentice's time for their academic module study.

The curriculum was also built on a spiral curriculum model with each year building on knowledge, understanding, application and skills taught and learnt the previous year.

Additionally, at each stage the curriculum was designed so that each module would complement and dovetail with each other, for example the content from applied radiographic knowledge would be applied in practice placement foundations and practice placement.

An example of where this has worked well includes facilitating a learning activity about reflective practice in the professional practice module and then asking the apprentices to use their chosen model of reflection for an event in practice placement and relating that reflection to the subject matter being taught in applied radiographic knowledge and practice placement foundations.

Pure pathology was taught in the applied radiographic knowledge module, and then in the practice placement foundations module how the pathological appearances manifest on medical images were explored. This could then be linked to the professional practice module where sociological and psychological theories about living with disease and illness or factors affecting health

*Table 9.1* Three-year module design

| Year/Module | Academic modules | | Work-based learning modules | |
|---|---|---|---|---|
| 1 | Applied Radiographic Knowledge 1 (30) | Professional Practice 1 (30) | Practice Placement Foundations 1 (30) | Practice Placement 1 (30) |
| 2 | Applied Radiographic Knowledge 2 (30) | Professional Practice 2 (30) | Practice Placement Foundations 2 (30) | Practice Placement 2 (30) |
| 3 | Applied Radiographic Knowledge 3 (30) | Professional Practice 3 (30) | Practice Placement Foundations 3 (30) | Practice Placement 3 (30) |

were explored. Finally in the practice placement module, the skills required to obtain the images for these pathologies/diseases were practised and learnt and practical communication skills were developed.

Another example of linking the modules was in stage 3, where the apprentices learned research skills, including audits and service evaluations, and then undertook a service evaluation or audit within their employing institution.

### Applied Radiographic Knowledge

In this strand of the pure academic curriculum, all of the knowledge and understanding of the content a radiographer is required to practice was included; this meant that in stage 1 anatomy and physiology, radiation protection and basic physical principles of imaging were taught; these were then built on in year 2 with the introduction of pathology, radiobiology and more complex physical principles until, in the final year, stage 3, image interpretation skills, digital imaging and complex physical principles including artificial intelligence (AI) were delivered.

### Professional Practice

In this another pure academic module, professional practice encompassed evidence-based practice and reflective practice alongside introduction to sociological and psychological theories and frameworks in year 1, which were built on in stage 2 with more complex theories and research skills until in the final year, stage 3, a research project, audit or service evaluation was undertaken. Also included in the final year were theoretical models and policy around professional practice.

### Practice Placement Foundations

In the first of the work-based modules, practice placement foundations was the theory-to-practice module where the knowledge and understanding gained in applied radiographic knowledge (ARK) was applied in clinical practice. This means taking the content of ARK and investigating how that manifests itself in the workplace. This module's content mirrors and complements that of ARK.

### Practice Placement

In the final module, another work-based module, the skills and theories learnt in the other three modules were applied and radiographic skills developed, each year getting more complex in terms of patient needs and also equipment used in practice. These modules closely mirror the practice placement modules of the full-time undergraduate provision but were conducted over a longer time span of ten months.

Alongside any curriculum design, the delivery team need to be aware of assessment of the module content and learning outcomes. The team when designing the programme were mindful of this as well as the knowledge, skills and behaviours (KSBs) of the apprenticeship standard so that assessment could be used to evidence some or all of the standard's KSBs.

Additionally, the variety of assessment needed to be considered to ensure that it reflected the diverse apprentice population and was inclusive of all learning styles. As a result, the assessment profile possessed a number of different types of assessment from written and multiple-choice examinations to coursework, presentations to professional discussions/vivas, as well as practical clinical skills examinations and portfolio building.

### *Evidence of Knowledge, Skills and Behaviours*

As previously mentioned, when designing the curriculum, the team needed to be mindful of the knowledge, skills and behaviours of the apprenticeship standard and how these must be achieved and evidenced for the apprenticeship award to be awarded. In order to lessen the burden on the apprentices, the intended learning outcomes (ILOs) from each module were carefully mapped to the knowledge, skills and behaviours of the standard and the assessment profile of the programme designed from there. This allowed the apprentices to use evidence from their assessments and assessment preparation to map to the KSBs.

Examples of this include the structured objective assessment of practice assessments used in the practice placement modules. The wording within the paperwork for these particular assessments often mirrors that of the standard or is similar and can be mapped directly to specific KSBs. As an example, skill 27 states the apprentice must adhere to the professional duty of confidentiality. This wording is used in the practice assessment paperwork and if the assessor feels that the apprentice has maintained confidentiality throughout the assessment period, then this may be used as evidence for the portfolio. Other skills have been compiled in a proficiency and skills booklet which needs to be signed off by an appropriate qualified healthcare professional and provides evidence for both the apprenticeship standard and the HCPC that specific radiographic skills have been met.

In terms of knowledge areas, many of these were encompassed in the applied radiographic knowledge module and assessed via progress testing which utilises multiple choice questions to test the knowledge and understanding of key concepts. As the questions for the exams were mapped across a number of knowledge areas, this plus their revisions could be used to show achievement of many of the knowledge areas of the standard. Knowledge is equally explored in the professional discussions where apprentices can be questioned to explore the extent of their knowledge and understanding of key concepts and practices related to radiographic practice.

Research skills and knowledge of research practice as defined in the standard are assessed through a practical data handling examination as well as the apprentices undertaking an audit or service evaluation within their employing departments. This not only allows the apprentice to gain the evidence and skills they require for the apprenticeship and professional regulatory requirements but also allows the employing department to audit or evaluate local practices.

The behaviours of the standard are probably the most difficult to evidence achievement, although a few are encompassed within the structure objective assessment of practice within the practice placement modules.

However, a drawback of having this system is that the apprentices need to pass every element of assessment without compensation or condonement allowed as per normal university assessment regulations. Reflective practice that is part of the e-portfolio requirements of the programme also serves to address some of the behaviours and therefore can be used as evidence for behaviours. Witness statements are also employed to gain evidence of these behaviours.

**Delivery Design**

Once the curriculum and module content was finalised, the next thing to consider was delivery.

In the consultations and workshops with interested stakeholders it was clear that a blended learning approach was the preferred method of delivery. This resulted in the apprentices coming to the campus three times a year for a week of intensive teaching and the remainder of the programme delivered online and through work-based learning activities.

Therefore, the team had to next consider pedagogical models of online and blended learning. After researching several options, including an online collaborative model and connectivism, and with advice from the technology-enhanced learning team at the university, the community of enquiry model was opted for.

The team decided this model was most appropriate because of the inclusion of social presence. As a team, we were conscious that many of the apprentices would not be local to the university and also may be the only apprentice in their employing department. We therefore wanted to ensure that peer support would be available to everyone on the course and that each individual could personalise their learning and socialisation as they felt suited themselves; it was also felt that this model would give a more holistic educational experience to those enrolled on programme.

The community of inquiry model was introduced in 2000 by Garrison, Anderson, and Archer to facilitate teaching and learning in pure online or blended learning format (Khodabandelou *et al.*, 2024). The model is based around three key presences, social, teaching and cognitive, in order to produce a positive, meaningful educational experience (Garrison *et al.*, 2000; Khodabandelou *et al.*, 2024).

In the social presence delivery design needs to consider how the online activity will allow the learner to bring their own personality to the community and how they will and can engage with the teacher or facilitator and also with fellow peers. In this presence the activity needs to encourage learner–learner interactions as well as teacher–learner interactions (Garrison *et al.*, 2000; Rourke *et al.*, 2001).

In the second presence, teaching, the design of the activity needs to consider how an active learning community is achieved and maintained as well as how the content of the learning is administered and achieved.

In the final presence, cognitive, the activity needs to consider how knowledge and understanding is achieved. Garrison *et al.* (2001) further explains that the cognitive presence can be broken into four discreet categories.

1. Triggering event
2. Exploration
3. Integration
4. Resolution

In the first category, the trigger, it is related to an issue of problem being identified which requires further investigation, this leads to exploration (category 2) where the issue is explored in more depth either as a group or individually. In the third category, integration, the learners start to understand the issue and will form their own ideas, knowledge and understanding. Finally in the final resolution stage, the learning has occurred and the issue is resolved.

In order to ensure that the programme embedded the community of inquiry model, workshops and training sessions were provided for staff delivering on the programme.

Finally, when designing and building the content for each module, some thought was given to the weekly content required under each of the following.

*Structure* of content: ensuring that it was easy for each learner to know what they had to do, by when, what it was worth and how the content fitted into the 'bigger picture'; additionally, staff had to be mindful that students did not work through the content at the same rate.

*Quantity* of work to be achieved: staff needed to consider how many learning hours the learners had each week for their individual module.

*Resources*: what workbooks, text books, other readings, other subscriptions, online databases or professional websites the content needed to link to or encompass as part of the activity.

*Activities*: ensuring that signposting to different types of learning activities that run through all modules was clear and that different activities were being used in each module and were not always the same.

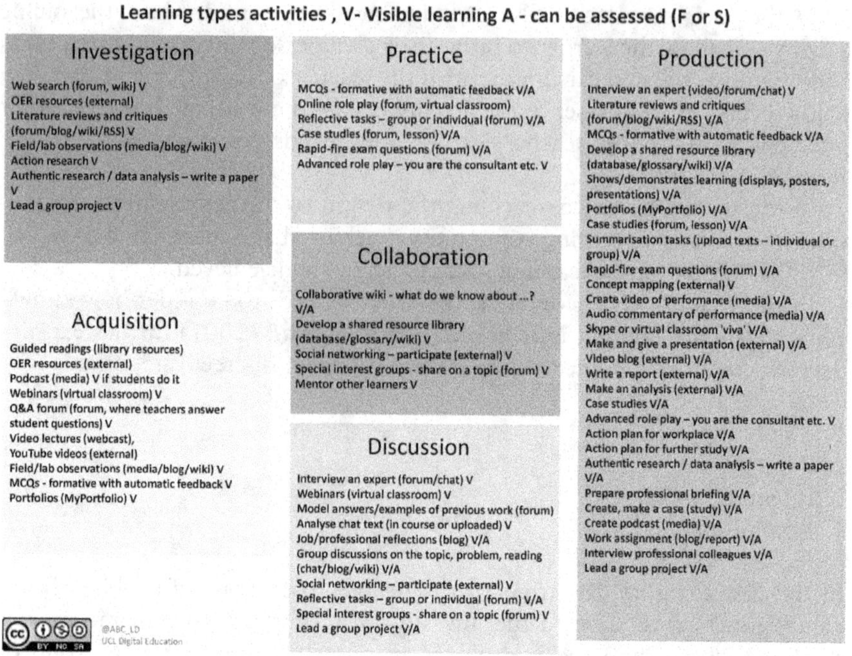

*Figure 9.1* UCL connected curriculum blended learning activities (University College London).

## Supporting Apprentices

Another key consideration when designing the programme was to consider support for the apprentices in terms of academic, pastoral and peer support.

In line with the apprenticeship guidance, each apprentice had a named mentor from the university and another in the workplace. The university mentor was the key link between the university and the workplace/employer and offered pastoral support to the apprentice as well as monitored progress on the apprenticeship and ensured that off-the-job time was adhered to. As the programme has developed, it has become apparent that the university mentor also offers support to the employers and the work-based mentor, especially when an employer is new to having apprentices within the radiography department.

The university mentor is there to support and signpost the apprentice but does not offer pure academic support; instead, their role is to signpost appropriately, whether to university central study skill support, module leads or programme leads. In addition, at every touchpoint, whether that be face-to-face campus attendance or online seminars, university academic staff 'check in' with the apprentices as a whole and offer cohort level support.

Pastoral support is offered by the university mentors but can often also mean signposting to university central wellbeing and welfare services. Pastoral support can also be gained from employer-based mentors or line managers and through each apprentice's employer wellbeing services.

The workplace mentors are the other key link between the employer and the university. In addition to ensuring that the apprentices are receiving adequate learning in the workplace, they need to be aware of how the programme is structured and any amendments/updates to delivery so that the employing departments stay current. The workplace mentors also need to ensure that the apprentices gain the correct experiences in order to meet the requirements of the course and consequently the apprenticeship and regulatory body.

Peer support both within cohorts and across cohorts/stages has also shown to be invaluable. For many of the apprentices, they are the only apprentice learner in their workplace and as such have no one to discuss programme matters with. The programme team therefore have set up a formal peer mentoring scheme for those who want to partake. Informally the programme team encourage and help organise social gatherings when the apprentices attend campus as well as encouraging the apprentices to set up their own social media groups/chats.

During the induction week, group activities and icebreakers are also scheduled to allow the apprentices to start bonding as a cohort from the start, as it is known that they will require distance support from their peers as they progress through the programme.

## Lessons Learned as the Programme Began, and Continues to Be, Delivered

### Academic Content

In terms of the content of the programme the intentions were clear and the modules carefully mapped and planned to encompass all the statutory professional requirements, the apprenticeship requirements and the community of inquiry model of delivery. However, due to many factors but mainly time pressures, the spiral curriculum and cross curriculum subject linking has been lost in places as the programme has grown and expanded; work is now to be done to ensure that the modules link as planned originally and that different learning activities are embraced and utilised across all the modules. In some cases, also due to time pressures, existing content from the full-time undergraduate programme was repurposed instead of specifically designed to fit with a blended learning delivery of community of inquiry. It is easy to take the existing content and use it, but this does not always work in a blended learning format. Also, if using similar or the same content and activity across programmes, it is important to ensure that any reference to the alternate programme is erased, as the learners could feel they were duped out of their own personalised learning material. In a similar vein, the team soon learned not to time stamp/date any material as this then needed to be updated or redone the following year, which could take a significant amount of time. If recording a podcast or vodcast to be used on both programmes, staff have become very aware to ensure that it is generic enough to be purposeful to both programme deliveries. It is also acknowledged with the rapid developments in technology and healthcare that having material and activities that are easy to update and change is preferable, as this allows the programme to remain current and as such fit for purpose.

With constant fluctuations in the staff delivering on the programme there has also been some duplicated content instead of complementary material which crosses the module topics/subject; where this has been identified module teams have had to look and redesign material and associated activity so that the ethos of the programme and delivery design is maintained.

It was also clear that even though the team had planned and designed the off-the-job academic content with the time allocation of 20% (7.5 hours) in mind, many apprentices were requiring more time than anticipated to complete and fully understand and comprehend the content. It then became necessary to support the apprentices to have conversations with their employers about additional study time, bearing in mind the government mandates a 20% *minimum* off-the-job requirement. In truth the apprentices average around 35% off-the-job time across the three-year programme. If we were to redesign the programme again, we would not try to religiously stick to 20% and would build in additional study time so that apprentices and employers are aware from the outset the actual amount of off-the-job time required to complete the programme.

### Qualification and Status

One of the first major misconceptions that the team had to quash in the early stages both during development and with the first cohorts was the level of the qualification. For many there was a misunderstanding around the level of the qualification and also the difficulty of the programme.

It was a common belief that the apprenticeship was at a lower level than the conventional full-time bachelor of science (BSc) undergraduate programme that has been the route to qualified status since the 1990s. Therefore, the rhetoric of same qualification/different route was created. Both cohorts, regardless of programme, graduate with a BSc degree, and the university expects the same level of academic rigor across both programmes. This is not an uncommon belief as Mulkeen *et al.* (2017) also found in their investigation that unlike our European counterparts who regard apprenticeships highly, within the UK degree apprenticeships are often considered to be a lower-class education. Both programmes are also approved and accredited by the Health and Care Professions Council (HCPC), who hold the same standards for all their programmes that lead to professional registration; therefore, the level of knowledge, understanding and skill upon completion and graduation needs to be equivalent in order to meet the HCPC standards of proficiency.

The other major misconception was that the degree apprenticeship was in fact an easier route than the BSc, due to the work-based element and training-on-the-job nature of the delivery.

The truth is that each programme has its own challenges with many of the apprentices juggling external responsibilities, including financial and family pressures as well as working and studying full time. The apprentices have less time to learn the academic content, whereas the full-time undergraduates have less time to become clinically proficient. To that end it was noticeable that the apprentices become clinically competent very quickly and often the theoretical underpinning of their practice comes much later in the programme.

Also due to the yearlong modules of the apprenticeship instead of semester modules, the apprentices have some major pinch points where many assessment deadlines come within a relatively short period of time. This is not too dissimilar to the undergraduate programme, but the apprentices have the extra pressure of needing to pass every assessment of every module without compensation and also a short referral period if they do not pass an assessment at first attempt.

This would probably be something that would be designed differently if starting from concept again.

## Workplace Activity

It became clear in the early stages of the programme that due to both misconceptions and lack of understanding of the degree apprenticeship training route that effort was needed to educate the wider radiography workforce regarding the nature of degree apprenticeship education. Apprentices were often reporting back that they were not getting workplace time to complete their workplace activities but also that they were often not being given the opportunities to learn and be taught as students on the full-time route were. Therefore, the rhetoric of the degree apprentices being paid to learn, rather than being paid to work, was created and reinforced at every opportunity. It was also clear that in times of short-staffed departments the apprentices were sometimes being used as support staff instead of in their apprentice role, again leading to lack of learning on the job. Clear messaging was needed that the apprentices had to be considered supernumerary and investment in terms of time and skills, and knowledge input was required in order to help them achieve and be successful.

There was also an expectation that the apprentices would spend their workplace time always patient facing and a misunderstanding around the concept that apprentices may be in the workplace but they would have to be completing the work-based learning activities which often were not patient facing. It was also reinforced that even though radiography staff were not required to formally teach their apprentice colleagues, they still needed to support and teach them the skills and underpinning theory they would impart to a full-time student who was in their department on placement. This included supporting and assisting the apprentice(s) to complete their work-based learning activities and correcting any misconceptions.

Initially, because the apprentices were employees, the university did not dictate the way in which apprentices were rostered; however, it soon became clear that a more structured approach was required, and a suggested roster was produced. This laid out clearly for the departments the topic areas in which the apprentices needed to gain experience, and these topics were closely mapped to the content being delivered.

Additionally, community of practice groups were set up and developed to support the clinical-based staff supporting their apprentices. In these groups ideas of good practice are shared alongside sharing of issues encountered in the work-based delivery of the programme. This then hopefully leads to a more uniform approach across multiple employers, ensuring parity of experience for all those registered on the programme.

It is recognised that the employer partners the programme works with are key in ensuring the success of the degree apprentices and the programme as a whole. Without this partnership and investment in the work-based learning training element of the programme the apprentice would not thrive and be able to complete the requirements of the programme and apprenticeship standard. It is also recognised that the programme and the employing departments need to be able to have some flexibility in the approach to the work-based training element, including the 'theory underpinning practice' elements, and adapt to meet the needs of each individual apprentice.

It is noted that named staff mentoring and supporting the apprentices need dedicated/protected time to perform this role in order for the apprentice to achieve their potential; anecdotally in the departments where this is enabled either through time off the roster or through dedicated practice educators, the apprentices have a better experience with fewer issues or problems. So even though the university cannot insist on a practice educator or equivalent being in role, they can highly recommend that it is considered as part of the future development of staffing within a radiology department.

### *Peer Support*

More needs to be done to develop our existing peer support, both informal and formal, as we still have apprentices who can feel isolated and flounder alone. Induction week is key to help in building up the informal networks of support, and we have introduced a social session during the face-to-face induction week to help enable this to occur.

It is hoped as more individuals undertake this training route and graduate there will be more placement support from people who understand the differences and pressures of the apprenticeship.

## Contract and Responsibilities

Despite it being clear in the apprenticeship contract between the university and the employer where responsibilities lie in terms of conduct, mandatory training, uniform and other employer-related policy, there were still some questions around these responsibilities.

In the early stages of the course the employing departments also expected the university to supply uniform for the apprentices, but this is an employer responsibility.

The employer equally needs to lead on all performance-related issues including lack of progress on the course, performance and conduct including sickness management and lateness; however, in a few cases the employing departments have expected this to be dealt with by the university as it would be with an undergraduate student. Therefore, conversations have been needed to clarify who leads on what matter(s) but with an agreement that information will be shared between both parties. An example being in a case of fitness to practice concerns an employer would lead on anything that occurs in the workplace or offences that involve police or external authority involvement, whereas the university would lead on concerns that occur on university premises or if academic misconduct offences are proven.

Where performance-related issues relating to lack of progress have occurred, both parties have been involved with supporting the student and devising action plans, but the university will follow the employer's policy on performance management.

## Challenges

From our observations there are still some challenges that need to be addressed and discussed further. Firstly, there is still some confusion and misunderstanding regarding where certain responsibilities lie in terms of performance management and progression on the course. Despite this being clearly articulated in the contract, the practical implementation when an issue arises is not always clear; however, what is apparent is that there must be continuous dialogue between the Higher Education Institution (HEI) and the employer and that the best interests of the apprentice is always kept at the heart of the discussions that may need to occur.

Another challenge is that the apprentices require an active teaching environment when in clinical practice, and this does not always occur. As discussed previously, there are still misconceptions around being paid to work versus being paid to learn, and this in some cases translates to the apprentice not receiving active teaching when undertaking work-based learning activities. Additionally, the apprentices need support to be able to challenge the situation when they are not receiving active teaching.

As the cohorts emerge from diverse backgrounds with unique individual needs, this can also post a challenge. Being able to support such a diverse cohort requires additional input from wider university services that promote wellbeing and help to improve study skills.

Finally, it is essential that the apprentices are supported in their learning and academic work as well as their clinical skill development. This often means that the departments have to be prepared to allow the apprentices additional study time above and beyond the mandated 20% minimum off-the-job time. Apprentices therefore need support from the academic team and their mentors to recognise when they may be struggling with the content or an assignment and also support to have conversations with their workplace to negotiate additional study time.

## Conclusion

Despite only being in practice for four years, it has become very apparent that having this additional and alternative route into radiography has benefited the profession. The apprentices registered on the programme do not all come from traditional educational backgrounds, with 50% entering the course through a non-standard route; with consideration given to experiential learning as well as standard academic qualifications. Not only does this open up opportunities to a wider pool of candidates, but it also serves to diversify the workforce which in turn is beneficial for the service and patients.

Upon qualification, it has been noted that the apprentices are quickly progressing to specialised roles or gaining promotion in a relatively short space of time. It is not yet apparent if this is due to the pre-programme experiences of the apprentice or the degree apprenticeship itself.

Employer partners are reporting back to the university team that the apprentices are quickly imbedded within the radiology departments and their radiographic skills develop rapidly, although the theory often follows much later. They have also learnt that investing time and energy into the training and supporting of the apprentice results in high-quality radiographers which are valuable members of the healthcare team. It has equally been noted that the apprenticeship has been a successful way to recruit more people into the profession either by upskilling and developing existing staff or recruiting outside the department and the NHS or healthcare setting.

For many apprentices the creation of the degree apprenticeship in radiography has been life and career changing, and many are expressing huge gratification for the opportunity afforded to them. The team have noticed that the apprentices have a similar degree award profile to that of the full-time undergraduates, hence reinforcing our message of same qualification/different route. This has also been noticed by the wider profession, with international interest in work-based models of learning to help address vacancies.

Since the launch of the University of Exeter's programme in 2020, as of June 2024 there are 13 HCPC-approved diagnostic radiography programmes, including pre-registration masters provision and 18 month top up from level

5 courses, and two HCPC-approved therapeutic radiography courses across England, with a number of additional higher education institutes looking at providing radiography apprenticeship provision. In the apprenticeship enrolment data from the pre-registration survey for the 2022–2023 academic year conducted by the Society of Radiographers, there were 133 diagnostic radiographers and eight therapeutic radiographers enrolled on apprenticeship pre-registration training programmes (The Society and College of Radiographers, 2024).

Although in its infancy, it has become equally apparent that this alternate route into the profession has aided in increasing the numbers of newly graduating radiographers entering the workforce, and in addition has afforded access to the profession to a much wider range of applicants. The recently published NHS workforce plan 2023 equally recognises the value of apprenticeships at all levels, stating, 'Apprenticeships will help widen access to opportunities for people from all backgrounds and in underserved areas to join the NHS' (NHS England, 2023). It is widely recognised that degree and higher-level apprenticeships are alternative education routes which allow opportunities for individuals to undertake degree-level study with the aim of addressing skills gaps within the workforce and increasing social mobility (Mulkeen *et al.*, 2017; Smith *et al.*, 2021; Fabian *et al.*, 2021). This has also been noticed by the wider profession, resulting in international interest in work-based models of learning to help address vacancies.

The NHS workforce plan also sets a target of 22% of clinical staff to be trained via apprenticeships, an increase of 15% from today's current opportunities, meaning that healthcare-related apprenticeships look like they are here to stay and will continue to develop and grow.

## Acknowledgements

The author would like to thank Christine Heales, who was co-lead on the development of the degree apprenticeship and provided valuable insight on this chapter.

## References

Fabian, K., Taylor-Smith, E., Smith, S., Meharg, D., and Varey, A. (2021). An exploration of degree apprentice perspectives: A Q methodology study. *Studies in Higher Education*, 47(7), pp. 1397–1409. Available at https://doi.org/10.1080/03075079.2021.1897094

Foster, W. (2021). *Increasing Training Capacity in Radiography Training*. AAEC University College.

Garrison, D. R., Anderson, T., and Archer, W. (2000). Critical inquiry in a text-based environment: Computer conferencing in higher education. *The Internet and Higher Education*, 2(2–3), pp. 87–105. Available at https://doi.org/10.1016/S1096-7516(00)00016-6

Garrison, D. R., Anderson, T., and Archer, W. (2001). Critical thinking, cognitive presence, and computer conferencing in distance education. *American Journal of Distance Education*, 15(1), pp. 7–23. Available at https://doi.org/10.1080/08923640109527071

Green, D., Heales, C. J., Hughes, D., Marsden, A., and Mills, J. A. (2022). Exploring current undergraduate student perspectives on the introduction of the degree apprenticeship scheme in diagnostic radiography – a single institution study. *Radiography*, 28(4), pp. 1058–1063. Available at https://doi.org/10.1016/j.radi.2022.08.002

Guest, D. E., Michie, J., Conway, N., and Sheehan, M. (2003). Human resource management and corporate performance in the UK. *British Journal of Industrial Relations*, 41(2), pp. 291–314. Available at https://doi.org/10.1111/1467-8543.00273

Heales, C. J., and Green, D. (2020, June/July). The degree apprenticeship route into diagnostic radiography – implications for the workplace. *UKIO Online, Virtual*. (Accessed May 16, 2024).

Khodabandelou, R., Vahdani Asadi, M. R., Ghasemi, M., and Amerian, M. (2024). More than two decades of community of inquiry research: A comprehensive bibliometric analysis. *E-Learning and Digital Media*, 0(0). Available at https://doi.org/10.1177/20427530241239418

Mulkeen, J., Abdou, H. A., Leigh, J., and Ward, P. (2017). Degree and higher-level apprenticeships: An empirical investigation of stakeholder perceptions of challenges and opportunities. *Studies in Higher Education*, 1(2), pp. 333–346. Available at https://doi.org/10.1080/03075079.2017.1365357

NHS England. (2023). *NHS Long Term Workforce Plan*. NHS England, NHS Long Term Workforce Plan. (Accessed April 20, 2024).

Price, R. (2009). Diploma to degree 1976 to 1993. *Radiography*, 15(Supplement 1), pp. e67–e71. Available at https://doi.org/10.1016/j.radi.2009.10.007

Richards, M. (2020). *DIAGNOSTICS: Recovery and Renewal*. Independent Review of Diagnostic Services for NHS England, NHS England. Available at www.england.nhs.uk/publication/diagnostics-recovery-and-renewal-report-of-the-independent-review-of-diagnostic-services-for-nhs-england/

Rourke, L., Anderson, T., Garrison, D. R., and Archer, W. (2001). Methodological issues in the content analysis of computer conference transcripts. *International Journal of Artificial Intelligence in Education*, 12, pp. 8–22.

Smith, S., Taylor-Smith, E., Fabian, K., Zarb, M., Paterson, J., Barr, M., and Berg, T. (2021). A multi-institutional exploration of the social mobility potential of degree apprenticeships. *Journal of Education and Work*, 34(4), pp. 488–503. Available at https://doi.org/10.1080/13639080.2021.1946494

The Society and College of Radiographers. (2022). *Diagnostic Radiography Workforce UK Census 2022*. Available at Diagnostic-Radiography-Workforce-UK-Census-2022-report.pdf (sor.org)

The Society and College of Radiographers. (2024, May). Radiography apprenticeships in the UK – why would we? The future of the workforce and pre-registration degree apprenticeships. *ASMRIT 2024*. Available at https://conference.asmirt.org/2024/

White, H. (2017). Apprenticeships are here. *Radiography*, 23(Supplement 1), pp. S5–S6. Available at https://doi.org/10.1016/j.radi.2017.05.008

Chapter 10

# Quality Metrics
## Navigating the Quality Landscape of Degree Apprenticeships in Higher Education Institutions

*Samantha Reive Holland and Ernest Edem Edifor*

## Introduction

### Background

Degree apprenticeships (DAs) were introduced by the UK Government in 2015 with the aims of enabling employers to recruit and retain their workforce, boosting economic productivity, improving social mobility, and developing transferrable and lifelong learning skills (QAA, 2019). To meet funding requirements set by the Department for Education through the Education Skills Funding Agency, apprenticeships must last a minimum of 12 months, with an 80%/20% split of work-based development and structured "off-the-job" learning, to develop competence in an occupation (Institute for Apprenticeships, 2017). Universities involved in the provision of DAs in England navigate multiple accountability frameworks, with several non-ministerial departments and agencies overseeing various aspects in addition to the accountability frameworks already in place for higher education institutions in the UK, including the QAA Quality Code (QAA, 2023) and the Teaching Excellence Framework. Due to the devolved nature of education in the UK, the regulatory frameworks of graduate apprenticeships in Scotland, higher apprenticeships in Northern Ireland, and degree apprenticeships in Wales are outside the scope of this chapter.

Some DA courses are also required to adhere to additional regulatory requirements from professional, statutory, and regulatory bodies (PSRBs); for example, the British Computer Society (for Digital and Technology Solutions Professional/Specialist Degree Apprenticeship), the Chartered Manager Institute (Chartered Manager Degree Apprenticeship), and Social Work England (Social Worker Degree Apprenticeship). Table 10.1 provides a summary of the regulatory framework (Office for Students, 2023a). With the tenth anniversary of DAs in England approaching, there is increasing recognition of the burden that the complex, overlapping regulatory landscape places on HEIs engaged with DAs, and consequently the barriers and risks to HEIs of engaging with DAs (QAA, 2024).

DOI: 10.4324/9781003496779-10

*Table 10.1* The regulatory framework for degree apprenticeships

| Area of oversight | Agency responsible |
| --- | --- |
| Overall accountability for quality, including the occupational standard and the end-point assessment | The Department for Education (DfE) acting through the Education and Skills Funding Agency (ESFA) |
| Apprenticeship standards development, review, and approval | Institute for Apprenticeships and Technical Education (IfATE) |
| Quality of training provision | Office for Standards in Education, Children's Services and Skills (Ofsted) |
| Quality of qualifications in Register of Regulated Qualifications | Office of Qualifications and Examinations Regulation (Ofqual) |
| Standards of higher education qualifications awarded by degree-awarding bodies | Office for Students (OfS) |

Source: Office for Students, 2023a

### Chapter Aims

The quality landscape of DAs is defined by its regulatory framework. Therefore, this chapter will review the formal and informal quality metrics imposed by regulatory frameworks and discuss their impact on DAs. Secondary data and published documents of multiple formal and informal quality metrics will be analysed and evaluated for their impact on teaching pedagogy and programme design of DAs. The result of this research will produce a series of practical and pedagogical recommendations for existing HEIs involved with the teaching and administration of DAs and serve as a useful resource for new HEIs seeking to engage with DAs.

### Formal Quality Metrics

This section will discuss the key formal DA regulatory requirements and their impact on quality. The section ends with a summary of these requirements and how they align with the learners' journey from pre-enrolment to post-gateway.

### IfATE Apprenticeship Standards

To meet the government's stated aim for "employers to be at the centre of the process for designing and delivering apprenticeships" (Institute for Apprenticeships, 2017), IfATE collaborates with groups of employers (known as trailblazers) to develop and review apprenticeship occupational standards (AOS). Trailblazers are required to include a wide range of employers that reflect the range of workplaces available within the profession, including at least two small and medium enterprise (SME) employers. This ensures the AOS address the most relevant skills and knowledge needed in the current job market. DA providers must ensure their courses directly address the knowledge, skills, and behaviours outlined in the relevant AOS. This guarantees apprentices gain the competencies employers seek. Providers are also required to engage with an end-point assessment organization (EPAO) to ensure proper evaluation of apprentices' knowledge and skills. This could be an external EPAO (as in the case of Chartered Management Institute (CMI) being the EPAO for the Chartered Manager Degree Apprenticeship), or the provider could run an integrated programme, in which they also serve as the EPAO. Each of these EPAO scenarios brings its own regulatory and administrative burden for the provider. It is also important for academic representatives to be involved in trailblazer groups, in order to ensure that AOS frameworks are translatable within provider contexts.

## *The Quality Assurance Agency (QAA) Quality Code*

The QAA Quality Code (QAA, 2023) plays a crucial role in ensuring high-quality DAs in the UK, although adherence to the code is voluntary rather than regulatory. The code provides a common set of expectations and fundamental principles for quality for all higher education providers and degree programmes in the UK, including those delivering degree apprenticeships (QAA, 2023). This ensures consistency in the design, delivery, and assessment of university programmes. In 2022, QAA announced that it would no longer act as the designated quality body (DQB) for DAs in England, ceding that role to the Office for Students (OfS) in recognition of L6 and L7 apprenticeships coming under the new Ofsted inspection framework for the first time (QAA, 2022). Prior to this, QAA had regulatory oversight of L6 and L7 apprenticeships, while Ofsted monitored L2–L5 apprenticeship provision. It is hoped that this change will address concerns over the lack of clear auditing purposes and alignment between the dual quality assurance systems in place previously of QAA having oversight of DAs under the umbrella of the university sector, and Ofsted having responsibility for Level 4 and Level 5 apprenticeships (which in some cases were also delivered by HEIs) (Linford, 2018; Felce, 2019). However, it also constitutes a new challenge for training providers, who, while they may have had prior experience of Ofsted inspection of Level 4 and Level 5 apprenticeship provision, are limited in their experience of readying departments for inspection and the additional resource this requires, as well as how to balance the dual concerns of maintaining existing academic standards to satisfy degree-awarding bodies alongside these new frameworks (Felce, 2019).

## *Ofsted Education Inspection Framework (EIF)*

Ofsted assumed responsibility for the monitoring and inspection of L6 and L7 DAs provision in 2021, meaning that all university providers would now be subject to the new Education Inspection Framework (EIF) (Office for Students,

2023a). Preparing for Ofsted inspection is a key area of focus for HEIs, who previously may have had limited exposure to EIF monitoring, necessitating a significant investment of resources into reporting, auditing, and compliance. Ofsted inspectors grade the quality of education and training; leadership and management; behaviour and attitudes; and types of provision offered. Ofsted reports of HEIs engaged in the provision of DAs involve five major areas of focus:

1. Functional skills provision and oversight
2. Support for the development of work-based behavioural standards
3. Appropriate scaffolding of learning and progression routes
4. Consultation with employers to adequately address skills shortages in the development of DAs
5. Safeguarding and support of apprentices

Providers are then assigned a grade point along a scale of 1. Outstanding; 2. Good; 3. Requires Improvement; 4. Inadequate. Any provider found to be inadequate will have their funding withdrawn by the ESFA once any apprentices remaining with the provider have completed their training (Powell, 2023). To date, only two universities have achieved an "outstanding" rating of their DAs provision: Manchester Metropolitan University (Manchester Metropolitan University, 2022) and the University of Huddersfield (University of Huddersfield, 2023).

### *Education and Skills Funding Agency (ESFA)*

In England, the DfE regulates apprenticeship provision at all levels through the ESFA. The ESFA is responsible for setting funding rules (which are updated annually), reviewing quality indicators, and auditing providers, including HEIs. Key quality indicators within the ESFA regulatory framework include Ofsted reports, retention rates, and the annual quality achievement rates (QAR) of each provider. QARs use the Individualised Learner Record (ILR) data to calculate what proportion of learning has been successfully completed, and the result is shown as a percentage figure for each programme (ESFA, 2024). Providers can then use this data for self-assessment purposes, or to benchmark themselves against other providers in the sector. QARs of less than 50% and retention rates of less than 52% are considered "at risk" under the ESFA framework, while QARs of 50%–60% and retention rates of 52%–62% are assessed as "needs improvement" and will be subject to a review and potential interventions (DfE, 2024). In addition to these indicators, there are several other supplementary indicators the ESFA uses to assess provider performance, including off-the-job training records, withdrawals, the percentage of apprentices who continue their training beyond their planned learning end date, and the percentage of apprentices who have temporarily suspended their studies (known as breaks in learning).

## Endpoint Quality Assessment (EQA)

Since taking over as the designated quality body for DAs, the Office for Students conducts external quality assurance monitoring of all EPAOs which deliver end-point assessment (EPA) for integrated higher and degree apprenticeships (QAA, 2022). An integrated degree apprenticeship is defined as one where the assessment relating to the degree is fully integrated with the EPA, meaning that the provider delivering the degree also acts as the EPAO. This means that HEIs who engage with integrated DAs must also seek registration as an EPAO and prepare for and participate in OfS EQA monitoring. During an EQA monitoring visit, the OfS will focus on the following areas:

1. The EPAO is providing high-quality, relevant assessment
2. The assessments are in line with the assessment plan
3. EPAs are consistent across all EPAOs delivering on that apprenticeship standard

Following the monitoring visit, the EPAO will be assigned a grade that follows the EIF grading scale used by Ofsted, from 1 – Outstanding to 4 – Inadequate. Preparation for an EQA visit will therefore involve a range of academic and support staff to provide adequate data and feedback regarding assessment planning, delivery, and examination, as well as whether the EPAO has appropriately mapped the EPA assessment activities to the knowledge, skills, and behaviours (KSBs) on the AOS.

## Teaching Excellence Framework (TEF)

The Teaching Excellence Framework (TEF) was introduced in 2017, with a stated aim to "encourage excellence in higher education and help [students] make more informed choices" (Office for Students, 2023b). TEF measures excellence in three areas: teaching quality, learning environment, and the educational and professional outcomes achieved by students. It does not measure teaching quality itself, but it is a range of measures that the government views as related to teaching quality (Circuit, 2023). In addition to meeting the existing national quality requirements, UK universities and colleges are awarded either a Gold, Silver, or Bronze TEF award (see Table 10.2). TEF awards are judged by an independent panel of students, academics, and experts, using a range of official data (including admissions data, student satisfaction, award outcomes, and graduate employment data) and a submission from each university or college to assess the quality, environment, and outcomes of teaching at the institution.

Similarly to the QAA Quality Code, the TEF aligns with Ofsted's framework for inspection in that it assesses the quality of teaching based on student understanding of the expectations of their course, as well as the learning engaged with on the course and the environment in which students are taught.

*Table 10.2* TEF categories

| | |
|---|---|
| Gold | The student experience and outcomes are typically outstanding. |
| Silver | The student experience and outcomes are typically very high quality, and there may be some outstanding features. |
| Bronze | The student experience and outcomes are typically high quality, and there are some very high-quality features. |
| Requires Improvement | The provider was assessed in TEF and no rating was awarded. Improvement is required for a TEF rating. |

Source: Office for Students, 2023b

Currently, it is optional to include DA provision in submissions to TEF (Office for Students, 2023b). If this was made mandatory, the data could serve a dual purpose, in supporting institutional submissions to TEF as well as demonstrating quality and outcomes to Ofsted inspectors.

### Professional, Statutory, and Regulatory Bodies (PSRBs)

PSRBs are professional bodies regulating key industries and roles within the UK. In DAs, they are involved in the trailblazer stage of creating and agreeing to an AOS and have an ongoing role in reviewing any changes to course delivery and design. This ensures that AOS align the knowledge, skills, and behaviours requirements of the occupational role with the demands of professional membership (Dawson and Osborne, 2018). Some PSRBs are also responsible for conducting EPAs; for example, the CMI is the EPAO for all Chartered Manager Degree Apprenticeship programmes in England. Once learners on relevant courses have completed their studies and successfully passed their EPA, they become members of their accompanying PSRB. On the one hand, this alignment also enables arrangements put in place by PSRBs to be used as a proxy for other quality assurance responsibilities; on the other, it inserts another layer of complexity and requires HEIs to submit to quality monitoring from yet another entity (QAA, 2024). For example, changes to social worker degree apprenticeship delivery must be approved by Social Work England. The role of PSRBs in curriculum review and as EPAOs is therefore critical when HEIs are planning their curricula and their compliance activities.

### Informal Quality Metrics

In addition to the multiple formal quality metrics detailed earlier, informal quality metrics can be as crucial to the success and perceived esteem of HEIs engaged in degree apprenticeship delivery. Informal quality metrics allow stakeholders (employers and apprentices) to "rate" their DA course and provider in a subjective way and are generally publicly available to anyone searching for DAs. The authors will outline two of the most high-profile informal metrics next.

## Apprenticeship Service Provider Reviews

In 2018, the ESFA launched an employer feedback tool for all employers registered with the Apprenticeship Service. This allows employers to give feedback on their experience with their training provider(s) via a high-level rating of various aspects of the service they receive. Reviews are then shared with training providers and employers through the *Find an Apprenticeship* website. Providers are rated by each employer on a four-point scale, ranging from "excellent" (four stars) to "very poor" (one star). However, while the tool has been dubbed a "Trip Advisor-style review tool" (Camden, 2023), these reviews are not simply used as an informal metric for employer satisfaction with their training provider. Critically, the ESFA use the provider reviews as part of their accountability framework, and any provider with an overall rating less than 2.5 stars is subject to enhanced monitoring and checks (ESFA, 2024). It is worth noting that the ESFA also publish apprentice feedback on the *Find an Apprenticeship* website, and from June 2024 this will also have an impact on the accountability framework, with the same threshold as the employer feedback rating (below 2.5 triggering "Needs Improvement") (DfE, 2024).

## Rate My Apprenticeship (RMA)

The Rate My Apprenticeship website is a resource for young people seeking an apprenticeship which collates employer and training provider reviews alongside apprenticeship job vacancies. On the site, current apprentices can review both their training provider and their employer, awarding each a rating out of 10. Using an algorithm, RMA then publishes an unofficial league table of the 100 "best" employers and 50 "best" training providers. Unlike the Apprenticeship Service provider reviews, RMA is a private enterprise and heavily promotes its review services to apprentices at apprenticeship fairs and online. Up until the 23/24 academic year, they also provided a small financial incentive to

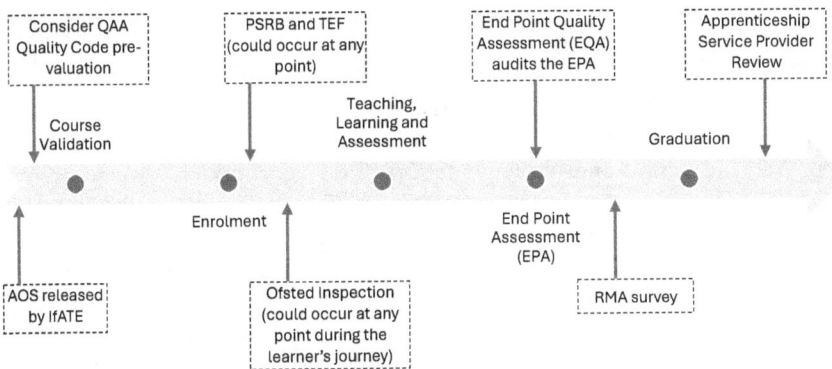

*Figure 10.1* Apprentices' learner journey.

apprentices to complete a review. Training providers and employers will often use their position on the RMA league table in marketing and outreach events to promote their programmes.

In summary, Figure 10.1 depicts the apprentices' learner journey with points at which the quality of provision is implemented and/or assessed.

## Quality Impact on Degree Apprenticeships

A high-quality DA that is compliant with regulatory bodies comes at a high cost. DA is acclaimed as "one of the most significant higher education inventions of the 21st century" (Nawaz, 2023) and is making a significant impact in many sectors (Nawaz et al., 2022). However, its quality delivery comes at a cost; training providers wrestle with its complex and multifaceted regulatory environment in addition to the demands of creating, delivering, and assessing high-quality degree courses (Aptem Ltd, 2022). In this section, the authors discuss the impact of quality metrics required by the regulatory framework on DAs using a holistic framework they call DAPPER, an acronym for design, assessment, pedagogy, processes, engagement, and resources.

### Design

Designing DA courses are, in many ways, different from designing non-DA courses (Cleaver, 2022; Office for Students, 2022); this has led institutions like the University College London to create bespoke DA frameworks (University College London, 2023) that cover how DA should be designed. The AOS document produced by trailblazer groups describes what apprentices are expected to achieve throughout their course, including KSBs. It also contains the EPA plan. Although the AOS provides "what" needs to be covered by apprentices, it does not spell out the details of "how" it must be implemented and achieved by each HEI. Therefore, educators are strongly recommended to actively involve employers in designing new or reviewing/refining existing courses (Bravenboer, 2016; Rowe et al., 2017; Nawaz et al., 2024). After all, the new apprenticeship reform requires employers to be in the "driving seat" for "developing and implementing new Apprenticeships" (Department of Business Innovation and Skills, 2013).

This means employers must contribute to, usually through validation and approval, the design and implementation of delivery models, course design, module summaries, and assessment strategies. Sometimes, multiple stakeholder groups from employers may have to be consulted via separate means to arrive at a holistic and robust curriculum. For example, employer stakeholders at strategic levels or in the apprenticeship recruitment teams in their organizations could be consulted for the delivery model and its feasibility while those at the operational and tactical levels in the technical roles could be consulted for an in-depth scrutiny into the indicative content, assessment, and delivery schedule/model. This provides a great opportunity for training providers to enrich their courses and make them fit for industry.

What complicates this process is when multiple employers have different strong opinions (Mulkeen *et al.*, 2019). It is not helpful for the "big" and powerful employers to have a stronger say than their smaller counterparts have. Another aspect of programme design that is heavily affected by the regulatory burden (for the sake of quality and coverage) is the volume of mapping documents that need creating. In addition to module learning outcome (MLO) mappings and course learning outcome (CLO) mappings, educators must have a KSB mapping showing how the KSBs align with their MLOs, CLOs, and to some extent every assessment element. This can be a significant piece of work since there are several KSBs to consider in every AOS. For example, an educator wanting to deliver all six specialisms of the Digital and Technology Solutions Professional (DTSP) Version 1.2 (IfATE, 2023), AOS would have to contend with 68 knowledge, 63 skills, and eight behaviour elements. Mapping these 139 KSBs to five or more CLOs and 36 or more MLOs (assuming there are 12 modules with at least three MLOs each) is an enormous amount of work on top of the usual mapping required for non-apprenticeship courses. This mapping is compounded when the said DTSP must be subject to the QAA Subject Benchmark for Computing and possibly the British Computer Society and Tech Industry Gold accreditations.

The requirement to involve employers and use the AOS in the design of DA courses is vital for improving the quality of DA so should be encouraged. However, it can have a significant impact on the time and resources needed during the course design phase.

### Assessment

There are several ways that regulatory requirements impact the quality of DAs assessments. Positively, it fosters "authentic assessments" (Swaffield, 2011) and ensures that learners attain the knowledge, skill, and behaviour required for them to be occupationally competent. DA assessments go beyond being an academic piece of work; an overwhelming 90% of academics relate their assessments to individual workplace experiences or problems (Nawaz *et al.*, 2024). This means apprentices' assessments are having an impact on real-world businesses across England. However, they come at a cost; new systems and structures must be implemented to make them work (Hughes and Saieva, 2020).

Although it is expected that DA assessments are authentic by nature, that is not always the case (Mulkeen *et al.*, 2019; Camden, 2022); this has led to the proposal of the PRACTISE framework (Edifor *et al.*, 2024). Developing authentic assessments for apprentices can be as simple as developing work-related and/or work-based assessments. Unlike non-apprenticeship courses where an authentic assessment can be a simple case study in a specific sector, authentic assessment for apprentices who may be from multiple employers (from different sectors) requires careful planning and consideration. Authentic assessments must be created in such a way that all learners on the course/module can engage with them without being disadvantaged due to the sector, scale, size, or setting of their employer.

Secondly, although setting assessments can be challenging, assessing them can also pose some challenges. Some assessments (especially in closed cohorts) run on bespoke systems on the employer's premises, which requires assessors to visit the premises physically to perform the assessment. Thankfully, due to the global migration to remote/virtual operations during the COVID-19 pandemic, such demands for visiting employer premises have been minimized. However, what remains is the need for confidentiality and/or non-disclosure agreement (NDA) processes from some employers whose businesses need them. These requirements, although necessary, place an extra layer of complication on the assessment process and sometimes produce more work for the educator.

Finally, every apprentice must demonstrate how they have achieved the KSBs, towards the end of their studies. This requires course teams to have ways of safely capturing how each learner has met the KSBs and an electronic portfolio system – this bundle of evidence would be assessed as part of the EPA. The EPA itself poses challenges for educators; they must seek "independent assessors" and ensure that the "degree" requirements are met while they meet the "apprenticeship" requirements, especially if it is an integrated degree. Typically, the educator must have parallel and synchronized systems for handling the degree and apprenticeship aspects simultaneously. This can be challenging, time consuming, and resource intensive. On top of this, educators must ensure quality and have the whole process properly documented for the endpoint quality assessment which is undertaken by the Office of Students as a way of quality assurance.

## *Pedagogy*

Pedagogies for delivering DA must be bespoke/tailored (Rowe, 2018; Lillis and Bravenboer, 2020). Again and again, tutors of DA modules unanimously and anecdotally agree that teaching their modules is rewarding and has some positive impacts. Firstly, teaching DA courses often mandates the integration of academic learning and workplace practices resulting in a more applied pedagogy where learners learn by doing real-world tasks and projects. This process usually requires a strong link between theoretical knowledge and practical experience gained; this very often requires blended learning approaches to be effective. Secondly, the pedagogy for DA modules requires the use of current industry-standard tools and frameworks; this is a result of the careful work of trailblazer groups made up of employers. This means the pedagogy should not be a "rebadging" or "rebranding" of non-apprenticeship courses (Camden, 2022). Finally, the active engagement of employers in the design, delivery, and evaluation of DA courses produces pedagogies that are employer informed, learner centred, and data driven (Nawaz et al., 2024).

Even though the regulatory structure that ensures high-quality DA delivery can lead to a more relevant, practical, and employer-driven approach to teaching, it presents some negative impacts. Quality DA learning should be "planned and delivered to impart vocational knowledge and skills [and behaviour per the AOS]" (Voeller, 2023). Regulations seek to provide some form of standardization, but this sometimes imposes some level of limitations that prevents tutors from being as flexible as they can be in providing a tailored pedagogy to specific disciplines and employer needs, especially in an open cohort condition. Secondly, handling the tension between academic rigour and practical experience can be challenging (Hughes and Saieva, 2020; Evans and Cloutier, 2023). Tutors have to work extra hard in developing innovative teaching and learning approaches to find the right balance between providing a robust academic underpinning and equipping learners to undertake their practical tasks.

Finally, DA courses have very diverse cohorts (Storer-Church Brooke, 2020); for example, a course may contain 18-year-olds coming from college and existing employees with 18 years of experience who are seeking to reskill or upskill. This introduces unique challenges in the development of a pedagogy that is inclusive, equitable, and effective. Tutors must ensure they have varied learning resources that engage/challenge experienced learners and are appropriate for inexperienced learners to develop their knowledge, skills, and behaviour. Tutors must be aware of some non-traditional demographic differences present in DA that could affect pedagogy such as family status, socio-economic background, employer sector, and so on.

### *Processes*

The regulatory landscape of DAs, which enforces a high standard of quality, can impact the processes of training providers in several ways. There are unique requirements emanating from various regulations that, at a very high level, require the standardization of processes across all providers. For example, training providers make provision for DA-specific accreditation of prior learning (APL), break in learning, tripartite reviews, electronic portfolios, and the like. Due to the employer dimension of DAs, processes are expected to be in place to ensure that there is active engagement with employers. Finally, due to regulatory requirements, educators must establish processes that foster a robust regimen for monitoring and evaluating DA courses.

However, these benefits have associated challenges. According to Cleaver (2022), the process changes associated with running DA include (1) quality assurance processes including discussions, recording, and reporting procedures, (2) learning and teaching opportunities that are appropriately and thoroughly tested wherever academic judgement is applied and are subject to academic governance, and (3) academic governance arrangements adapting to respond to DA differences. All these pose challenges for training providers. Firstly, although most regulatory bodies provide high-level prescriptions of processes, the implementation of some of the processes could be ambiguous, time consuming, and/or resource intensive. Training providers must adhere to multiple regulatory standards and requirements. This may involve developing and implementing processes to ensure compliance with specific program criteria, assessment guidelines, and quality assurance measures. In some cases, regulatory changes trigger major changes in processes. For example, the recent changes in the ESFA funding rules require training providers to make necessary adjustments in their processes to accommodate the "active learning" requirement/changes.

DAs typically involve a significant portion of work-based learning alongside academic study. Training providers may need to establish processes for coordinating with employers, identifying suitable work projects, and monitoring apprentices' progress in the workplace (Cleaver, 2022; Nawaz et al., 2024). They are often under pressure to demonstrate the quality and effectiveness of their courses; this leads to the implementation of processes for internal quality assurance, such as regular program reviews, staff development initiatives, and student feedback mechanisms (Nawaz et al., 2024). Finally, several regulatory bodies require training providers to monitor and report on various aspects of their provision of DAs, including apprentices' progress, completion rates, and employer satisfaction. Establishing robust processes for data collection, analysis, and reporting is essential for meeting regulatory requirements and identifying areas for improvement.

### Engagement

Regulatory frameworks enforce quality DA delivery across various jurisdictions but commonly emphasize the importance of engagement/partnerships between training providers and external stakeholders (Mulkeen et al., 2019; Nawaz et al., 2024). These frameworks outline requirements for collaboration, quality assurance, and alignment with industry standards to ensure the efficacy of DA courses. Through such engagement/partnership, educators are exposed to the needs and practices of industry. This helps tutors to stay current with topical industry practices, technologies, skills, and requirements. Such knowledge is usually transferred to other students in non-apprenticeship courses. Such partnerships allow training providers to tap into external resources, including facilities, expertise, and networks of their employer partners. Collaboration with further education colleges provides smoother progression pathways for those with non-traditional academic backgrounds. Partnerships with organizations specializing in supporting underrepresented groups can enhance outreach efforts and create a more inclusive delivery of DAs. These are the benefits of the sort of engagement DA fosters.

Although such engagements or partnerships are intrinsically beneficial, they require enormous effort and resources. Establishing and maintaining partnerships requires significant investments of time, resources, and expertise from training providers and external organizations. Limited funding, staff capacity, and administrative support may impede effective collaboration, particularly for smaller providers or in less economically advantaged regions. Ensuring alignment of interests and goals between training providers and external partners is crucial for successful collaboration. Conflicting priorities, differing organizational cultures, and power imbalances may pose challenges to effective partnership working and require careful negotiation and communication. With multiple partners involved, ensuring consistency in curriculum delivery and quality assurance across the program requires careful planning and joint monitoring strategies. The risk of fragmented approaches necessitates robust frameworks to guarantee all apprentices receive a high-quality and standardized educational experience.

DAs require additional engagements and partnerships beyond the scope of employer partners. Some training providers have to engage the services of third-party organizations for the provision of functional skills for their learners who require them (Allen, 2023). This can be a complex, challenging, and expensive process. A number of training providers have to engage the services of organizations or practitioners to support them through a regulatory inspection/audit. For example, some training providers pay thousands of pounds for others to assist them with the development and monitoring of their Quality Improvement Plan (QIP) and Self-Assessment Report (SAR) in preparation for an Ofsted visit. Some training providers, especially those from the further education sector, have to partner and collaborate with HEIs with degree-awarding powers for the delivery of DA courses. Other educators have to work with EPAOs to deliver their EPAs. All these engagements and/or partnerships require commitment and resources.

## Resources

The resource implications of delivering quality DAs are arguably the most significant factor for training providers (Mulkeen *et al.*, 2019; Cleaver, 2022). It is said, "there are other factors affecting the success – and underpinning the quality – of degree apprenticeships . . . the first of these relates to the additional costs of this area of provision" (Stroud, 2024). It is common (Nawaz *et al.*, 2024) for HEIs delivering DAs to have a bespoke department/unit that handles DA-specific duties. Such departments recruit staff to handle quality assurance, IT, recruitment, portfolio management, employer engagement, regulatory compliance, learner engagement monitoring, and sometimes tuition. The size and shape of such DA-specific staff vary considerably from one HEI to another. For example, while some HEIs may have a handful of staff (due to their small number of learners), others, for example Manchester

Metropolitan University, have over 100 members of staff in their Apprenticeship Unit. Other expertise resources required are DA-knowledgeable practitioners for course verification and external examination. HEIs sometimes must pay for externals to serve as their independent end-point assessments examiners/assessors.

Some traditional HEI infrastructures are not suitable for delivering quality DA courses (Rowe, 2018; Lillis and Bravenboer, 2020; Voeller, 2023). Bespoke systems are required for monitoring learners' engagement and achievement, e-portfolio, break in learning, and the like. Such software resources are necessary not only for delivering quality DAs but also to be compliant with the regulatory requirements. Some HEIs have had to invest in high-quality IT equipment to help deliver high-quality hybrid or blended models. A final resource required for delivering quality DAs is training. Training of staff, employer partners, and learners must be a necessity for educators (Nawaz et al., 2024). It is incumbent on training providers to provide training for their staff, apprentices, and to some extent, their employer partners on all aspects of their provision (such as EPA, off-the-job, etc.)

## Case Study

In this section, the authors demonstrate the dimensions of DAPPER in a real-world case study using the Digital and Technology Solutions Professional (DTSP) DA at the Manchester Metropolitan University (McrMet). DTSP at McrMet started when DA was launched in 2015 with just under 60 learners but now enrols over 150 learners annually from over 80 employer partners from England. It runs across three academic faculties at McrMet and focuses on only four (Data Analyst, Cyber Security Analyst, Software Engineer, and IT Consultant) of the six pathways in the DTSP AOS. It has one specialist closed cohort (Mainframe) for one specific employer which is a variant of the Software Engineer pathway. Table 10.3 shows selected interventions using the dimension of DAPPER to ensure effective, equitable, and high-quality delivery of McrMet's DTSP provision.

## Conclusion

There is evidence that DAs are contributing to social mobility and providing some form of levelling up or social equity. Delivering DAs also requires an equitable mindset from educators. Training providers such as universities have established structures for delivering non-apprenticeship courses. This means that there is the temptation to use these same structures for delivering DAs to be economical and to gain a competitive edge. However, various DA regulations forbid such practices. Delivering high-quality DAs comes with several benefits but is also laden with a myriad of challenges. The authors recommend

Quality Metrics 173

Table 10.3 Implementation of DAPPER in McrMet's DTSP

| Dimension | Intervention | Quality Implication |
|---|---|---|
| Design | • Two groups of employer partners were involved in revalidation. One group consisted of senior management who reviewed the delivery model and the other group consisted of staff with technical expertise who scrutinized each pathway via a deep-dive session. Some ex-learners were involved in the deep dives.<br>• All employer contacts were invited to join input into the revalidation process via an Employer Advisory Board.<br>• All indicative content and delivery schedules were made available to employers.<br>• In addition to compliance with the QAA Subject Benchmark and other standard higher education regulatory requirements, accreditations for the Tech Industry Gold (TIG) and British Computer Society (BCS) were renewed. | The topics and contents to be delivered meet the needs of the employer partners and the requirements of the AOS, TIG, and BCS. |
| Assessment | • Almost all assessments are work-based via a variety of assessment methods (including exams, reports, portfolios, projects etc.)<br>• All assessments are mapped to the KSB elements of the DTSP AOS.<br>• There are bespoke systems to monitor engagement and performance with a specific focus on learners at risk.<br>• Assessments are designed to be as generic as possible to allow all learners from various industry backgrounds to complete them.<br>• There are agreements with some employers for submission of assessments via non-McrMet portals. | Assessments are set and assessed to a high standard with various levels of verification, standardization, and moderation. All assessments comply with the regulatory standards. |
| Pedagogy | • To overcome the prevalent experience/education inequality, there is a one-week coding boot camp at the start of the course to provide a "level playing field".<br>• Some tutors work very closely with employers to deliver sessions (e.g. Mainframe).<br>• Teaching and learning are carefully designed to ensure that students engage and they are supported. | Teaching and learning activities to ensure that students thrive and flourish are implemented. |

(Continued)

174  Approaches to Work-Based Learning in Higher Education

Table 10.3 (Continued)

| Dimension | Intervention | Quality Implication |
|---|---|---|
| Processes | • Bespoke processes have been put in place to support DTSP learners who enrol on a day-release model.<br>• Appropriate exemptions (which require tailored structures and processes) are made in student regulations where necessary to factor in the work-and-study dynamics of apprentices (especially in terms of assessment mitigations). | These processes ensure that there is an equitable delivery of degree apprenticeships that capture the particular needs of learners. |
| Engagement | • Each employer partner is assigned a dedicated Apprenticeship Development Manager, who meets with them occasionally.<br>• There are Employer Advisory Boards which meet multiple times a year.<br>• All learners attend a tripartite meeting with their line managers and a dedicated McrMet skills coach.<br>• The sequencing of DTSP was changed recently in response to evolving employer needs. | The DTSP provision is closely monitored with employer input to ensure that their needs are met. |
| Resources | • There are bespoke IT systems and infrastructure to support all apprenticeships in terms of learning, quality assurance, learner attendance, engagement, monitoring, and so on.<br>• McrMet has set degree apprenticeships as a strategic priority; it has a dedicated Apprenticeship Unit that has over 100 staff working in various capacities.<br>• DTSP has a dedicated programme director (responsible for strategic and tactical issues) and a programme leader (responsible for operational issues)<br>• Tutors receive two inductions: one institutional induction on degree apprenticeships and an annual tutor's induction. | Provision of appropriate resources ensures that regulatory requirements are met and the standard of delivery is of high quality. |

that to overcome these challenges and put in place robust quality assurance methods, HEIs engaged in DAs put the following practices in place:

1. Centralize the oversight of apprenticeship delivery, creating bespoke systems and employing staff familiar with DA-specific funding rules and regulatory requirements.
2. Establish robust processes for data collection, analysis, monitoring, and reporting.
3. Actively involve employers in designing (and delivering where possible) new or reviewing/refining existing DA courses.
4. During course design, providers should ensure that they map AOS KSBs to both module and course learning outcomes.
5. Develop parallel and synchronized systems for handling the "degree" and "apprenticeship" aspects of DA simultaneously.
6. DA courses should not be a "rebadging" or "rebranding" of non-apprenticeship courses, and should integrate academic learning with work-based practices.
7. When developing external partnerships, HEIs should ensure that interests and goals are aligned and put in place robust frameworks to ensure standardization and success.
8. Provide training to all DA staff (academic tutors, professional services, etc.) on the requirements of DAs and their equitable and quality delivery.
9. Collaborate and work with other providers to share practice and contribute to the evolving landscape of DAs.
10. Rather than viewing quality standards as geared towards an inspection or monitoring visit, HEIs should strive to embed quality standards in the "day-to-day" delivery of DAs.

The authors have discussed the impact of delivering quality DAs in terms of design, assessment, pedagogy, processes, engagement, and resources. These dimensions require careful consideration and investment from training providers. Having bespoke and/or siloed interventions to make room for apprenticeships can seem disjointed and unhelpful; therefore, the suggestions and recommendations in this chapter must be streamlined and holistic for a quality delivery of DAs.

## References

Allen, S.H. (2023) *Apprenticeships: Overcoming the Functional Skills Hurdle*. Available at: www.personneltoday.com/hr/apprenticeships-functional-skills-hurdle/ (Accessed: 21 May 2024).

Aptem Ltd (2022) *Are Degree Apprenticeships 'Over-Regulated'?* Available at: www.aptem.co.uk/wp-content/uploads/2022/11/Aptem-Degree-Apprenticeships-Regulation-eBook-1.pdf (Accessed: 23 January 2023).

Bravenboer, D. (2016) 'Why co-design and delivery is "a no brainer" for higher and degree apprenticeship policy', *Higher Education, Skills and Work-Based Learning*, 6(4), pp. 384–400. Available at: https://doi.org/10.1108/HESWBL-06-2016-0038/FULL/PDF.

Camden, B. (2022) *Degree Courses Rebadged as Apprenticeships at University, Ofsted*. Available at: https://feweek.co.uk/ofsted-finds-degree-courses-rebadged-as-apprenticeships-at-university/ (Accessed: 15 January 2024).

Camden, B. (2023) *Employer and Apprentice Feedback Ratings for Providers Revealed, Apprenticeships*. Available at: https://feweek.co.uk/employer-and-apprentice-feedback-ratings-for-providers-revealed/ (Accessed: 20 May 2024).

Circuit, P. (2023) *What's the Teaching Excellence Framework (TEF)?, The Complete University Guide – Choosing Where to Study*. Available at: www.thecompleteuniversityguide.co.uk/student-advice/where-to-study/teaching-excellence-framework-tef (Accessed: 20 May 2024).

Cleaver, L. (2022) *Academic Governance and Degree Apprenticeships in England – Getting It Right | Advance HE, News and Views*. Available at: www.advance-he.ac.uk/news-and-views/academic-governance-and-degree-apprenticeships-england-getting-it-right (Accessed: 20 May 2024).

Dawson, S. and Osborne, A. (2018) *Reshaping Built Environment Education: The Impact of Degree Apprenticeships*. Available at: https://nrl.northumbria.ac.uk/id/eprint/36461/1/CHOBE%201617%20Reshaping%20Built%20Environment%20Education%20Report%20FINAL%20(002).pdf (Accessed: 20 May 2024).

Department of Business Innovation and Skills (2013) *The Future of Apprenticeships in England: Implementation Plan*. Available at: https://assets.publishing.service.gov.uk/media/5a7c95aded915d12ab4bbc19/bis-13-1175-future-of-apprenticeships-in-england-implementation-plan.pdf (Accessed: 6 May 2024).

DfE (2024) *Apprenticeship Training Provider Accountability Framework, Education, Training and Skills*. Available at: www.gov.uk/government/publications/apprenticeship-training-provider-accountability-framework (Accessed: 20 May 2024).

Edifor, E. et al. (2024) *Chartered Association of Business Schools Learning, Teaching & Student Experience 2024*. Birmingham. Available at: https://charteredabs.org/events/ltse2024.

ESFA (2024) *Introduction to Qualification Achievement Rates (QARs), Education, Training and Skill*. Available at: www.gov.uk/guidance/introduction-to-qualification-achievement-rates-qars (Accessed: 20 May 2024).

Evans, M. and Cloutier, L.M. (2023) 'Integrating higher degree education with practice: Exploring the value proposition of executive MBA apprenticeships', *Higher Education, Skills and Work-based Learning*, 13(2), pp. 283–298. Available at: https://doi.org/10.1108/HESWBL-10-2022-0207/FULL/PDF.

Felce, A. (2019) 'Managing the quality of higher education in apprenticeships', *Higher Education, Skills and Work-Based Learning*, 9(2), pp. 141–148. Available at: https://doi.org/10.1108/HESWBL-10-2018-0106.

Hughes, C. and Saieva, G. (2020) 'The journey of higher degree apprenticeships', *Applied Pedagogies for Higher Education: Real World Learning and Innovation across the Curriculum*, pp. 243–266. Available at: https://doi.org/10.1007/978-3-030-46951-1_11/TABLES/1.

IfATE (2023) *Digital and Technology Solutions Professional, Apprenticeships*. Available at: www.instituteforapprenticeships.org/apprenticeship-standards/digital-and-technology-solutions-professional-v1-2?view=standard&option=All (Accessed: 20 May 2024).

Institute for Apprenticeships (2017) *'How to' Guide for Trailblazers, Media*. Available at: www.instituteforapprenticeships.org/media/1033/how_to__guide_for_trailblazers_-_v2.pdf (Accessed: 16 May 2024).

Lillis, F. and Bravenboer, D. (2020) 'The best practice in work-integrated pedagogy for degree apprenticeships in a post-viral future', *Higher Education, Skills and Work-Based Learning*, 10(5), pp. 727–739. Available at: https://doi.org/10.1108/HESWBL-04-2020-0071/FULL/PDF.

Linford, N. (2018) *Cambridge University and Greggs Among 354 Organisations Added to Register of Apprenticeship Training Providers*, *News*. Available at: https://feweek.co.uk/cambridge-university-among-354-new-organisations-on-register-of-apprenticeship-training-providers/ (Accessed: 20 May 2024).

Manchester Metropolitan University (2022) *Manchester Met rated Ofsted 'Outstanding' for Degree Apprenticeships*, *News and Events*. Edited by G. Balint et al. Manchester Metropolitan University. Available at: www.mmu.ac.uk/news-and-events/news/story/?id=15579#:~:text=Manchester%20Metropolitan%20has%20been%20recognised,regulator's%20new%20Education%20Inspection%20Framework (Accessed: 16 May 2024).

Mulkeen, J. et al. (2019) 'Degree and higher level apprenticeships: An empirical investigation of stakeholder perceptions of challenges and opportunities', *Studies in Higher Education*, 44(2), pp. 333–346. Available at: https://doi.org/10.1080/03075079.2017.1365357.

Nawaz, R. (2023) 'Degree apprenticeships need better nurture', *The Times Higher Education–Opinion*. Available at: www.timeshighereducation.com/blog/degree-apprenticeships-great-uk-invention-needs-better-nurture (Accessed: 6 May 2024).

Nawaz, R. et al. (2022) 'The impact of degree apprenticeships: Analysis, insights and policy recommendations', *Transforming Government: People, Process and Policy* [Preprint]. Available at: https://doi.org/10.1108/TG-07-2022-0105.

Nawaz, R. et al. (2024) *Degree Apprenticeship: Voices from the Frontline – Impact, Policy and Good Practice Guide 2024*. Available at: www.qaa.ac.uk/docs/qaa/members/degree-apprenticeships-voice-from-the-frontline-impact-policy-and-good-practice-guide-2024.pdf?sfvrsn=6682b481_10 (Accessed: 23 April 2024).

Office for Students (2022) *Degree Apprenticeships in England: Current Practices in Design, Delivery and Quality Management*. Office for Students. Available at: www.officeforstudents.org.uk/media/f9e2b239-1ad0-4b8a-8a34-4f1f2ecf3543/degree-apprenticeships-thematic-review-final-for-web.pdf (Accessed: 20 May 2024).

Office for Students (2023a) *Degree Apprenticeships: A Guide for Higher Education Providers*, *Degree Apprenticeships*. Available at: www.officeforstudents.org.uk/advice-and-guidance/skills-and-employment/degree-apprenticeships/degree-apprenticeships-for-providers/checking-the-quality-of-apprenticeships/ (Accessed: 16 May 2024).

Office for Students (2023b) *The TEF – a Guide for Students, Teaching Quality and TEF*. Available at: www.officeforstudents.org.uk/for-students/teaching-quality-and-tef/the-tef-a-guide-for-students/ (Accessed: 20 May 2024).

Powell, A. (2023) *Apprenticeships Policy in England*, *House of Commons Library*. Available at: https://researchbriefings.files.parliament.uk/documents/SN03052/SN03052.pdf (Accessed: 16 May 2024).

QAA (2019) *Characteristics Statement: Higher Education in Apprenticeships*. Available at: www.qaa.ac.uk/docs/qaa/quality-code/characteristics-statement-apprenticeships.pdf.

QAA (2022) *QAA Demits DQB Status to Focus on Sector and Students in England*, *News & Events*. Available at: www.qaa.ac.uk/news-events/news/qaa-demits-dqb-status-to-focus-on-sector-and-students-in-england (Accessed: 16 May 2024).

QAA (2023) *The UK Quality Code for Higher Education*. Available at: www.qaa.ac.uk/docs/qaa/quality-code/revised-uk-quality-code-for-higher-education.pdf (Accessed: 16 May 2024).

QAA (2024) *Degrees of Difference: Delivering on the Ambition of Quality Degree Apprenticeships in England*, *Policy Series*. Available at: www.qaa.ac.uk/docs/qaa/

news/delivering-on-the-ambition-of-quality-degree-apprenticeships-in-england. pdf?sfvrsn=66a8b481_12 (Accessed: 16 May 2024).

Rowe, L. (2018) 'Managing degree apprenticeships through a work based learning framework: Opportunities and challenges', *Enhancing Employability in Higher Education through Work Based Learning*, pp. 51–69. Available at: https://doi.org/10.1007/978-3-319-75166-5_4.

Rowe, L. *et al.* (2017) 'The challenges of managing degree apprentices in the workplace: A manager's perspective', *Journal of Work-Applied Management*, 9(2), pp. 185–199. Available at: https://doi.org/10.1108/JWAM-07-2017-0021/FULL/PDF.

Storer-Church Brooke (2020) *Looking Beyond: Celebrating the Value and Diversity of Apprenticeships, Office for Students Blog*. Office for Students. Available at: www.officeforstudents.org.uk/ (Accessed: 21 May 2024).

Stroud, R. (2024) *The Quality of Degree Apprenticeships, Higher Education Policy Institute*. Available at: www.hepi.ac.uk/2024/03/26/the-quality-of-degree-apprenticeships/ (Accessed: 21 May 2024).

Swaffield, S. (2011) 'Getting to the heart of authentic assessment for learning', *Assessment in Education: Principles, Policy & Practice*, 18(4), pp. 433–449. Available at: https://doi.org/10.1080/0969594X.2011.582838.

University College London (2023) *Chapter 11: Degree Apprenticeships Framework, UCL Academic Manual 2023-24*. Available at: www.ucl.ac.uk/academic-manual/sites/academic_manual/files/chapter_11_degree_apprenticeships_framework_2023-24. pdf (Accessed: 21 May 2024).

University of Huddersfield (2023) *Huddersfield Awarded Outstanding Ofsted Apprenticeships Rating, News*. Available at: www.hud.ac.uk/news/2023/november/ofsted-apprenticeships-outstanding-rating/ (Accessed: 16 May 2024).

Voeller, J. (2023) 'New higher education model? Degree apprenticeships as a strategy to modernize apprenticeships: Rationale, current development in the U.S., and a conceptual framework', *International Journal for Research in Vocational Education and Training*, 10(2), pp. 220–238. Available at: https://doi.org/10.13152/IJRVET.10.2.4.

# Chapter 11

# The Role of Reflection in Effective Work-Based Learning and Assessment

Syed Waqar Nabi and Derek Somerville

## Introduction

Work-based learning (WBL) is not a new concept; in fact, the association between learning and work predates more structured, classroom-based pedagogies by centuries. However, a more formal view of WBL contrasts it with simple, experiential learning by defining it as a pedagogy based on a formal partnership between an educational institution and an external organization, combining classroom learning with learning in a workplace setting (Boud and Solomon, 2001).

WBL is a type of experiential learning, where much of the learning happens in the absence of a structured learning environment, may not be intentional, and may even be unconscious (Boyd and Fales, 1983). Such learning can make the learning proficient at one particular kind of behaviour, but it is reflection on the experience that helps create and clarify meaning from workplace experiences. John Dewey was instrumental in shaping a view of education that gave experiential learning a central place, a means of growth that changes a person's perspective in a fundamental sense, a goal that is achieved when experience is accompanied by reflection (Rodgers and LaBoskey, 2016).

Reflection is thus a key component of the WBL pedagogy that helps consolidate learning in the workplace. One conceptualization of WBL and the role reflection plays in this pedagogy was presented by Raelin in a model he proposed in 1997 (Raelin, 1997). While introducing the model, Raelin notes:

> knowledge necessary to perform useful work cannot be a body of information to be learned, and learned once. Rather work-based learning is acquired in the midst of action and is dedicated to the task at hand.... In work-based learning, *theory*, for instance, may be acquired in concert with *practice*.... *Explicit knowledge* is the familiar codified form that is transmittable in formal, systematic language. *Tacit knowledge* is the component of knowledge that is normally not reportable since it is deeply rooted in action and involvement in a specific context [emphasis added].

The Raelin model of work-based learning thus incorporates two dimensions: the theory–practice learning dimension and the explicit–tacit knowledge dimension. Raelin further classifies tacit knowledge into two types, the *technical* part relevant to specific settings, and the *cognitive* part which relates to more general mental models of people's perception and definition of the world around them. We can construct a matrix from the two learning modes and knowledge forms discussed earlier resulting in four types of learning, all of which according to Raelin should be constructed in the learner.

In this framework, the learning journey starts with *conceptualization* in the classroom: theoretical learning and explicit knowledge. Experimentation in a university lab adds context. Such university labs are a stepping-stone towards learning in the workplace. Thuné and Eckerdal (2019) highlight experimentation in labs as it "reflects the students' evolving understanding". Practical experiments in a lab environment allows students to practice their skills and see results. Eckerdal *et al.* (2024) demonstrate the importance of lab work to "to gain both a more complete theoretical understanding or programming and a more complete mastery of practical programming skills".

While the efficacy of labs is unarguable, the learning is still effectively theoretical, in that it is decoupled from real-world contexts. It is the workplace that provides a practical, real-world dimension to the learning where the theoretical knowledge can be *cemented* via experience. However, this learning is still *tacit* and will remain so until the loop is closed by *reflection*. This then creates the space to convert at least some of the tacit learning into explicit knowledge, which can thereon be called upon in a more deliberate manner. Raelin for example notes, "reflection is required to bring the inherent tacit knowledge of experience to the surface. It thus contributes to the reconstruction of meaning". This conversion of tacit to explicit knowledge can also be viewed as *continuity* from one experience to another, as Rodgers and LaBoskey (2016) note: "Continuity described the connectedness between experiences, where understanding from one experience prepared one to understand the next experience in fuller and more complex ways".

Another way to look at this model is as follows: Access to a combination of classroom and workplace allows movement along the theory–practice dimension. Experimentation in the classroom and then experience in the workplace both enable tacit learning. Reflection finally enables the more subtle and often ignored component of this learning journey: taking tacit knowledge – intangible by definition – and transforming it to explicit knowledge.

Kolb's *experiential learning model*, developed in 1984 and forming the basis of "The Kolb Learning Style Inventory" (Kolb and Kolb, 2013), is similar to Raelin's model, and it too involves reflection – specifically, "reflective observation" – as a key component of the so-called cycle of experiential learning. The role of reflection in this model is very similar to Raelin's tacit–explicit framing: "reflections are assimilated and distilled into abstract concepts from which new implications for action can be drawn".

At an abstraction, whether we consider Raelin's model of work-based learning or Kolb's experiential learning model, the message is the same: Practice should be followed by reflection to realize its potential for the kind of learning that creates a permanent, fundamental change in perspective. While practice will inevitably lead to *some* learning, that learning will remain tacit and implicit, unless brought to the surface via reflection. Without this deliberate act of reflection, the learning will be less useful, less available for recall and re-use, and less likely to be recorded, transferred, and shared in written or spoken words. Simply put, not reflecting on practice is a valuable opportunity lost.

**Structured Reflection**

Reflecting on one's own actions, to varying extents, happens naturally. However, in the context of a more formal work-based learning pedagogy – an example of which we present later in this chapter – a more structured approach to reflection may be needed. To understand why, we refer to Griffiths and Tann (Griffiths and Tann, 1992), who call this kind of organic reflection "act-react", or "rapid reaction"; that is, instinctive and immediate reflection and reaction. This is the first level of their five-level model of reflective practice, followed by what they call "repair" (react-monitor-react/rework-plan-act) which – even though involving "pause for thought" – is also quite fine-grained, on the spot, and may be habitual. These two lower levels are lumped together as "reflection-*in*-action". While such reflection is very important, on its own it does not close the WBL loop, as there is no "reconstruction of knowledge" (Raelin, 1997). This is where the following three higher levels of reflection as described in Griffiths and Tann (1992) come in, which together are categorized under "reflection-*on*-action":

- Review (act-observe-analyse and evaluate-plan-act),
- Research (act-observe systematically-analyse-rigorously-evaluate-plan-act), and
- Retheorize and reformulate (act-observe systematically-analyse rigorously-evaluate-retheorize-plan-act).

Interestingly, this higher-level reflection-on-action, which should result in a fundamental change of perspective, can be thought of as means of getting better at the lower-level reflection-in-action (Rodgers and LaBoskey, 2016), and one can visualize this as a growing spiral of learning that cycles between reflection-in-action and reflection-on-action.

The higher-level, more critical reflection-on-action is unlikely to happen naturally, and a structured mechanism can encourage it. Structure is also important as, while the utility of deliberate reflection on practice seems unarguable, it must be done at the right time. A gymnast in the middle of a complex routine, a teacher building a narrative to convey a complex concept, a method actor acting out a difficult scene; it is easy to see how pausing for deliberate reflection will do more harm than good for all these circumstances, and many more examples can be imagined.

## Instruments for Higher-Level Reflection

Reflection should not be considered just a technique, but an orientation towards education (Rodgers and LaBoskey, 2016). It is still however useful to have knowledge of some practical instruments to encourage and structure higher-level reflection-*on*-action, which can take many forms.

Maintaining a workplace journal is one practical instrument for encouraging, documenting, and sharing higher forms of reflection. As Lukinsky notes (Lukinsky, 1990), "Another complementary tool to help participants reflect more on their individual development is the journal. Journal writing provides an opportunity for participants to break their habitual ways of thinking and doing through reflective withdrawal and re-entry".

Conversations between teachers and students can also be used to encourage reflection. One form of such an exercise is *descriptive feedback*, which sits at the overlap of *listening* and *description*, and was first described by Rodgers (Rodgers, 2006) as "a reflective conversation between teacher and students wherein students describe their experiences as learners, with the goals of improving learning, deepening trust between teacher and student, and establishing a vibrant, creative community on a daily basis".

A more formalized approach to reflection is the *5R framework*, which was the outcome of a research project to enhance reflective writing and thinking in the context of student teachers (Bain *et al.*, 2002). The 5R framework gets its name from the five-component scale that it proposes: reporting, responding, relating, reasoning, and reconstructing, with a number of distinct levels within each scale. The model is useful for structuring the process of reflection itself and of writing it up. *Reporting* is descriptive in nature, where you describe the context without offering any interpretations. *Responding* is where the learner can note their response or reaction to the learning experience, and it is quite closely coupled to *reporting*. *Relating* is the first scale where the student steps outside the situation of the learning experience, and relates it to knowledge and skill from outside the context. *Reasoning* is a step towards higher abstraction, where the learner makes sense of the situation, focussing on the significant factors underlying the incident, bringing in alternative explanations and multiple perspectives. The final scale, *reconstructing*, can be related to our earlier discussion on transforming tacit knowledge to explicit knowledge in Raelin's model, where conclusions are drawn, and plans for future tasks and actions, real or hypothetical, are connected to reflection on current learning experience. This final scale is the fundamental change in perspective that higher-level reflection is eventually about.

Another similar model is Roger Greenways's 4F model of reflection, based on the idea of students working through four levels of the model: fact, feeling, finding, and future (Anam *et al.*, 2023). We can see strong resonances between this model and the 5R model. The *fact* level is descriptive in nature, simply narrating what happened and what the learner did. *Feelings* is about the learner's reaction to the experience, the "unmistakable 'gut' feelings as well as intuitive sensing – feelings on the fringes of perception" (Greenways, n.d.). *Findings* is the level corresponding to the tacit–explicit transition, focussing on the concrete takeaways, created through interpretations and judgements. Finally, the *futures* level is organizing learning such that it can be used for future growth and yet unknown possibilities.

There are other similar models of reflection, any of which can be adopted in an experiential learning setting. The CARL framework is a simple model of reflective learning that takes the student through context, action, results, and learning (*The CARL Framework of Reflection*, 2018). Gibb's reflective cycle breaks the process into description, feelings, evaluation, analysis, conclusion, and action plan (Gibbs, 1988). The integrated reflective cycle frames the reflective learning process as experience, reflecting on action, experience (again), and preparation, before starting the cycle again (Bassot, 2015).

While the exact instruments adopted to encourage reflection will vary with context, the case for having some kind of scaffolding to aid students in higher forms of reflection is in our view compelling. One interesting finding of the authors of the 5R framework we discussed earlier (Bain *et al.*, 2002) is relevant here, where they found that when students were not assisted or instructed beforehand, there was a wide range of scope and depth in their reflections. The most common type of reflection was simple descriptions, what they refer to as reporting in their 5R model. That is, most students would be unlikely to improve their level of reflective writing unaided.

To illustrate how reflection could be integrated formally into a WBL degree program, we next present the case study of a graduate apprenticeship program in software engineering, where the authors have been deeply involved from its inception to delivery. Our model is based mostly on Raelin's framing, but it incorporates the key stages of the more fine-grained models we described here.

## Case-Study: A Graduate Apprenticeship Program in Software Engineering

The School of Computing Science at the University of Glasgow, where the authors are based, offers a degree-level apprenticeship program in software engineering that is of academic standing equivalent to a standard-route degree. Employers recruit apprentices before the start of the program, and around 80% of apprentices' time over four years is spent at work. The remaining 20% is reserved for academic courses in the classroom. This course was designed

|        | Autumn | Spring | Summer |
|--------|--------|--------|--------|
| Year 1 | How to Learn a New Lang' | | Workplace Assessment 1 |
|        | Foundations of Professional Software Engineering | | |
| Year 2 |        |        | Workplace Assessment 2 |
| Year 3 | Workplace Assessment 3 | | |
| Year 4 | Workplace Assessment 4 | | |

*Figure 11.1* The modules in our graduate apprenticeship program where reflection is integrated into the assessments.

following a consultation with industry (Barr and Parkinson, 2019). The model for an apprenticeship presented different challenges and opportunities (Fabian and Taylor-Smith, 2021); while the workplace setting provides an opportunity for experiential learning that is simply not possible in a regular academic environment, there is a risk that such learning will remain implicit, relevant and useful only to specific tasks and contexts, unable to create a shift in conceptual perspective. Reflective learning was thus integrated as a key educational process in this degree programme, recognizing its crucial role in completing the work-based learning cycle as it helps in "creating and clarifying the meaning of experience" (Boyd and Fales, 1983).

The considerable amount of time our graduate apprentices spend in the workplace organically creates the space for implicit, tacit learning, which we can presume is accompanied by reflection-*in*-action reflection. Valuable as that is, we wanted to make ensure that the learning cycle is completed by a structured, deliberate reflection-*on*-action that enables tacit-to-explicit knowledge conversion. Reflection is deeply integrated throughout the program in various forms, and we discuss it next under three main categories:

A. As part of first-year courses *Foundations of Professional Software Engineering* and *How to Learn a New Language*.
B. As part of *Workplace Assessment* modules in the junior years of the program (years 1 and 2).
C. As part of similar *Workplace Assessment* modules in the senior years, where the structure differs from the first two years, pivoted towards professional development and accreditation.

### Reflection as Part of the Course Foundations of Professional Software Engineering

The graduate apprentices (GAs) start their first year with a course "Foundations of Professional Software Engineering". The aim of this course is to give the students a grounding in software engineering for when they go back to the workplace for two months. The consultation with industry (Barr and

Somerville, 2020) was a driver for the content of this course. This course contains two reflective assignments, in addition to a formative assessment that takes the form of fortnightly reflection.

*Fortnightly Reflection*

The GAs at the University of Glasgow have a block model for teaching (Schulte, 2008). In an eight-week semester the teaching is broken into four two-week sprints. Each two-week sprint has eight days of "block teaching" in the classroom, followed by two days where the students are back in the workplace. This is to help with collaboration in the workplace and keep bonds with work colleagues stronger. The importance of collaboration has been highlighted by Drake and Chen (2023) and is a key learning method in this course.

In these two days back in the workplace, the students reflect on one or two topics from the university teaching in the current sprint. They will set up meetings with their coaches to discuss the highlighted topics. The aim is to gain an understanding of how these practices are implemented in the workplace. The students are then encouraged to create a formative log reflecting on their learning at university and what they have discussed in the workplace. The topics covered are toolsets, codebases, development process, security, quality assurance, and clean code and refactoring.

On the first day of the subsequent sprint, the students have a retrospective to reflect and share their experiences from their discussions in the workplace with their coaches. The students split into groups to discuss each topic using active learning (Settles, 2009). They have an assigned chair and scribe (Lawal et al., 2021). The scribe will then summarize the discussion of the group for each point of discussion. The lecturer reviews the formative logs from the meetings with coaches and introduces key points if not highlighted from the team discussions.

The students' learning is reinforced for each topic as similar workplace approaches are mentioned or new, different approaches taken are discussed. The students justify why certain tools, processes, or practices have been adopted.

*Workplace Report*

After the first semesters at university and their second period in the workplace, the students are asked to create a summative reflective essay on their experience in the workplace, balanced with what they have learnt at university. The workplace report is worth 25% of the 30-credit course. The students provide an introduction with background on what they have learnt at university and via workplace practices. The students then describe the development process in the workplace, and this is balanced against learning prior to starting university, university learning, and any self-knowledge they have gained since starting the course. The students describe the specific tasks they worked on at their workplace, captured in the abstraction of a "ticket" in the context of software engineering, and give context by describing other processes that led to their task, as well as the processes that follow on from and depend on their task. The security implications used for their applications are covered. A section then covers the quality assurance or testing that has been employed to ensure their completed ticket has met the requirements or goals of the task. This is finished by a conclusion to demonstrate their depth of insight into the workplace and its relevance to the software engineering practice.

### Reflection as Part of the Course How to Learn a New Language

The aim of this course is to give the students the skills to learn new programming languages themselves. It is designed to teach the fundamentals of programming in such a way that students will very easily be able to pick up new languages and then be able to use them quickly in their respective workplaces.

This assignment asks them to give an overview of the projects they have been working on in the workplace. It covers the tools and the programming languages being used. They have to give a critical evaluation of the programming practices encountered and provide programming concepts that have been covered in class. It will also show examples of code that has been written, including an explanation of what the code does. They discuss how the code they have seen in the workplace differs from similar code they have seen before. They finish the report by reflecting on what they have learned about programming while in the workplace.

### Reflection as Part of Workplace Assessment – Junior Years

The apprentice students on our program spend a substantial time over four years at the workplace, and what they learn there is a crucial component of the degree program. In order to integrate this workplace learning into a formal degree program, it is assessed via bespoke courses called "Workplace Assessment" that run every year, with relatively increasing credit weightage as they progress through the program, adding up to 180 credits of a total of 480 credits of a four-year undergraduate course. Reflection on workplace learning, practices, and experiences forms a significant portion of these workplace assessment courses.

### Workplace Assessment – Level One

After they finish semester two in level one, by which time apprentices have completed three periods in the workplace, they write two workplace reports, two reflective workplace reports, and a reflective workplace report on *meta-skills*.

The first workplace report is geared towards the technical (as opposed to cognitive) aspect of their tacit learning and has the students select a topic from a number of suggestions provided to them as prompts:

- Describe how you identified code to be refactored, the challenges involved in refactoring, and how these were resolved.
- What are the advantages and disadvantages of the web application framework(s) you use in the workplace?
- To what extent have agile development methods been adopted in your workplace?
- Describe the object-oriented principles you have observed being put into practice in your workplace.
- Describe how requirements gathering is carried out in your workplace.
- Describe how and why a design pattern is used in your workplace.
- Describe how computer misuse is prevented in your workplace.

The selected topic is assessed on level of knowledge, comprehension, and evaluation of workplace practices.

The apprentices are also asked to write a second, more reflective report, with a topic of "What have you learnt about software engineering in the workplace?" This is assessed on quality of reflection carried out, level of knowledge, comprehension and evaluation of workplace practices, and quality of academic communication.

The students then write a report on "meta-skills". This report asks the question "How have you developed your meta-skills in the workplace?" These meta-skills are defined by Skills Development Scotland and include focussing, integrity, adapting, initiative, communicating, feeling, collaborating, leading, curiosity, creativity, sense-making, and critical thinking (*Meta-Skills Toolkit – Skills Development Scotland*, n.d.). This report loosely maps to the *cognitive* (as opposed to *technical*) aspects of their tacit learning at the workplace. It is assessed on the following marking criteria: quality of reflection carried out; level of knowledge and understanding of relevant meta-skills; quality of academic communication.

*Workplace Assessment – Level Two*

The level two workplace assessment is done after completing the second year at university and the students have had a few months in the workplace. The same block model of two eight-week semesters is delivered for level two. The first submission for the workplace assessment is around 21 months after starting at the university, with the GAs having had several long periods in the workplace. This course has four assessments: portfolio, presentation, meta-skills report, and final report.

The students use a tool called Mahara to create a workplace portfolio.[1] They are encouraged to add to this portfolio throughout their summer back in the workplace. They must add eight pieces of work to the portfolio and create an accompanying report. They also have to reflect on the IEng competencies and how these have been achieved in the portfolio of work.

The students record a five-minute presentation on a piece of work from their portfolio. The presentation should relate to at least one of the intended learning outcomes:

- Demonstrate the development or extension of a substantial software product which displays technical achievements in computer science.
- Analyse software engineering best practices to write easy-to-read and suitably formed software.
- Create software that include well-justified data structures and test coverage.

The students are asked to describe the work undertaken, reflecting on why the work was required, how they went about it, and how it turned out.

They write a meta-skills report which is an expansion on the level one meta-skills report. This reflection is double the length at 1,500 words. Then a final report asks the students to reflect and demonstrate how they have met the first three intended learning outcomes of the course. The report is expected to provide evidence of critical, evaluative judgement (what has worked well and what hasn't) and reflections on what the student has learnt in the workplace.

## Reflection as Part of Workplace Assessment – Senior Years

In the senior years, the reflection takes on a slightly different structure and tenor, with the focus on maintaining a workplace journal that revolves around a professional competency framework. We have incorporated a workplace journal-based assessment as a crucial component of the workplace assessment module to encourage higher forms of reflection. The journal is meant to bring closure to the unique and individual learning journey of each apprentice. Given that reflection of this nature is meant to translate knowledge from a tacit form to an explicit one, we decided to add some structure to the reflection, basing it around a competency framework which we describe next.

### A Competency Framework

One way to perceive a WBL program is to frame it as the delivery and assessment of *professional competencies*. Since our apprenticeship program is deeply embedded in the local industrial ecosystem and aims primarily to produce a high-quality software engineering work force for the local industry, it makes sense to optimize the program for UK-oriented competency frameworks. With this view, we have chosen to base our competency framework on the UK Standard for Professional Engineering Competence (UK-SPEC) (*Engineering Council*, n.d.), which describes the competence and commitment requirements that must be met to be registered as an incorporated engineer (IEng) or a chartered engineer (CEng). This approach aligns the goals of the program to professional competence and commitment standards developed collaboratively by a breadth of industry professionals and academics.

The competency framework for this assessment, following the UK-SPEC framework and terminology, spans five dimensions: knowledge and understanding; design and development of processes, systems, services, and products; responsibility, management, or leadership; communication and interpersonal skills; and professional commitment.

Coming back to the reflective workplace journal, the competency framework provides the seed for reflecting on tacit learning at the workplace and a skeleton for building a reflective narrative. Apprentices are encouraged to revisit their workplace experiences against the backdrop of this competency framework, noting what progress they feel they made for each of the various components of the framework. The framework is such that it covers both the technical and cognitive aspects of tacit learning, as can be seen from its five dimensions listed previously.

### The Workplace Journal

The apprentices are asked to maintain a workplace journal throughout the year and are then required to submit a reflective essay based on their journals. There are two milestones for this assessment: a formative peer review process around halfway through the year, and then a final essay submitted towards the end of the year for summative assessment. The report is assessed on quality of the reflection carried out, how well it accounts their journey towards gaining competencies from the competency framework, and quality of academic communication.

As discussed earlier, to make the journal essay more structured and to encourage the tacit-to-explicit knowledge transformation, they are asked to write the journal with reference to the competency framework. They submit a separate portfolio that records what competencies they have achieved along with any relevant artefacts, but the journal asks them to note personal reflections of their journey towards building those competencies. In their narratives, they are asked to make explicit references to competencies from the framework, where appropriate.

Apprentices are also encouraged to reflect on competencies that may not be captured by the framework, as all such frameworks are a generalization that can and often do miss specifics and idiosyncrasies of individual circumstances. For the same reasons, they are not required to ensure they are covering *all* competencies from the framework; the guiding principle is that they should aim for achieving a preponderance of competencies.

To encourage deep and authentic reflection that is not made superficial by the use of a structured competency framework, apprentices are given a list of leading questions, which they can use to frame their reflective narratives:

1. Can you look back at your past years as a GA in general, and now describe competencies you may have gained implicitly, without deliberately planning for them?
2. What knowledge do you feel you gained while carrying out your unique roles at your workplace? How does it compare qualitatively with the knowledge you acquired at university?
3. Can you think of specific instances of knowledge acquired at university and then applied at the workplace? Can you contrast it with knowledge from university that you feel has not found utility at work?
4. Can you think of skills that you acquired at university (e.g. programming in a certain language, writing documentation, presenting, time management, people skills, etc.) that you found useful at your workplace?
5. What are the skills that you feel you have acquired solely or largely based on your workplace experience? How do these compare, qualitatively and quantitatively, with any skills you developed at the university?
6. Can you reflect on your professional dispositions coming into this program, and how they have changed and evolved over the years?
7. Can you think back at dispositions and attitudes that you feel you have acquired, or would wish to acquire, because you observed them in colleagues you interacted with at work?
8. Do you have any other general comments about your journey towards any of the competencies from the framework (or even from outside it) not specifically covered by the previous questions?

These questions are meant to strike a balance between a structured approach that maps to a relevant competency framework and a personalized and organic reflective account.

### Examples of Student Reflections

We have some excellent examples of reflective accounts from the assessments integrated into our program that we described earlier. We feel such examples vindicate the view that reflection is a crucial part of the work-based learning journey, that it enables the translation of tacit knowledge – technical and cognitive – to explicit knowledge resulting in a shift of perspective, and that having an assessed, structured reflective exercise can play an important role in this context.

For example, here a student reflects on technical knowledge that they learned implicitly, and which they then acknowledge in their reflective writing (text in square brackets added by authors):

> At first, working on a monthly sprint [a software engineering practice] was not something I was familiar with, as we previously built applications from scratch. I quickly learned the "rules of the road" to help support the team such as the workflow of the applications, the code review format, the flow of the JIRA Kanban board [a tool for managing software engineering projects] and lastly performing agile ceremonies (sprint planning, stand-up, sprint review and retrospectives).

Another similar example shows a student describing the learning of a new technical skill: "Between my old team and university, I have learned a lot about the delivery pipeline and how it should be carried out".

Here a student reflects on an appreciation for correctness and efficiency when developing software:

> However, soon after taking on more complex work projects, like [redacted], I realised that despite not applying the algorithms exactly as explained in lectures, a profound understanding of correctness and efficiency in algorithm design is a requisite for building performant and scalable software.

This example illustrates how reflection on workplace experiences can cement connections between theoretical knowledge from the classroom and practical application in the workplace:

> An unexpected amount of theoretical knowledge has use within the applied setting of the workplace. At first glance, one would not expect knowledge of B+ Trees [a special type of algorithm] to immediately translate into a task for a [redacted] webapp; yet it can.

Another example from the Level 1 course we discussed earlier shows a similar connection:

> Drawing upon principles discussed in our academic coursework, particularly in the Foundations of Professional Software Engineering course, I recognise the importance of addressing certain concerns. Specifically, optimizing the efficiency of our meetings, prioritizing crucial issues, and establishing clearer testing protocols are paramount.

We have another good example where the learning is not of a specific technical subject, but of realizing the importance of learning that subject:

> As I recognise that this manner of operating would not be suitable for [my company's] fast-paced and client-centred product turnover, I will now aim to maintain and expand my machine learning knowledge through side projects and other relevant university courses.

Here we have a good example of a student reflection on their evolving understanding of a technical term: "From discussions with other apprentices, I've found coding in my team means something slightly different".

A similar reflection on coding, undoubtedly a key skill for an aspiring software engineer, shows a shift in perspective from the somewhat naïve view that being a software engineer is all or mostly about coding, to a more mature view that, like any other profession, there is much more to it than the core technical skill:

> I've learned that in professional software engineering teams often it's not about writing lines and lines of code but instead discussion and planning taking place to write just what is needed.

This student reflects on their learning in the workplace and demonstrates self-awareness by highlighting the need to improve further:

> The work I have done in the workplace has greatly contributed to my learning as a software engineer, but I could still improve – I could review my older code to look for potential improvements, and I could be more careful in the design stage of my projects.

While the previous examples could be said to relate to the *technical* aspect of learning, the following is a good example of *cognitive* learning, where the learning is more subtle, for example in the form of a "shift from one perceptual perspective to another"(Boyd and Fales, 1983):

> However, having learned that I could not do this on my own and that I needed to reach out more than I initially thought I would have to, I now feel much more confident in taking ownership of tasks and accepting responsibility for organising discussions around finding a solution.

There are many more such examples highlighting the cognitive aspect of learning. For example, this student reflects on how they learnt the importance of communication from an experience where communication was not taking place as well as it could have:

> This [an incident at work] caused me having to stay on late at work to fix others code. Having experienced this, I now know that communication

is a key part in a development team to manage pressure and timescales effectively.

Another similar example shows that the learning the importance of communication skills, separate from the communication skills themselves, is a valuable tacit learning that the workplace can enable:

> Having a natural affinity to the technical side of things greatly helped me perform the practical side of my role, but my dispositions in regard to inter-personal situations was less than ideal, as I tended to remain quiet during meetings and discussions. This obviously was not good for my position, as communication amongst a team is essential to the effective delivery of a project. And so, with the need to share information and ideas being so prevalent, I gained exposure and experience of situations in which I had to do exactly that. This allowed me to become more accustomed to inter-personal communication, and my disposition of usually staying quite gradually shifted to me being more vocal and setting forth any relevant thoughts I have on a matter.

We also found examples of reflections on subtle aspects of communication, demonstrating self-awareness, and explicit articulation of a learning experience which, in the absence of the requirement of writing a reflective journal, would possibly have remained tacit. For example:

> When originally joining the program, it was noted that my disposition was too passive and nervous. Not wanting to be an inconvenience to my team members when requiring assistance and reassurance on communication with higher ups. This has been developing over the years. This year for example I am now fully comfortable approaching others in the team for assistance and even provide such assistance to others myself. I no longer require reassurance on my tone when interacting with people out with my team due to feedback that my tone has been consistently polite and professional.

The examples just noted, and many others we came across in such journals, indicated to us an authentic and earnest engagement from our apprentices when they wrote up their reflective assessments. We saw evidence of the tacit to explicit knowledge conversion that reflection is meant to achieve, and we saw indications of both technical and cognitive learning.

Whether such reflective exercises should be based around competency frameworks, as we do in the latter two years of our program, is in our view a more open question still. It is possible that this may have pre-empted some lines of reflection, and we saw some evidence of what might be called "overfitting" the reflective essay to the framework. While we did try to mitigate this tendency by prompting the students with open-ended questions, as noted earlier, we cannot yet say if that balanced out the possible restrictive effects of the framework. Having a structure has its benefits too that we discussed earlier, and we expect to continue adapting our assessments on this spectrum of highly structured reflection on one end, and highly open-ended reflection on the other.

## Conclusion

Reflection is a crucial component of any work-based learning framework. While it is trivially true that work experience will lead to *some* learning, without deliberate, reflection-*on*-action, the learning will remain tacit, implicit, not always available for recall and re-use in circumstances where they might have added value. This is because tacit knowledge gained via experiential learning remains inaccessible for contexts outside which they were developed, unless they also result in a shift in perspective, which is unlikely to happen without deliberate reflection-on-action. Hence, for effective work-based learning, reflection-on-action is essential.

In view of the crucial role of reflection-on-action in a WBL paradigm, which is unlikely to happen automatically, a structured approach that incorporates reflection as part of its assessment is important. We have presented one such example of structuring reflection in a WBL software engineering program which has been running effectively for a few years. It incorporates reflection through courses in the classroom, but mostly through bespoke *workplace assessment* modules developed for the program. Based on the reflections we have seen so far through these assessments, a few examples of which we have noted in this chapter, we feel that our structured approach to encouraging reflection-on-action to complete the WBL loop has worked quite well. While the exact structure would vary from program to program, we suggest that some manner of structure to encourage deliberate reflection-on-action should be incorporated into any WBL program, while noting the possibility of introducing too much structure which might discourage earnest reflection and authentic learning.

## Note

1 https://portfolio.gla.ac.uk/.

## Bibliography

Anam, F., Muharlisiani, L. T., Soewardini, H. M. D., & Purnomo, A. (2023). Reflections on 4F Model Learning for Professionalism Development of Prospective Teachers: Evidence from Teacher Professional Education. *Journal of Education Research*, 4(4), Article 4. https://doi.org/10.37985/jer.v4i4.740

Bain, J. D., Ballantyne, R., Mills, C., & Lester, N. C. (2002). *Reflecting on Practice: Student Teachers' Perspectives*. Post Pressed.

Barr, M., & Parkinson, J. (2019). Developing a Work-Based Software Engineering Degree in Collaboration with Industry. *Proceedings of the 1st UK & Ireland Computing Education Research Conference*, 1–7. https://doi.org/10.1145/3351287.3351292

Barr, M., & Somerville, D. (2020). Preparing Software Engineering Apprentices for Industry. *Proceedings of the 2020 ACM Conference on International Computing Education Research*, 310–310. https://doi.org/10.1145/3372782.3408116

Bassot, B. (2015). *The Reflective Practice Guide: An Interdisciplinary Approach to Critical Reflection*. Routledge.

Boud, D., & Solomon, N. (2001). *Work-Based Learning: A New Higher Education?* Maidenhead, UK: McGraw-Hill Education (UK).

Boyd, E. M., & Fales, A. W. (1983). Reflective Learning: Key to Learning from Experience. *Journal of Humanistic Psychology*, 23(2), 99–117. https://doi.org/10.1177/0022167883232011

*The CARL Framework of Reflection*. (2018, November 9). The University of Edinburgh. www.ed.ac.uk/reflection/reflectors-toolkit/reflecting-on-experience/carl

Drake, R., & Chen, W. D. (2023). Rethinking Workplace Collaboration – an Old Topic with a Practical View. *Management Decision*, 61(12), 3637–3643. https://doi.org/10.1108/MD-01-2023-0044

Eckerdal, A., Berglund, A., & Thuné, M. (2024). Learning Programming Practice and Programming Theory in the Computer Laboratory. *European Journal of Engineering Education*, 49(2), 330–347. https://doi.org/10.1080/03043797.2023.2294953

*EngineeringCouncil*. (n.d.). www.engc.org.uk/standards-guidance/standards/uk-spec/

Fabian, K., & Taylor-Smith, E. (2021). *How are We Positioning Apprenticeships? A Critical Analysis of Job Adverts for Degree Apprentices*. Society for Research in Higher Education.

Gibbs, G. (1988). *Learning by Doing: A Guide to Teaching and Learning Methods*. Further Education Unit.

Greenways, R. (n.d.). *The Active Reviewing Cycle | Reviewing Skills Tutorial*. https://reviewing.co.uk/learning-cycle/the-active-reviewing-cycle.htm

Griffiths, M., & Tann, S. (1992). Using Reflective Practice to Link Personal and Public Theories. *Journal of Education for Teaching*, 18(1), 69–84. https://doi.org/10.1080/0260747920180107

Kolb, A., & Kolb, D. (2013). *The Kolb Learning Style Inventory 4.0: Guide to Theory, Psychometrics, Research & Applications*. Experience Based Learning Systems, Inc. https://www.researchgate.net/profile/David-Kolb-2/publication/303446688_The_Kolb_Learning_Style_Inventory_40_Guide_to_Theory_Psychometrics_Research_Applications/links/57437c4c08ae9f741b3a1a58/The-Kolb-Learning-Style-Inventory-40-Guide-to-Theory-Psychometrics-Research-Applications.pdf

Lawal, O., Ramlaul, A., & Murphy, F. (2021). Problem Based Learning in Radiography Education: A Narrative Review. *Radiography (London, England: 1995)*, 27(2), 727–732. https://doi.org/10.1016/j.radi.2020.11.001

Lukinsky, J. (1990). Reflective Withdrawal through Journal Writing. *Fostering Critical Reflection in Adulthood: A Guide to Transformative and Emancipatory Learning*, 213–234.

*Meta-SkillsToolkit – Skills Development Scotland*. (n.d.). www.skillsdevelopmentscotland.co.uk/what-we-do/scotlands-careers-services/education-team/meta-skills-toolkit

Raelin, J. A. (1997). A Model of Work-Based Learning. *Organization Science*, 8(6), 563–578.

Rodgers, C. R. (2006). Attending to Student Voice: The Impact of Descriptive Feedback on Learning and Teaching. *Curriculum Inquiry*. www.tandfonline.com/doi/abs/10.1111/j.1467-873X.2006.00353.x

Rodgers, C. R., & LaBoskey, V. K. (2016). Reflective Practice. In J. Loughran & M. L. Hamilton (Eds.), *International Handbook of Teacher Education: Volume 2* (pp. 71–104). Springer. https://doi.org/10.1007/978-981-10-0369-1_3

Schulte, C. (2008). Block Model: An Educational Model of Program Comprehension as a Tool for a Scholarly Approach to Teaching. *Proceedings of the Fourth International Workshop on Computing Education Research*, 149–160. https://doi.org/10.1145/1404520.1404535

Settles, B. (2009). *Active Learning Literature Survey [Technical Report]*. University of Wisconsin-Madison Department of Computer Sciences. https://minds.wisconsin.edu/handle/1793/60660

Thuné, M., & Eckerdal, A. (2019). Analysis of Students' Learning of Computer Programming in a Computer Laboratory Context. *European Journal of Engineering Education*, *44*(5), 769–786. https://doi.org/10.1080/03043797.2018.1544609

# Chapter 12

# Advancing Work-Based Learning in Higher Education

*Matthew Barr*

The 11 chapters in this book collectively offer a comprehensive exploration of the current landscape, challenges, and innovations in work-based learning (WBL) within higher education. From the inception and design of WBL programmes to their delivery, assessment, and quality assurance, the contributors provide valuable insights that enhance our understanding of this evolving field. As we reflect on the diverse perspectives and case studies presented, several key themes emerge that highlight the significance of WBL in contemporary higher education and its potential to bridge the gap between academia and industry.

**Integration of Theory and Practice**

A recurring theme across multiple contributions is the importance of integrating theoretical knowledge with practical experience. This integration is at the heart of WBL and is seen as crucial for developing well-rounded, work-ready graduates: we have seen, for example, how live briefs and real-world projects provide students with authentic learning experiences that connect academic content to industry needs. Similarly, practice-based models in various disciplines allow students to apply theoretical knowledge in real-world settings, enhancing both their understanding and their employability.

The book also presents examples of carefully designed curricula that blend academic learning with workplace training. These approaches not only meet regulatory requirements but also ensure that graduates are well prepared for their professional roles.

**Reflection as a Key Component**

Many contributors highlight the critical role of reflection in WBL. There is a consensus that structured reflection can transform tacit knowledge gained through work experience into explicit, transferable knowledge. Without deliberate reflection, much of the learning that occurs in the workplace may remain implicit and underutilised.

This emphasis on reflection is echoed throughout the book, with various authors discussing how reflection helps students consolidate their learning and develop professional identities. In apprenticeship models and other WBL programmes, regular reflection is built into the learning process to help students make connections between their academic studies and workplace experiences.

## Partnerships and Collaboration

The success of WBL initiatives often hinges on effective partnerships between higher education institutions, employers, and in some cases, professional bodies. This theme is prominent in several chapters, with authors emphasising the need for close collaboration to ensure that programmes meet both academic standards and industry needs.

These partnerships not only enhance the relevance and authenticity of the curriculum but also provide students with valuable industry connections and insights. Indeed, the importance of engaging with external stakeholders to create authentic learning experiences is a common thread throughout the book.

## Challenges and Opportunities

While the benefits of WBL are clear, the contributors also acknowledge the challenges involved in implementing and maintaining effective programmes. Common challenges include balancing academic rigour with workplace demands, ensuring consistency in learning experiences across different workplace settings, managing administrative complexities, addressing diverse learner needs, and navigating complex regulatory landscapes.

Despite these challenges, we have identified numerous opportunities presented by WBL. These include enhancing student employability and career readiness, addressing skills gaps in various industries, promoting social mobility, fostering innovation through cross-pollination of ideas between academia and industry, and developing more agile and responsive degree programmes.

## Pedagogical Innovations

Throughout the book, various pedagogical innovations that support effective WBL are described. These include the use of live briefs and industry-sponsored projects, structured reflection activities, competency frameworks that align academic outcomes with professional standards, flexible delivery models, and the integration of digital technologies to support learning in both academic and workplace settings. Such innovations demonstrate the dynamic nature of WBL and its potential to transform traditional approaches to higher education.

## Quality Assurance and Assessment

Ensuring the quality and consistency of work-based degrees is a concern addressed by several contributors. The complex regulatory landscape in various countries and the challenges it presents for higher education institutions are examined, revealing a need for an holistic approach to quality assurance that considers the unique nature of WBL.

Assessment in WBL contexts also emerges as a key theme, with discussions on the need for authentic assessment methods that can capture the complexity of workplace learning. The use of portfolios, reflective journals, and competency-based assessments, for example, are highlighted as effective approaches.

## Contributions and Future Directions

This book makes several significant contributions to the field of work-based learning in higher education. It provides a comprehensive overview of current approaches to WBL across various disciplines and contexts, offering valuable insights for practitioners, policymakers, and researchers. The case studies and examples presented offer practical guidance for institutions looking to develop or enhance their work-based degree programmes.

The book highlights the importance of reflection and integration in WBL, providing theoretical frameworks and practical strategies for embedding these elements into programme design. It addresses the complexities of quality assurance and assessment in WBL contexts, offering suggestions for navigating these challenges. Collectively, the contributors make a strong case for the value of WBL in enhancing student employability, addressing skills gaps, and promoting social mobility.

Looking to the future, several areas for further research and development emerge from the discussions here. These include longitudinal studies on long-term career outcomes, exploration of emerging technologies in WBL, investigation of WBL's role in addressing global challenges, research on social mobility and diversity impacts, and development of more sophisticated quality assurance frameworks.

## Conclusion

What ties these themes together is the transformative potential of work-based learning in higher education. *Approaches to Work-Based Learning in Higher Education* presents WBL as a powerful approach that can make university degrees more relevant, responsive, and effective in preparing students for the complexities of modern professional life, while also addressing broader societal and economic needs.

As higher education continues to evolve in response to changing societal and economic needs, work-based degree programmes should play an increasingly important role. By bridging the gap between academia and industry, WBL has the potential to create more relevant, engaging, and impactful learning experiences that prepare students for the complexities of modern professional life.

The contributors here collectively argue for a more integrated approach to higher education, one that recognises the workplace as a valid and valuable site of learning. They challenge traditional notions of what constitutes "higher" education and make a compelling case for the recognition of diverse forms of knowledge and expertise.

At the same time, we acknowledge the challenges inherent in implementing effective WBL programmes. The book highlights the need for careful design, strong partnerships, robust quality assurance mechanisms, and a commitment to reflective practice. The authors here provide valuable guidance on navigating these challenges, drawing on their own experiences and research.

As we look to the future, it is clear that WBL will continue to evolve and adapt to changing circumstances. The COVID-19 pandemic, for instance, has accelerated the adoption of digital technologies in both education and the workplace, creating new opportunities and challenges for WBL. Future research and practice in this field will need to embrace these changes, exploring how work-based degrees can remain relevant and effective in an increasingly digital and globalised world.

In conclusion, *Approaches to Work-Based Learning in Higher Education* makes a significant contribution to our understanding of work-based learning in higher education. It provides a solid foundation for future research and practice, offering both theoretical insights and practical guidance. As higher education continues to grapple with questions of relevance, accessibility, and impact, the approaches to WBL outlined in this volume offer promising pathways for creating more responsive, inclusive, and effective learning experiences. By bridging the worlds of academia and industry, WBL has the potential to transform not only individual learners but also the institutions and industries in which they work and study.

# Index

Note: Page numbers in *italics* indicate figures, **bold** indicate tables in the text, and references following "n" refer notes.

Aberdeen Software Factory 77
active blended learning 91
active learning 91, 170
adult learning theory 33
Agile Software Factory 77
alignment: apprenticeship 5–7, 19; conceptualising 7; constructive 25
Anderson, T. 148
andragogy 33
apprenticeship occupational standards (AOS) 160–161, 164, 166–167
apprenticeship(s): alignment 5–7, 19; assessment 13–16; collaboration 8–9, 11; communication 9–10, 18; compassionate approach 27–28; employability 87; employer needs 12–13; flexible delivery 17; identifying appropriate tasks 10, 12; institutional challenges 19–20; integrated programmes 129; integration 7–8; mentoring 11, 17–18; pastoral support 17; tailored support 18–19; traditional learning *vs.* 26–27; tripartite relationship 16–17, 25, 27, 31–32; workplace experience 12; *see also* degree apprenticeships (DAs); diagnostic radiography degree apprenticeship
Apprenticeship Service Provider Reviews 165
apprentices' learner journey *165*, 166
Archer, W. 148
Armsby, P. 13, 14
assessment: apprenticeships 13–16; authentic 8, 13, 33, 36, 91, 167–168; challenges 13–14; degree apprenticeship 167–168; end-point assessment 21n1; flexible and innovative strategies 14; formative 35; parity of 14–16; peer 35; self-assessment 35–36; summative 135; in WBL 199
assessment for learning (AfL) 25, 35–36, 38, 40
augmented reality (AR) 37
Austria 61n8; dual study programmes 58–59
authentic assessment 8, 13, 91, 167–168; tasks 33, 36

Baaken, T. 82, 98
Baden-Württemberg Cooperative State University (DHBW) 46, 50–51, 53
Ball, I. 85
Barr, M. 11, 33
Barrows, H.S. 34
Bell Academy, IRE 111; career development 114; culture of community 114–115; facilitation 112–113; international students 114; program features 111–112; program operation 112
Berufsmaturität 59
Betts, M. 27
Biggs, J. 25
Billett, S. 7, 134
blended learning approach 148, *150*
Bloom's Revised Taxonomy 90
Boud, D. 25
Bovill, C. 25, 90

Boz, M. 82, 86
Bravenboer, D. 11, 13, 14
Brown, J. 98
Bungay, M. 7, 8, 12, 14, 16, 18, 19
Bureau 507 (B507) 116–117

career development 114
care theory 28
CARL framework, of reflection 183
case studies 15
Chartered Management Institute (CMI) 164
Chase, J. D. 77
Chen, W. D. 185
Choy, S. 136
Clarke, M. 87
Cleaver, L. 169
co-creation 8, 20, 25, 89
code reviews 74
cognitive presence 149
collaboration 2, 8–9, 11, 15, 27, 198; *see also* partnerships
colonisation 130
communication: apprenticeships 9–10, 18; technology 18
compassionate approach 27–28, 38
compassionate empathy 28
compassionate pedagogy 28
competency 188–189
constructive alignment 25
contracts 155; learning 15; study 49, 50
Costley, C. 13–15
COVID-19 pandemic 199

Dalrymple, R. 134
DAPPER 166–172; assessments 167–168; design 166–167; engagement 170–171; McrMet's DTSP 172, **173–174**, 175; pedagogy 168–169; processes 169–170; resources 171–172
Daun, M. 98, 99
degree apprenticeships (DAs) 159–163, 175; alignment challenge 5–7, 19; assessment 13–16; collaboration 8–9, 11; communication 9–10, 18; diagnostic radiography 142–157; employer expectations 12–13; flexible delivery 17; identifying appropriate tasks 10, 12; institutional challenges 19–20; integration 7–8; mentoring 11, 17–18; pastoral support 17; quality impact on 166–172; regulatory framework 159, **160**; tailored support 18–19; tripartite relationship 16–17; in UK 87; workplace experience 12; *see also* DAPPER; quality metrics
descriptive feedback 182
Deuer, E. 131
Dewey, J. 179
diagnostic radiography degree apprenticeship 2, 142–157; academic content 151–152; applied radiographic knowledge **145**, 146; blended learning approach 148, *150*; challenges 155–156; contract 155; conventional undergraduate degree *vs.* 143–144, 152; delivery 148–149; design 144–148; inception and drivers 142–143; KSBs 147–148; peer support 151, 154; practice placement **145**, 146–147; practice placement foundations **145**, 146; professional practice **145**, 146; qualification and status 152–153; responsibilities 155; support 150–151; workplace activities 153–154
Digital and Technology Solutions Professional (DTSP) DA [McrMet] 172, **173–174**, 175
digital pedagogies 135–136
Doherty, O. 14
Dollinger, M. 98
Drake, R. 185
dual degrees 128–129
Duale Hochschule Gera-Eisenach (DHGE) 51
Duale Hochschule Schleswig-Holstein (DHSW) 51
dual study programmes, in Germany 2; companies involvement in 51–52; conventional degree programmes *vs.* 47, 49; criticism 55–58; development of 52–55, **54**; drop-out rate 57–58; emergence of 45–46; financial aspects 52, 58; governance aspects 55–56; interlocking theory and practice 49–51; marginalisation of dual VET 55; practice-integrated 47, **48**; providers 51; quality assurance 56–57; social aspects of students 57–58; subject structure 51; training-integrated 47, **48**; types of 47–49; work-integrated 47, **48**

Dual Study Quality Network 57
dual training system 46, 55
dual VET system 46, 55, 56

Eckerdal, A. 180
Edifor, E. 6, 8–12, 14, 15, 17–20
Education and Skills Funding Agency (ESFA) 162, 165
Education Inspection Framework (EIF) 161–162
Education Skills Funding Agency 159
educator–employer partnerships 8–9, 11, 15
emotional intelligence 87
employability 81, 86–88
employer advisory boards 11
employer needs 12–13
end-point assessment (EPA) 21n1
end-point assessment organization (EPAO) 161, 163
Endpoint Quality Assessment (EQA) 163
engagements 170–171; *see also* partnerships
Eraut, M. 130
expansive workplace 134
experiential learning 34, **40**, 91
experiential learning model 180
explicit knowledge 180

facilitator 109, 112, 113, 114–115
Falchikov, N. 25
Federal Institute for Vocational Education and Training, Germany 56
Fergusson, L. 85
5R framework of reflection 182
Fletcher-Brown, J. 87
formative assessment 35
4F model of reflection 183
freelancers 65
Fuller, A. 24
Furness, S. 11, 12

Gambin, L. 17
Garrison, D. R. 148, 149
generative AI (GenAI) 96–97
German Council of Science and Humanities 57
Germany: dual study programmes in 45–58; tertiary sector 61n2; *see also* dual study programmes, in Germany
Gerstung, V. 131
Gibbs, G. 183

Gibbs, P. 28
Gilligan, P. 11, 12
Glasgow University Software Service (GUSS) 64; agile practices 73; code reviews 74; dealing with customers 71–73; experiences of project management 76–77; finance administrator 68; history of development 66–68; lack of marketing 71; maintenance period 73; objectives 65; project delivery 72; project manager 68; retrospectives 68–69; technical skills 73; *see also* student software engineers (SSEs)
Graduate Apprenticeship program [University of Glasgow] 183–194; *see also* University of Glasgow, GA program
Green, D. 142
Green, R. C. 77, 78
Green, S. 6, 9, 14–16, 19
Greenways, R. 183
Griffiths, M. 181

Hagenauer, G. 89
Harrington, K. 88
Hase, S. 131
Hattie, J. 25
Health and Care Professions Council (HCPC) 152–153, 156–157
higher education apprenticeships 24–40; assessment for learning 35–36, 38; collaborative partnership 38; compassionate and inclusive learning environment 38; compassionate approach 27–28; expanding the pedagogical lens 34–35; multifaceted pedagogical approach 37, 39; pedagogical approaches 32–33; reflective practice 31–32, 34, 38, 39; stretch and challenge 36–37; student partnerships 28–30; support systems 29–30; technology-enhanced learning 33, 35, 37–39; traditional and institutional partnerships 31; traditional *vs.* apprenticeship learning 26–27; tripartite relationship 31–32; understanding learners 25
higher-level reflection 182–183
historically black colleges and universities (HBCUs) 120–121
Hughes, C. 16, 17, 26

IfATE apprenticeship standards 160–161
imposter syndrome 27, 74
integrated model 125–126
integrated professional programmes 3; apprenticeship 129; competence and readiness to practise 129–130; continuum 126, *127*; digital tools 135–136; dual degrees 128–129; issues in 129–132; learners 136; learning design 135; learning-integrated work 136–137; nominal *vs.* deep integration 131–132; nursing 128; organisations and partnerships 132–133; pedagogies 134–136; teaching 128; theory/practice tension 130–131; work-space 134
integration 7–8; of theory and practice 197
internships 35, 49
Iron Range Engineering (IRE): Bureau 507 116–117; CS program 118–119; IRE v2.0.110; practice-based model 110–115; project-based model 106–110; Project Maverick 115–116; SE program 119–120

Jackson, D. 10, 12
Jackson, J. 6, 8, 13, 14, 20
Jarvis, J. 89
Johnson, D.W. 29
Joseph T. C. 77, 78
journal writing 182, 189–190
Joyce, L. 5, 7–9, 12, 19, 20

Kenyon, C. 131
Knight, P. T. 87
knowledge, skills, and behaviours (KSBs) 26–27, 147–148
Kolb, A. Y. 91
Kolb, D. A. 131; experiential learning 34, 91, 180
Kyndt, E. 86

LaBoskey, V. K. 180
labs, experimentation in 180
large language model (LLM) 97
Lave, J. 134
learning: active 91, 170; active blended 91; blended 148, *150*; contracts 15; design 135; experiential 34, **40**, 91, 180; life-long 87; peer 29, 73–74; problem-based 32, 34, 36–37, **40**, 91; project-based 36, 91; self-directed 33; social and emotional 91; team-based 90; technology-enhanced 33, 35, 37–39; traditional 26–27; work-integrated 83, 85, **85**, 86, 126, 136–137; work-related 85, **85**; workplace 85, **85**, 86
Lester, S. 11, 13, 15, 126, 134, 135
Lillis, F. 13, 14
live briefs 2, 82–83; challenges 98–99; commercial 94; education 94–95; ethical factors 97–98; examples of 92–95, **93**; GenAI 96–97; health 94; literature on 83, **84**; pedagogical underpinnings 90–91; social 92–94; sources of 95, **96**; student-staff-stakeholder partnership 88, 88–90
Lukinsky, J. 182

Macklin, R. 82
Manwaring, G. 85
Marsden, F. 17, 18
Maverick Software 115
Maxwell, N. 28
McrMet's DTSP DA 172, **173–174**, 175
MediLingo live brief 94–95
mentoring: apprenticeships 11, 17–18; IRE program 113
Messmann, G. 7
Minnesota's Iron Range *see* Iron Range Engineering (IRE)
Minton, A. 8, 13–18, 20
misalignment 5, 13
MN Tech Workforce Summit (2022) 119
Mulder, R.H. 7
Mulkeen, J. 14, 152
Muller, J. 131
multifaceted pedagogical approach 37

NHS workforce plan (2023) 157
nursing, integrated programmes 128, 130

Ofsted Education Inspection Framework (EIF) 161–162
Oliver, B. 81, 86

parallel model 125
Parkinson, J. 11
partnerships 27, 198; collaborative 38; definition 88; organisations and 132–133; staff-stakeholder 89; strategic 133; student-staff 89–90; student-staff-stakeholder 88; student-stakeholder 90; student 28–30; traditional and institutional 31
pastoral support 17, 151
pedagogical innovations 198
pedagogy: compassionate 28; DAPPER 168–169; integrated professional development 134–136; signature 134; transformative 90
peer assessment 35
peer learning 29, 73–74
peer support 148, 151, 154
Perrin, B. 87–89
Perusso, A. 14
practice-based model, IRE *110*, 110–115
practice-integrated dual study programmes 47, **48**
problem-based learning (PBL) 32, 34, 36–37, **40**, 91
Professional, Statutory, and Regulatory Bodies (PSRBs) 164
project-based learning (PjBL) 36, 91
project-based model, IRE 106–110, *108*; design curriculum 107; professionalism curriculum 107–108; technical curriculum 108–110
Project Maverick 115–116

quality achievement rates (QARs) 162
quality assurance 56–57, 199
Quality Assurance Agency (QAA) Quality Code 159, 161
quality metrics 2–3; Apprenticeship Service Provider Reviews 165; Education and Skills Funding Agency 162; Education Inspection Framework 161–162; Endpoint Quality Assessment 163; formal 160–164; IfATE apprenticeship standards 160–161; informal 164–166; PSRBs 164; QAA Quality Code 161; Rate My Apprenticeship 165–166; Teaching Excellence Framework 163–164, **164**; *see also* DAPPER

Raelin's model 179; explicit–tacit knowledge dimension 180; theory–practice learning dimension 180
Rate My Apprenticeship (RMA) 165–166
Reflecta live brief 95
reflection 179–180; CARL framework 183; 5R framework 182; 4F model 183; GAs at University of Glasgow 183–194; Gibb's reflective cycle 183; higher-level 182–183; as key component 197–198; structured 181–182
reflective observation 180
reflective practice 31–32, 34, 38, 39
remuneration 52, 56, 58
Revans, R. 131
reverse colonisation 130–131
Roberts, A. 11
Rodgers, C. R. 180
Rowe, L. 10, 32

Saieva, G. 16, 17, 26
Sara, R. 89, 98
Sauli, F. 5, 7, 8
Saville, K.-M. 14, 17
Scholtz, D. 13
Schön, D. 131
Schonell, S. 82
Scott, D. 130
self-assessment 35–36
self-directed learning 33
self-efficacy 136
sense of belonging 27, 38, 81
sequential model 125, 130, 131
Shaw, M. 87
signature pedagogy 134
Siqueira, F. L. 78
situated cognition strategies 32, **40**
skills coach 12, 18
small and medium-sized enterprises (SMEs) 12, 17
Smith, R. 27
Smith, S. 27
social and emotional learning 91
social constructivism 90
Software Factory model 78
staff-stakeholder partnerships 89
Stephenson, J. 136
Stephens, S. 14
structured reflection 181–182
student partnerships 28–30

student software engineers (SSEs) 65, 75–76; exit interviews 70; imposter syndrome 74; peer learning 73–74; prior learning 74–75; recruitment 67, 70; turnover 70–71; *see also* Glasgow University Software Service (GUSS)
student-staff partnerships 89–90
student-stakeholder partnerships 90
Stuttgart Model 46
summative assessments 135
Switzerland, dual study programmes in 59

tacit knowledge 180
Tann, S. 181
Teaching Excellence Framework (TEF) 163–164, **164**
teaching, integrated programmes 128
team-based learning 90
technology-enhanced learning 33, 35, 37–39
theory–practice divide 130–131
Thuné, M. 180
Timperley, H. 25
trade unions 55–56, 58, 60
traditional student learning 26–27
trailblazers 160
training-integrated degree programmes 47, **48**
transformative pedagogy 90
tripartite relationship 16–17, 25, 27, 31–32

UK Standard for Professional Engineering Competence (UK-SPEC) 189

University of Exeter programme 2, 142–157; *see also* diagnostic radiography degree apprenticeship
University of Glasgow, GA program 183–194; *see also* Graduate Apprenticeship program [University of Glasgow]
Unwin, L. 24

van der Laan, L. 85
virtual learning environments 18
virtual reality (VR) 16, 18, 37
Vocational Training Act 56, 60

Wagenaar, R. 14
Weiß, R. 136
Wenger. E. 134
Wenham, K.E. 16–18
Williams, D. L. 98, 99
Wink, J. 90
Woolmer, C. 90
work-based learning (WBL) 85, **85**; *see also individual entries*
work-integrated degree programmes 47, **48**
work-integrated learning (WIL) 83, 85, **85**, 86, 126, 136–137
workplace experience 12
workplace journal 182, 189–190
workplace learning (WPL) 85, **85**, 86
work-related learning (WRL) 85, **85**
work-space 126, 134

Yorke, M. 86, 87
Youde, A. 17, 18
Young, M. 131